THE TEST MATCH CAREER OF
WALTER HAMMOND

Derek Lodge

Foreword by Brian Johnston

THE NUTSHELL PUBLISHING CO. LTD.
TUNBRIDGE WELLS

In the Spellmount/Nutshell Cricket list:
The Test Match Career of Geoffrey Boycott
by C D Clark
The Test Match Career of Sir Jack Hobbs
by Clive W Porter
Cricket Anthology
by Samuel J Looker
Cricket at Hastings
by Gerald Brodribb
The Test Match Career of Ted Dexter
by Derek Lodge
Kent Cricketing Greats
by Dean Hayes
Gloucester Cricketing Greats
by Dean Hayes
The Lord's Test
by Steven Lynch

First published in the UK in 1990 by
THE NUTSHELL PUBLISHING CO LTD
12 Dene Way, Speldhurst
Tunbridge Wells, Kent TN3 0NX

© Derek Lodge 1990

British Library Cataloguing in Publication Data
Lodge, Derek
    The test match career of Walter Hammond
    (Test match career series).
    1. Cricket. Hammond, Walter
    I. Title II. Series
    796.358092
    ISBN 1-871876-10-9

Printed in Great Britain by
The KPC Group, London and Ashford, Kent

DEDICATION

To R. C. M., a sensitive and inspirational biographer, and a hard act to follow.

ACKNOWLEDGEMENTS

This book was to have been written by the late David Burnett James, and I am indebted to him for his research and ideas, which have been an enormous help to me. For the figures, I have drawn heavily on the work of David Goodyear, and on the invaluable study written by David Moore; I have drawn also on two most admirable biographies of Walter Hammond, written by Ronald Mason and Gerald Howat. I had the pleasure of introducing these two gentlemen to each other at Lord's one day, and sitting back to listen to a fascinating discussion on the business of biography; it was a great deal more interesting than the Test Match we were all supposed to be watching.

My thanks, as always, to Stephen Green at Lord's and to the courteous and efficient staff of the Newspaper Library at Colindale. During Hammond's career, newspapers, both in England and in Australia, gave a lot of space to their cricket writers, and my enjoyment of the work of Neville Cardus, Douglas Jardine, Major R. B. Vincent and many others will be apparent to the reader.

David Frith was, as ever, most helpful in my search for pictures; his collection yielded some fresh and evocative studies, to accompany the classic pictures of the master-cricketer.

Finally, my thanks to Sandra Forty for her editorial work, and to Ian Morley-Clarke for giving me the opportunity to write a book that I, at least, have enjoyed.

CONTENTS

CONTENTS (cont)

FOREWORD

I was lucky to see Wally Hammond play with special memories of his superb 240 in the Lord's Test of 1938.

It must be difficult for anyone who never saw him to appreciate fully the magnificent power and majesty of his stroke play. It has been said that he was largely an off-side player, but remember that in *his* day bowlers bowled more on or outside the off-stump. It is however true that he always found Bill O'Reilly difficult to play because he used to concentrate on Hammond's leg-stump.

But Hammond played every stroke except the hook which he deliberately avoided. Because he used a light bat he was a superb cutter, both late and square. There was his famous cover drive, and those tremendous forcing strokes past mid-off and mid-on off both front and back foot. He also had his own particular sweep – more of a paddle – down to long-leg. This was later copied by Colin Cowdrey.

W. G. Grace was the colossus of the Victorian era. Hammond was his equivalent in the late twenties and throughout the thirties. He looked and was the supreme athlete. His every movement portrayed greatness. The whole ground would stir as he strode majestically to the wicket – 'like a ship in full sail' as R. C. Robertson-Glasgow so aptly described him.

He was a brilliant slip fielder and made it all look ridiculously easy. I never remember seeing him fall over nor fling himself at the ball. There is a story that when he made one of his many catches off Charlie Parker he would sometimes quickly slip the ball to B. H. Lyon at second slip, who would then be credited with the catch!

As a bowler Les Ames used to say that with his perfect action he got as much zip off the pitch as Maurice Tate.

The war in which he served in the R.A.F. seemed to take its toll of him and afterwards he was never again the masterly figure of old. Even so in 1946, his last regular season in first-class cricket, he managed to top the batting averages with 1783 runs in only 26 innings at an average of 84.90!

He was a comparative failure on the Australian tour of 1946-47 and at the end of it he retired from first-class cricket. (He made two appearances in 1950 and 1951.) He went to live in South Africa where he was a rather sad and lonely figure. At Durban in 1964 I met him for the very first time, although I had commentated for TV on the Tests against India in 1946. But in those days there were no media interviews with the captains. I saw him quietly watching Mike Smith's MCC Team practising in the nets before the Test. I introduced myself and alerted Mike of his presence. From that moment he became part of the MCC team. I shall never forget seeing him that evening in the hotel surrounded by all the players who were listening spellbound to the great man as he reminisced.

Greatness is a much over-used word, but Wally Hammond really was one of the greats. I like to think that this hero-worship from the MCC team made his last six months that much happier before he sadly died in July, 1965.

In front of me as I write is one of cricket's most famous photographs – Wally Hammond playing his glorious cover drive from a yard outside the crease, dark blue handkerchief showing out of his trouser pocket and Bertie Oldfield crouching behind the stumps, hoping for a stumping chance.

But Wally was in the perfect position for the stroke as he followed through with his bat, and I am sure it must have been a four.

Brian Johnston

1 The Man

Walter Hammond was, quite simply, the most graceful and majestic batsman who ever played for England. In the interest of strict accuracy, I stress graceful *and* majestic – Spooner and Gower may have been more graceful, and Neville Cardus would certainly have asserted that AC Maclaren was more noble, but Hammond's overall presence was pre-eminent. In a slender and now rather unjustly forgotten book about English cricket between the wars, *To the Wicket,* Dudley Carew wrote.

> 'There was some grand cricket played . . . and if our children and grandchildren condole with us in having lived in these dreadful times, we can at least answer "Ah, but we saw Chapman field, Larwood bowl, Hammond bat, and we are not so much to be pitied as you think" . . .'

It was no accident that Carew hit on these three names – Chapman the athlete, swooping on the ball wherever he was placed and catching everything above the ground, Larwood coming in off his carpet-slipper run and bowling the ball faster, it seemed, than man had ever bowled it or could ever bowl it (there are still those who swear that he was faster in absolute terms, than Holding or Jeff Thomson) and above all Hammond, hammering the ball at the speed of light into the covers, beating a packed field by the subtlest delay in the playing of the stroke or by the sheer power of stroke which turned even an Australian fielding side to stone.

Hammond began in county cricket as a brilliant young player with all the strokes – he was looked on by some as a bit of a dasher and not quite sound enough for Test cricket, but when he first went to Australia under Chapman, he decided to play the percentages a little and to concentrate on the strokes he could play with perfect safety. Essentially this meant the cover-hit, off either the front or the back foot, and immensely hard drives into the V between mid-on and extra-cover, varied with a cracking square-cut. He more or less left the hook out of the repertoire, although he was a notable exponent of the stroke, and he didn't play the late cut often. A chart of his great 251 in Sydney on

1

this tour (reproduced on page 00) tells the whole story with its sheaf of boundaries on the off-side. Such was his power that only the very best bowlers could contain him, even though he was restricting himself to a segment of the field. Grimmett and O'Reilly sometimes managed it by concentrating on his leg stump and pushing the ball through so that he could not step back and force them away on the off-side.

One or two comments on his style, from observers who saw more of him than I did, enhance the picture. Ronald Mason wrote:

> 'Nothing that he did was without grace; nothing that he did was without authority. He was orthodox, but he expressed his orthodoxy in rich chorded tones. His on-drive was right out of the book; his off-drive was right out of this world.'

and RC Robertson-Glasgow, in a perceptive essay in *Wisden* 1942:

> '. . . he has adorned cricket and entertained the public with a style of batting in which splendour of manner, grace of execution and muscular power of stroke have been combined to a degree rarely equalled . . . "Let's go and see Hammond" we used to say. It was worth a journey even to see him walk out to bat; for the true stamp of greatness was printed on him.'

It is tempting to go on and on, quoting his contemporaries, for his grandeur inspired much fine writing – but there is more to be said about his achievements. He was one of the finest fielders of his age, taking slip catches with deceptive ease; his anticipation was such that he moved to take catches two-handed that others would have been diving all over the place for. It is often asserted that he was never off his feet and that he never missed a catch. Neither statement is quite true; there are pictures of Hammond diving to take his catches and I have uncovered references to his missing catches, to the general consternation, but the consternation itself was a recognition of his exceptionally high standard.

Away from the slips, he was an easy, graceful mover, and this easy grace was evident too in his bowling. He could be distinctly quick – especially, it is said, when a batsman had upset him – and he was very accurate. In the Bodyline series, he was invaluable as a bowler, putting in long stints on very hot days and enabling Jardine to keep Larwood and the other fast men fresh to the end of the longest day. Later in his career, Hammond's suspect back prevented him from bowling as much as he would have liked, but his figures tell their own story – a persevering, economical bowler, making him a real asset particularly in matches of long duration.

2

Hammond, then, was a towering figure in English cricket, an automatic choice in nearly every writer's all-time England XI – one exception was EHD Sewell, who could see very little merit in any cricketer born in the twentieth century and actually preferred JT Tyldesley to Hammond in *his* all-time team. I will return to the analysis of Hammond's achievement in the final chapter, but it is useful to identify here three themes which run through the story.

The first is the great running saga of Anglo-Australian cricket – the fight for the Ashes. Hammond played in seven rubbers against Australia and these are the high spots of his story. It wasn't Hammond's fault that England only won two of the seven, and shared another. The England sides were generally competent, but the other side had Bradman, the one player of the age who was unarguably more valuable to his side than Hammond.

Bradman was in fact the greatest asset that any Test side has ever had. He was, quite literally, worth two batsmen to Australia, by which I mean that his career average of 99.94 was twice the collective average of the next three or four best Australian batsmen of his time. Moreover, he scored his runs at a great pace and gave his bowlers that much more time to bowl the other side out in time-limited matches. Great as were Hammond's achievements against Australia, he was consistently outdone by Bradman – even in the Bodyline series Bradman had the higher average, though that isn't the full story – and it must have been disappointing to him that he was universally regarded as the *second* best batsman in the world. It's something, of course, to be second only to a phenomenon.

The second theme is that of the emergence of the second group of the cricketing nations. At the beginning of Hammond's career, there were just three Test-playing countries – England, Australia and South Africa; five years later, they had been joined by the West Indies, New Zealand and India. England's matches against South Africa were hard-fought in Hammond's time and England won only five matches to South Africa's four, no less than 16 being drawn, but the games against the other countries were seen largely as preparation for the Australian games. Because of the introduction of these new contenders, Hammond was actually the most successful of Test players up to the time of his retirement; he participated in 29 wins, to Hobbs' 28. Once again, he was rapidly overtaken by Bradman, who was on the winning side 30 times, and others such as Cowdrey, Lloyd and Richards have overtaken even Bradman in these days when many more Tests are played.

Hammond's matches against the other countries coincided with the careers of some notable players, and it is fascinating to trace the course of his battles with certain bowlers, notably Learie Constantine, and,

3

very surprisingly, CL Vincent of South Africa, who dismissed him in Tests more often than anybody else except Bill O'Reilly. Each of them had him out ten times. The wins against the 'new countries' were not always easy ones.

Finally Hammond formed a link between two generations of England players. When he began, the leading batsmen were Hobbs and Sutcliffe, strongly supported by Hendren and Woolley. Hammond quickly took his place, and a leading place, among this fine array of batsmen, but by the mid-thirties the others had retired and he was surrounded in due course by the new generation – Hutton, Compton, Edrich, Leyland and Paynter. The latter was not always fully appreciated by the selectors, although he played throughout the period before the war when England generally had a goodish batting side. However, Hammond was pre-eminent, consistently at the top of the English first-class averages with some wonderful batting in county cricket. He was always the batsman that everyone wanted to watch as the epitome of classical batting. Which is where we came in – let us look at his career in detail.

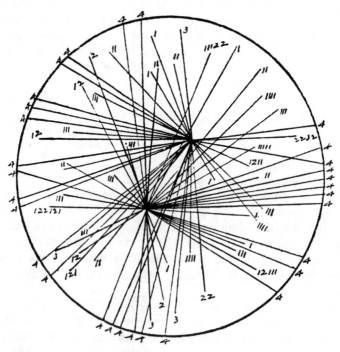

Diagram of Hammond's innings of 251 at Sydney, 1928-29.

4

2　The rise of a star in the sky

This is a book about Hammond's Test career and it is not for me to describe Hammond's early life and county career in any great detail – his two biographers, Ronald Mason and Gerald Howat, have covered the subject admirably. However, it is interesting to glance at one or two influences, and to note the comments of his contemporaries – some of them can claim to have recognised incipient greatness.

Walter Hammond was born in Dover on 19 June 1903. His father was a professional soldier, and we have no record of any family aptitude or affinity for cricket. Soon after Walter's birth, his father was posted to Malta, and mother and child followed the drum, as soldiers' families have always done. Young Walter's first introduction to cricket was therefore informal. He has told in his autobiography how he chalked a wicket on a door and played with a cut-down bat discarded by the soldiers.

There are those who would have us believe that players who have learned the game under difficult conditions are always likely to turn out better than those who are spoon-fed. But this is to over-simplify, to romanticise. True, Bradman learned the rudiments in solitary play, throwing a ball against a fence and hitting it as it rebounded, with a long tramp before him if he missed the fence in the first place. True, Hobbs picked up the game hacking about on the edge of Parker's Piece. We can never know, though, how many lads who practised away in unpromising surroundings never made any sort of mark. On the other hand many public schoolboys who enjoy every advantage of good wickets and professional coaching fail to learn even the basics, but Peter May, Colin Cowdrey and Ted Dexter are living proof that *this* path also can lead to Test cricket. The plain truth is that genius will out and that a player of real potential will develop that potential in one school or another; it is true also that nobody can put in what isn't there.

Hammond had the opportunity to develop his skills on the field when his family returned to England on the outbreak of war in 1914. They settled in Southsea and he went to Portsmouth Grammar School, but this doesn't seem to have worked out too well. He says that he was not the most assiduous of scholars and with his father away in France, he may well have lacked some direction at home. Consequentially his parents decided that he would do better at boarding-school and in April 1918 he transferred to Cirencester Grammar School. Within three weeks, he was called to the headmaster's study to hear the devastating news of his father's death in action.

One can easily imagine the shattering effect on a lonely boy – and Walter had to bear his grief alone, for he stayed at boarding-school. It may well have been at this time that the seeds of his moodiness, that withdrawn air that was to characterise him all his life, were sown. It may well have been then, too, that he formed in his mind the idea that he could make a career as a professional sportsman. He had to identify a career of some kind, for he now had to support his mother, and he had shown no great intellectual promise. Whether or not he was thinking along these lines, he soon made a sporting mark at his new school. In the 1918-19 season, he made his way into the football team, and in 1919, just before his sixteenth birthday, he was picked for the cricket XI.

Cirencester did not have a distinguished fixture list; although it was surrounded by well-known public schools, its team did not play even against their second XIs. The school played against other grammar schools, the nearby villages, even the Church Lads' Brigade. However, pitches were on the rough side, and in the circumstances Hammond's batting performance was noteworthy. Certainly, he far outshone his contemporaries, scoring over 500 runs and taking 86 wickets in 1919.

Another future Gloucestershire player, Billy Neale, was in the school side, and together they were too much for most of their opponents. Neale left in 1920 and Hammond carried the team in a way which is rare in any class of cricket. Mr Howat has extracted the appropriate and significant figures from the school magazine. In school matches, Hammond averaged 57.84; the next best average was 7.86! In house matches, he scored 613 runs for once out, his highest score 365 not out. We know very little about the quality of the opposition, but a score of 365 has always to be respected whatever the circumstances. The young man had done all that could be asked of him and more, and his deeds had not gone unremarked.

Upon leaving school, he joined the local Cirencester club, but he had already been recommended to Gloucestershire by his headmaster. Within a month of the end of term he had played for the Club and Ground, scoring 60, and been selected for the county side against Lancashire. It was a fairy-tale start, but there followed no instant success. He played four innings that year in three county matches, scored 27 runs and didn't bowl. No better and no worse than dozens of other young aspirants, but the county had seen enough to invest at least

6

something in him.

He was appointed as assistant to John Tunnicliffe, the old Yorkshire player who was the coach at Clifton College. It was clearly the intention that Tunnicliffe should coach young Hammond too, and Hammond acknowledges in his ghosted autobiography *Cricket My Destiny* how much he learned from the older man, but he hints that the relationship was not always smooth and that the time came when it was sensible for them to part. One can guess the tensions: most great players have a pretty good idea of their own worth and the young Hammond was certainly no exception. Tunnicliffe, brought up in a hard professional school, would have expected a young player with no record of achievement to accept teaching and criticism with eager gratitude. It says something about the county committee's view of Hammond's potential that they didn't write him off, but passed him on to George Dennett for further instruction. Dennett was a more patient instructor, or so Hammond implies, but he was also demanding and gave Hammond a very thorough grounding.

He played just twice for the county in 1921, in the two matches against Armstrong's powerful Australian side. This seemed an odd decision at the time and it seems so still; the Australians were one of the strongest sides ever to tour England, and it was not then the custom for the counties to rest their best players in non-competitive matches against the tourists. Why was not Hammond given a chance against one of the weaker counties? Perhaps somebody thought he should be thrown in at the deep end to sink or swim – just possibly there were already some misgivings about his county qualification. Whatever the reason, he played and he failed. He scored one run in three innings, and that was the whole of his first-class season.

Gloucestershire were still happy enough about his future to give him a prolonged run in the first team in 1922, but he didn't achieve very much. His best score in nine innings was 32, but several very good judges noted his obvious class and that 32, against Middlesex at Lord's, attracted a good deal of notice of the wrong kind. Sir Home Gordon, a most enthusiastic follower, who reckoned that a summer's day on which he was not watching cricket was a day wasted, saw the innings and, as we all do when we see a young player of talent, he sang Hammond's praises to all his acquaintances. Among his hearers was Lord Harris, one of the game's two fairly benevolent dictators (the other being Lord Hawke). Harris's benevolence did not extend to matters of county qualification and it was an automatic reaction for him to ask about the provenance of any new player. It would of course be a calumny to suggest that Harris's next action was influenced in any way by the undoubted fact that Hammond had been born in the county of which he was himself a leading light. He was at all times a zealous upholder of the qualification rules, but he certainly set the wheels in motion without delay and was totally unrepentant when accused of undue punctiliousness. The rules were as they were, he said, and made to be kept. Under those rules, it must be said that Hammond's occasional residence in Gloucestershire did not qualify him, and the county didn't fight the case. It must have been a bitter blow to Hammond just as he was beginning to settle. It probably seemed less of a blow to the county, his career figures to date being:

Innings	N.O.	H.S.	Runs	Average
15	1	32	117	8.37

He had held eight catches and taken no wickets.

Poor Hammond returned to the Gloucester City Club, for whom he had been playing in 1921, and averaged over 50 for them; he watched avidly the famous and less famous cricketers who came to play against Gloucestershire, and wondered if he would get another chance in 1923. The county put him straight back into the first team, as well they might, for their batting had been remarkably unsuccessful in 1922, only three men averaging more than 20. He made a sensational start, unleashing all his frustration on a pretty moderate Surrey attack and scoring 110 and 92 in his very first match. *The Daily Telegraph* correspondent made some relatively muted comments, describing it as: '. . . a very attractive display . . . hearty applause from a fairly large company.'

I think that rather more excitement would be voiced today if a 19-year-old took 202 runs off one of the leading counties in the first match of the season.

Young players in their first full season of county cricket often find the sheer physical effort of continuous play affects their form, and this seems to have happened to Hammond in 1923. After that first match he played 13 innings without getting past 35, although he took a most distinguished first wicket, in the person of Andrew Sandham. Then he got a couple of 90s, and things began to look up. He was picked for the Players at the Oval – where sides were seldom fully representative, counties not being asked to release their players as they did for the Lord's match – and he took 6 for 59 against Hampshire, dismissing four Test players in George Brown, Lord Tennyson, Phil Mead and Alec Kennedy. In the 1924 *Wisden*, Sydney Pardon singled him out for high praise, for one who had still only made one first-class 100:

'Irreproachable in style and not yet 21 years of age, Hammond has all the world before him, and there is no telling how far he may go.'

However, 1924 turned out to be a very poor season for batsmen, with rain-interrupted matches and wet wickets; one indicator is that 103 sides were put out for under 100, about twice the going rate between the wars. It wasn't the best outlook for a classical batsman trying to establish himself and unsurprisingly Hammond took a long time to get going. It was 7 June before he scored more than 31 in an innings and then he scored a lively 120 against Somerset, with only one chance. Then followed a string of mediocre scores – interrupted only by 72 against Essex and 96 against Cambridge – but Gloucestershire persevered with him, possibly because they hadn't many reserves.

Then on 25 August the breakthrough came in an extraordinary game against Middlesex at Bristol. It began on a rain-affected pitch, and Haig and Durston, taking full advantage, had the home side out for 31, Hammond making 5. Charlie Parker hit back with 7 for 30 and Middlesex were out for 74. It was Gloucestershire's last Championship match of the season and Hammond needed a success. He says in his autobiography that he felt the Committee had their collective eye on him and that he was in danger of dismissal. This is hard to believe as they had persevered with him thus far and there was little obvious local talent about to compete for his place. Anyway, he decided to chance his arm, probably the best tactic on that wicket. *Wisden* describes his innings as 'the batting display of the year'. He scored 174 in under four hours on a wicket on which 20 wickets had just fallen for 5 runs apiece. Gloucestershire won comfortably, Parker doing the hat-trick in each innings, and Hammond woke to find himself famous. *The Daily Telegraph* writer said:

'His gallantry, his confidence, the freedom with which he treated almost unplayable bowling recalled the days of Jessop with his back to the wall'.

At the end of the season, *Wisden* was again in prophetic mood:

'Not yet 22 . . . he is perhaps something more than the hope of Gloucestershire cricket.'

In short, all eyes were upon him, but once again he started poorly in 1925. He scored only 7 runs in his first 5 innings and made the third 'pair' of his career against Surrey. By June he was scoring more consistently and also doing a lot more bowling – he had filled out physically and no longer wilted under the strain of three-day cricket. Once again, he played just one stunning innings, this time at Old Trafford and before the enraptured eyes of Neville Cardus, who had a good deal to say about it.

Lancashire had an extremely strong bowling side, headed by McDonald, Parkin and Richard Tyldesley, all more or less at their peak, and Gloucestershire were 20 for 2 when Hammond came in to face McDonald at his fastest and best. In no time at all it seemed, Hammond and Dipper, an underrated batsman having a very good season, had reduced this powerful attack to shreds. They added 330 in 225 minutes. At this stage of his career, Hammond was still playing every stroke in the book and he hooked McDonald without mercy. The Australian kept going well and when Dipper was out, he and Sibbles were too much for the later batsmen, but Hammond strode on to the end, making 250 not out in a total of 456. Listen to Cardus:

'To be present at the rise of a star in the sky and to know that it is going to be glorious – here is a moment thrilling indeed to men who live their lives imaginatively . . . In years to come we will remember 19 August 1925, for when in good times Hammond carves history out of Australian bowlers . . . we shall be proud to say that we understood well enough he was born for the company of master batsmen.'

Cardus was allotted plenty of space in the *Manchester Guardian* of those days and he made the most of it. He took some six lines to describe a single stroke of this innings:

'Once he actually drove straight for four a ball that rose sharply after pitching; while it was in the air Hammond shaped for a forward drive with full arm-swing; then, quickly seeing the ball pitch and come from the turf at a rather awkward angle, he let all his weight full on the back foot and hit the ball powerfully by means of a short-armed thrust of his bat, wristwork adding its bloom in a fraction.'

Eloquent words, but a modern critic writing for readers who saw plenty of cricket analysed on television, would say, grossly enough 'he hit it on the up'. Even now, Cardus was not done with this innings. Next day, he resumed:

'For flexibility of style, his cricket went far beyond anything else I have ever seen from a player still in his twenties . . . Hobbs would have needed to recapture his finest arts to keep himself in the picture with this young England batsman of tomorrow.'

No holding back there – Cardus had never seen anything like it – but how fortunate were the cricket-lovers of the time to see Hammond in his youth and vigour, and then to read about it in the master's glittering prose! I haven't been able to resist these extended quotations which exemplify the general view of Hammond, though *Wisden* described him, justly but unromantically, as 'brilliant but somewhat inconsistent'. Nevertheless, he acquired his first representative honour – he had yet to play for the Players at Lord's – when he was chosen for the MCC side to tour the West Indies that winter.

The West Indies had not yet attained Test Match status and the strength of the touring side reflected this. It contained only four Test players and was best described as being of strong county standard. The games were mostly played on good batting wickets and were mostly drawn. Hammond distinguished himself, scoring 732 runs at an average of 48.80 and taking 20 wickets. He played a wonderful innings in the first representative match scoring 238 not out in five hours, and was always doing something useful.

It was on this tour that a certain rivalry sprung up between Hammond and Learie Constantine. Much of an age, they were players of a similar kind – both brilliant batsmen, lively bowlers and brilliant fielders. Each was his country's up and coming man. There is a suggestion that Constantine felt himself slighted by something that Hammond said, or didn't say, early in the tour, and he set out to show Hammond who was the master. Honours were about even on the tour – each dismissed the other twice – but they would be looking to renew their battle, two years later.

The tour is better remembered for the fact that Hammond contracted a disease which almost killed him. The details remain obscure, but it seems that he was stung by a mosquito on the site of an existing strain, however he still played in his final game even though he was unfit to do so, and came home with a very severe form of blood-poisoning. He spent most of the summer of 1926 in hospital, where it seemed for a while that his leg would have to be amputated to save his life. Fortunately for him and for cricket, this proved unnecessary, and he made a complete recovery. In a period when it is fashionable to emphasise the faults of some of the traditional rulers of the game, among them Sir Pelham Warner, it is pleasing to be able to record that Sir Pelham visited Hammond in hospital and heartened him by assuring him that he was destined to recover and to do great things yet against the Australians.

The Australians were in England that summer and lost the Ashes in the final Test to one of England's strongest sides. It is very probable that a fit Hammond would have played for that side and rendered it stronger still, but his illness had further delayed his Test debut. It must have seemed to him that he would never make that first Test appearance, but he was still only 23. If he could recover his health and strength, the ball was still at his feet.

Gloucestershire once again demonstrated their faith in Hammond, sending him to South Africa to recuperate. He both coached and played at the Green Point club in Capetown and came to love the country. He went on tour there three times, spent a large part of the war there, and ended his days in Durban.

Back in England for the start of the 1927 season, he started sensationally. Sporting memories are short and the public may well have already forgotten about him or assumed that his form had left him for ever. He may have sensed this and gone all out to make an early impact, or he may simply have been filled with frustration after this second interruption of his career. In any event, the bowlers paid. Before we come to his selected Test debut, let us take a look at the month of May 1927, for it was then that he established himself as the major English batsman of his generation.

It began at the unlovely Wagon Works ground in Gloucester. The opponents were Yorkshire, second in 1926 and champions in the four preceding years. Hammond had made only 213 in 12 previous innings against Yorkshire, and an attack made up of four Test bowlers – Rhodes, Macaulay, Kilner and Waddington – plus the formidable Emmot Robinson may not have expected too much trouble from him. He made 27 out of a first-innings total of 189, which was par for the course for most sides against Yorkshire. The visitors headed this small score before losing a wicket, and went on to make 468 for 5, with centuries from Holmes and Sutcliffe. Hammond, playing in restrained style, scored 135 and thus made his mark early in the season, even though his side lost by an innings.

Gloucestershire went on to the Oval and fielded out to a huge score of 557 for 7 declared, of which Tom Shepherd made a career best of 277. It would have been understandable and forgivable if Gloucester had now caved in, but this was not the way of Hammond, or of Alf Dipper. They made a century apiece, Dipper going on to 186, but they just failed to save the follow-on and it was all to do again. This time, Dipper did fail, but Smith and Sinfield backed Hammond up as he scored 128 in as many minutes and the game was saved. It was the first time Hammond had made two centuries in a match; he was to do so seven times in all, setting a record not broken until Zaheer did it in the 1980s.

There followed a double failure against Yorkshire at Dewsbury, and then a scintillating performance at Old Trafford, again before the approving eyes of Cardus. Gloucestershire were put out for 235 by the

12

county champions, but Hammond made 99 of these, scoring his first 50 in 70 minutes. Lancashire headed this score by 101, and then Gloucestershire took their strong attack apart. Lyon and Dipper made 90 in less than an hour, and Hammond 187 at a run a minute. Cardus rhapsodised:

'It was one of the greatest innings ever witnessed on the ground. No other living Englishman could have given us cricket so full of mingled style and power, an innings of strength, bravery, sweetness and light . . . in his own way, another Trumper in the making.'

There was no doubt where Cardus stood and he remained Hammond's most fervent admirer to the end. The match was drawn, Gloucestershire making 510; and people were now beginning to talk of the possibility of Hammond making 1,000 runs in May. Only Grace had ever done this, way back in 1895, though Tom Hayward in 1900 had scored 1,000 before the end of May, having started the season in April. It was only 20 May, and Hammond had scored 712. He had three matches to play, and to the uninitiated it seemed almost easy. But nothing is ever exactly easy in first-class cricket and Leicestershire brought him down with a bump, Geary and Skelding seeing him off for 4 and 30. Alec Skelding will be remembered as a popular and skilled umpire, but he was also a deceptively fast bowler and he beat Hammond for pace on this occasion. Hammond's aggregate was now 746, with two matches to go – a very different proposition. Against Middlesex he made a glittering 83 and was then out for 7, so that he came to Southampton on 28 May needing 164. Meanwhile, Charles Hallows of Lancashire had been scoring heavily, and at this point was 44 ahead in the race. It seemed that Hammond's thunder had been stolen.

Rowlands struck the first blow by winning the toss for Gloucestershire and then the Hampshire fielders collaborated, though quite unwillingly, by dropping every catch they were offered – the best estimate is five. Hammond was by all accounts batting rather frenetically, but he took full advantage of the missed catches and a short boundary, hitting 6 sixes and 27 fours in his 192. The deed was done; meanwhile poor Hallows was put out for 14 and 27 by Worcestershire, who were having a terrible season in which they won only one match. It looks as if Hallows' nerves got the better of him, but it is pleasant to be able to record that he made *his* 1,000 in May in the very next season.

Gloucestershire were also having a terrible season, for all Hammond's brilliance. To this point they had played seven matches without a win – indeed without even leading in the first innings. So it continued for the rest of the season, Hammond making heaps of brilliant runs, Gloucester making nothing of it. It is tempting to go on with the recital of Hammond's success, but this is supposed to be a book about his Test career. Let us merely note that his first nine innings in June were: 76, 63, 197, 58 not out, 29, 116, 110, 5, 105 not out, and that by 17 June he had scored 1,801 runs with nine centuries in 23 starts. If the fine weather had held and he had stayed on his feet, he must have had a good chance of breaking all records for a season, even of scoring 4,000 runs, but the monsoon season began in mid-June and he finished with 'only' 2,969. Nevertheless, he had been the sensation of the season and was rightly made one of *Wisden's* Five Cricketers of the Year. More importantly from our point of view, he was selected for the MCC side to tour South Africa, and embarked on his Test career at last, at the age of 24.

3 Test cricket at last

The England team which went to South Africa that winter was not a strong one and the critics at home said so, very outspokenly. Of the 15 players, only six had appeared in Test cricket, and several of the newcomers were to make no mark. GR Jackson of Derbyshire was picked as captain, but he declined for business reasons and was replaced by RT Stanyforth, a Yorkshireman who had never played in county cricket. Nor had Ian Peebles, who had only made his first-class debut in a Gentlemen-Players match towards the end of the 1927 season. All in all, it seemed that South Africa were being taken pretty lightly.

All went well to begin with. The MCC bowlers were too much for the opposition in the early matches and Sutcliffe, Holmes and Tyldesley made plenty of runs. Hammond took some time to get going and didn't pass 50 in an innings till his sixth match, against Transvaal. Then, however, he went on to 132, at a time when the MCC had got themselves into a bit of a hole. It is interesting to note that on the very same day a 19-year-old playing for New South Wales for the first time announced himself with a chanceless 100. The name was Bradman.

Hammond scored 61 in the next match, against a fairly strong South African XI and went into the first Test with some runs behind him. There had never been any question of leaving him out, even when he was struggling a little; apart from his batting, he was an important member of the attack and had taken 6 for 32 in that final match.

The teams for the first Test at Johannesburg, were unusually inexperienced – six men on each side were making their debut – and the course of the play reflected this. South Africa batted very unevenly on a pitch which always gave the fast men something to work on, and were all out for 196, of which Catterall made 86. George Geary took 7 for 70. Percy Holmes was out without scoring, but Sutcliffe and Ernest Tyldesley, the most experienced men on the England side, added 230 and England were well placed when Hammond came in. Tyldesley soon followed Sutcliffe, and from then on Hammond fought alone. He was last out for 51, the last seven batsman having made just 13 runs between them.

This was to be the pattern of the series, the good batsmen making enough runs, the less good being sunk without trace. Promnitz did the damage with his off-spins, but Hammond, hitting out when Peebles joined him, was caught at mid-on from the bowling of CL Vincent, a slow left-arm bowler. Vincent was to dismiss him ten times during his Test career, a remarkable feat for a player who is largely forgotten today. The explanation is probably not so much that Vincent had some mysterious power over Hammond as that few other South African bowlers had any power over him at all.

England led by only 117, but it was enough. The wicket was now faster than it had been in the first innings, and Hammond joined Geary in the attack to destroy South Africa. At one time, they were 26 for 6, and only a ninth-wicket stand of 80 by Coen and Vincent brought them to the semi-respectable total of 170. Geary, this time, took 5 for 60, and Hammond 5 for 36. This was to remain his best bowling performance in a Test innings. Their bowling was described as 'good but not unplayable' – the eight players dismissed for single-figure scores will have had their own opinion – and Hammond was described as occasionally achieving off-turn. In the modern jargon, we would speak of off-cutters. England needed only 54 to win, and Holmes and Sutcliffe got them without trouble.

The second Test at Capetown followed immediately and produced an altogether more interesting match. South Africa brought in Bissett, a young fast bowler, and he went through England in double quick time. Hammond made the top score, getting 43 out of a modest total of 133. He was described as playing 'perfect if subdued cricket' – he might well be subdued when, for the second time, his colleagues were falling all about him. The MCC had arrived with three experienced Test batsman in Sutcliffe, Holmes and Tyldesley, and it is interesting to note that the South African papers were already describing these three and Hammond as the Big Four. South Africa failed to capitalise on their success and were all out for 250. Geary had developed elbow trouble and was possibly not at his best, but Hammond and Freeman rose to the occasion, taking three and four wickets respectively.

England batted consistently in the second innings, Holmes, Sutcliffe and Tyldesley all coming off. Hammond came in at 233 for 2, tried to hit a full-toss out of the ground and was brilliantly caught on the leg boundary for 14. Palm, the catcher, was playing in his only Test and didn't make many runs, but as he leapt for the catch he may well have thought that he hadn't lived in vain. England had slipped back a little, but Bob Wyatt played his best innings of the series, making 91, and England totalled 428. Although England were now without Geary, they dismissed South Africa for 224 and went two up. Hammond again bowled well, taking 2 for 50 in 30 overs. He also took his first three catches in Test cricket, all off Freeman.

★ ★ ★ ★ ★

South Africa continued to chop and change for the third Test at Durban, bringing in three new caps. One of these, AL Ochse, was decidedly fast and their attack had a distinctly modern look with four fast or fast-medium bowlers. England were forced to make one change, bringing in Staples for the injured Geary. South Africa made the modest score of 246, and might not have made so many but for a bizarre piece of captaincy by Stanyforth. Wyatt, often underrated as a bowler, opened with a spell of 11-10-1-1, was taken off, and not brought back until the score was 241 for 7, whereupon he took two more wickets and finished with figures of 13-10-4-3. Inexplicable. England batted consistently and Hammond played his best innings of the tour. *The Rand Daily Mail* wrote that he played with

> 'none of the fierce aggression characteristic of his play in England, but with beautifully correct and perfect footwork and back-play.'

Since he scored 90 in 152 minutes, one wonders how fast he would have gone if he *had* displayed fierce aggression. He fell to Vincent, again, and England were all out for 430, 184 ahead. South Africa now came good, making 464 for 8 in a most consistent batting display, and Deane was able to make a token declaration. England scored 132 for 2, Hammond 1 not out.

★ ★ ★ ★ ★

Once again, one Test followed immediately on the one before. The fourth match was back at Johannesburg and England, still without Geary, played like jaded men. Hammond looked as tired as anyone, as he was entitled to – he had already bowled 108 overs as well as bearing his full load when batting. It was left to him to do most of the work thrown on the attack by Geary's absence. South Africa had recalled Alf Hall, a Lancashire-born left-arm fast-medium bowler who had last played for them five years earlier against Frank Mann's team, and he and Bissett effectively won the match. They took all the wickets in England's first innings of 265. Hammond looked more at ease than the other batsmen, but Hall had him caught at the wicket for 28. South Africa headed the England score by 63, the great Herbie Taylor making South Africa's first century of the series. Hammond and Staples bore the brunt of the bowling. Hammond took 3 for 62, and he was beginning to look a very tired man.

Hall and Bissett again led the way in putting England out for 215, but this time Hammond was lbw to Vincent for 25. South Africa needed only 153 to win and their chance was enhanced when Stanyforth was cut under the eye and had to go off. Freeman went behind the stumps and did pretty well. On the face of it, it seems odd that England sacrificed their leg-spinner in this way, but on a matting wicket the quicker men were probably a better bet and Peebles, the team's other leg-spinner, didn't bowl at all in the innings. South Africa faltered before Staples, but got home by four wickets. Hammond dismissed Taylor for the second time in the match, a considerable achievement.

★　　★　　★　　★　　★

England therefore had to save the last Test at Durban if they were to win the series, and it must be said that they never looked like doing so. Stanyforth was still unfit and Elliott came in to keep wicket, Stevens captaining England for the only time. England decided to strengthen their batting line-up by bringing in Dawson for Peebles. It is a policy that seldom works, and it didn't then. Dawson made 14 and 9, and Peebles' bowling was missed. The first day was washed out and Deane, who had to force a win, put England in. It was the first Test story all over again; Sutcliffe, Tyldesley and Hammond made 217 between them (Hammond 66) and nobody else made very many. England were all out for 282. Holmes was shot out by Bissett for nothing, and is said to have assured his team-mates that it wouldn't happen again because he could play Bissett with an adjectival broom-handle. They awaited the event, but had first to get South Africa out.

England started well enough, getting 4 out for 95, but Bob Catterall made a fine forceful 119 in two and a quarter hours, and Deane was able to declare at 332 for 7. Bissett justified his faith, getting Holmes for nothing again, to the considerable joy of the Englishmen, who seem to have been a particularly light-hearted bunch, and running through the rest, taking 7 for 29. England were all out for 118, Hammond very well caught at point off a bouncer for 3. South Africa won by 8 wickets and had deservedly squared the rubber.

Hammond had made a good, if not sensational start to his Test career. His batting had been widely acclaimed as sound and stylish, though even at the end of the series one South African critic was able

18

to write that Ernest Tyldesley was the most-feared batsman in the side
– and indeed Hammond was third in the averages, behind Sutcliffe and
Tyldesley. He had had a hard tour, doing a good deal of bowling, and
he was at least a probable for the full-strength team at home. If this
seems a slightly tentative judgment, we should remember that Hobbs,
Hendren and Woolley were still very much on the stage and that
whoever led the side at home would almost certainly be a batsman.
Hammond had still to make the place his own.

	Innings	N.O.	H.S.	Runs	Average	100	50
1927/28	9	1	90	321	40.12	–	3

	Balls	Runs	Wickets	Average
1927/28	968	399	15	26.60

4 A new Test nation

Hammond made a brisk start to the 1928 season, scoring 205 not out in the second match against Surrey, and 118 not out against Notts. In between, he took 10 for 134 against Sussex. The 118 began a sequence in which he made nine scores of 50 or more in 11 consecutive innings and, although he failed in the Test Trial, he was an automatic selection on form for the first Test at Lord's. The West Indies, playing in their first Tests, were not regarded as a threat and the selectors were clearly going to experiment in their search for the ideal side to defend the Ashes in the coming winter. Hendren and Woolley were not even picked for the Trial, in which Hobbs aggravated an injury and ruled himself out of the Test. Hallows came in to partner Sutcliffe, Chapman resumed the captaincy and Jardine made his Test debut.

The West Indies seem to have been a little out of luck in this match. Their fast bowlers had Sutcliffe and Hallows in all sorts of trouble at the start without actually getting them out, and Tyldesley was also in trouble early on. He survived this period, and he and Hammond got on top with some lively batting. They got some mixed reviews. Col Philip Trevor, in one of his less happy assessments, wrote that this was 'not quite the real Hammond', but Cardus thought that he 'mingled strength and charm in proportion'. They put on 77 in less than 50 minutes, Hammond's share 45, which looks very reasonable at this distance, whatever Col Trevor thought. One must of course remember that the West Indies were not highly rated. Tyldesley went on to score 122, and England were out for 401 early on the second day. The West Indians, understandably and collectively nervous, made no sort of showing in their first innings and were all out for 177, Jupp being the most successful bowler with 4 for 37. Hammond did not bowl.

Chapman now faced an awkward decision. With not much more than a day to go, he would normally have enforced the follow-on without hesitation, but Larwood had been injured during the first innings and would not take the field. However there was no great risk involved – there was hardly time for the West Indies to build up a lead and also to bowl England out, always supposing them capable of doing either. Chapman put them in again, though he can scarcely have been very

20

optimistic about forcing a win. It is always tempting, in a biography, to see one's subject at the centre of every incident but it is very probable that Hammond's bowling ability was a big factor in the decision. Certainly, he opened with Tate and took an early wicket; thereafter Jupp and Freeman did the business and England won by an innings.

★   ★   ★   ★   ★

Hobbs was fit again and came back for the Old Trafford Test. England paid Hammond a little compliment by replacing Larwood with a spinner, Jack White, leaving Hammond to open the bowling with Tate. In the event, he did little more than take the shine off, the spinners doing most of the damage. The visitors made a pretty good start, reaching 100 with only one wicket down, but they collapsed before Freeman who took 5 wickets, and were all out for 206. Hobbs and Sutcliffe made 119 for the first wicket – their tenth Test century partnership – and although three wickets then fell quickly, Hammond and Jardine, in their first substantial partnership, added 120, with Hammond making 63. Cardus has some interesting remarks on this. He comments that Hammond held his best strokes in abeyance for much too long and that he 'suffered the indignity of a silly mid-on' and allowed the slow bowlers to operate with no man in the deep. The batsmen scored their 120 in 130 minutes, and one is thankful that Cardus was spared the sight of modern Test cricket.

England hardly capitalised on their good beginning and were all out for 351, the only excuse being that Chapman had to retire hurt. The score was good enough to secure the second innings win of the summer with the West Indies collapsing again to the spinners, though Hammond chipped in with the wicket of George Challenor, the batting star of the team. He also took three catches, two of them brilliant, and altogether had a very good match.

★   ★   ★   ★   ★

In retrospect, the selectors of 1928 look an ungrateful lot, for they now dismissed three of the successes of the second Test. Jardine, Jupp and White were replaced at the Oval by Leyland, Hendren and Larwood. The explanation is that they were trying out every possible combination with Australia in mind – but surely they knew all they needed to know about Hendren?

Once again, the West Indies got away to a good start, and once again they failed to make the most of it. Challenor and Roach began with a brilliant stand of 91 in 70 minutes, before Larwood bowled Roach.

Chapman daringly introduced Leyland, not one of the great Test bowlers, and he had Challenor taken by Hammond at slip. The predictable collapse followed, the most remarkable incident being the dropping of a catch by Hammond – he didn't drop very many. Constantine was the lucky batsman and he made the most of it, adding 54 in half an hour with Wight, before Hammond made amends by having him caught by Chapman, running hard from deep mid-on to hold the ball on the off-side. Chapman was in great catching form, as he usually was, and finished the innings with two fine slip-catches off Tate.

Hobbs and Sutcliffe made yet another century stand, and England were not far behind the West Indies score of 238 at the end of the first day, with only one wicket down. On the Monday, Hobbs and Tyldesley made a brisk start, but heavy rain drove the players off in mid-morning and when play was resumed, the England batsmen found it difficult to force the pace on a freshened pitch. Hobbs was out for a very good 159, and then Hammond was brilliantly caught by Joe Small at third slip for 3. It needed a rather lucky stand of 61 in very quick time by Tate and Larwood to give England a lead of exactly 200, which proved much more than adequate.

The West Indies were all out for 129, and lost by an innings for the third time. Hammond made three catches. It had been a tough introduction to Test cricket – for which they were to take a terrible revenge in due course – and England had been able to get their side into shape for the tour. Hammond would be a key member of that side; though he had not made many runs, he had bowled usefully and had taken nine catches in the three games.

Hammond's private duel with Constantine was renewed this year. The West Indian was at this period an out-and-out fast bowler, as fast as anybody in the world, not excluding Larwood, and he seemed to find even more pace when he bowled at Hammond. He dismissed him twice in the three England innings, and once in another match. Again, Hammond reciprocated with a will. He only got Constantine out once in the Tests (he may not have had the chance in every innings, for Constantine made a string of small scores) but he had him twice in other games.

Hammond went straight from the Oval to Cheltenham for the greatest all-round performance of his career, arguably the best performance by any player in a single week's cricket. In the two games of the Cheltenham Festival, his figures were:

v Surrey	139 and 143. 1 for 71, ten catches
v Worcestershire	80. 9 for 23 and 6 for 105, one catch

These figures need no commentary, but they attracted more notice at the time than Hammond's rather ordinary achievements in the Tests, and he was acknowledged as a leading all-rounder, as well as being the rising batting star.

	Innings	N.O.	H.S.	Runs	Average	100	50
1928	3	0	63	111	37.00	–	1
To date	12	1	90	432	39.27	–	4

	Balls	Runs	Wickets	Average
1928	234	103	3	34.33
To date	1202	502	18	27.88

5 The world's greatest

Whatever the stars of other countries might achieve, *the* important clashes in Hammond's time were the battles for the Ashes, and Hammond was now to try his skill against Australia in Australia. It was to be the first of seven rubbers in which he was to figure, and distinctly the most successful. In his story, it deserves detailed consideration and I make no apology for treating the matches at some length.

The English team was by common consent one of the strongest ever. It is true that PGH Fender, a critic to be respected, made a strong case for Douglas' side of 1920-21 to be ranked above it, but old players have always tended to believe that the sides they played in were the strongest-ever, and we cannot get away from the fact that Douglas lost 5-0.

Chapman led an enormously strong batting side, including Hobbs, Sutcliffe, Hammond, Mead, Jardine, Ernest Tyldesley, Hendren and Leyland. The bowling was a little weaker and its make-up looks odd to our eyes in that there was only one fast bowler, Larwood, three fast-medium men – Tate, Geary and Staples – and two spinners in White and Freeman. Ames and Duckworth, the wicket keepers, completed the party. We would say today that the side was a bowler short, but it survived the early loss of Staples and lost only one match. It was a weakness that there was no genuine all-rounder, although Tate had done the double in the 1928 season and Geary could bat pretty well. Whatever side was selected for the Tests, Hammond would be the fifth bowler, and was undoubtedly in for a busy time.

The tour began with a rain-interrupted draw against Western Australia in which Jardine made a century and Hammond failed to get going. There followed a high-scoring draw against South Australia. This time, Hammond batted spectacularly, coming in at 93 for 2 and making 145 at a run a minute. The *Sydney Morning Herald* correspondent wrote approvingly of his 'running down the wicket daringly to Grimmett' which says a lot about his confidence and will be seen to be in stark contrast with his troubles against Grimmett in England. On a perfect pitch, Chapman also made 145, and MCC totalled 528, but South Australia came within four runs of this and critics began to wonder about the English attack. Staples had already fallen ill and gone home and Tate wasn't playing, but Larwood conceded 116 in 20 eight-ball overs and it was already apparent that the side would be relying heavily on White's ability to close up an end. That would be Hammond's job too, and he was to do it well.

Hammond was rested against Victoria, where Jardine and Hendren made 100s, and then came the most spectacular batting of the tour. MCC ran up 734 for 7 against New South Wales at five runs an over. Jardine made his third successive 100 and Hammond and Hendren ran riot. They added 333 for the fourth wicket, and Hammond made 225 in 324 minutes. This was Hammond's first encounter with Don Bradman, who was put on to bowl with the score approaching 600. Hendren hit him for 16 off four balls and was caught off the fifth. Hammond then took 24 off an over from him and was then run out – by Bradman.

If Hammond's autobiography is to be believed it was an absolutely superb return, but this doesn't quite agree with the *Sydney Morning Herald* whose writer simply recorded the throw as 'straight but rather high'. Some people are hard to please, but anyway Hammond was out. New South Wales made a brave reply, Bradman making 87 in their 349, and once he and Kippax had settled down in the follow-on, the cricket wasn't taken *too* seriously, Jardine, Hendren and Sutcliffe all taking unaccustomed exercise. It is worth noting that Hammond bowled 32 overs in the match, on top of his long innings. Chapman still regarded him as an all-rounder. He was rested for the next match and then failed against Queensland at a moment when it hardly mattered. The stage was now set for the first Test to be played at Brisbane, not at the Woollongabba ground, but on the Exhibition Ground, which was destined to be used only twice.

Both sides packed their batting for this match. The ploy is not unusual in modern times when both captains spar for an opening at the start of a series, but it was a risky business in a timeless Test. England's batting was enormously strong, Mead being preferred to Geary and Chapman coming in at No 7, but the bowling rested on Larwood, Tate, White – and Hammond. Australia, too, had only three specialist bowlers – Gregory, Ironmonger and Grimmett – and three all-rounders, none of them very penetrative, in Kelleway, Ryder and Hendry. On the other hand, they too were strong in batting, with Bradman coming in at No 7. The toss was going to be very important.

Not much went wrong for Chapman on this tour and he won the toss. Hobbs and Sutcliffe opened quite slowly on a pitch that offered a little lift early on. Just before lunch, Gregory tried Sutcliffe with a very short bouncer and he holed out, virtually at long-stop. Mead came in and saw Hobbs run out. This time, Bradman's throw certainly was a swift one, though Fender suggests that Oldfield had to 'fetch' it a long way to complete the job. Hammond came in for his first innings against Australia and almost at once Mead was lbw to Grimmett and at 108 for 3 on a good wicket, England were in trouble.

Hammond and Jardine were to share several important partnerships during the series, and this was one of them, unspectacular though it was. They went on to the defensive against all the bowlers. Jardine was the more assertive of the two and MA Noble, for one, felt that Hammond should have been taking the fight to the bowlers. He was going down the wicket to Grimmett, but doing little with the ball when he got there. However, they were pulling things round when Hammond propped at Gregory and was caught. He had scored 44 off 126 balls and some of the criticism of his negative play may have been justified. Jardine followed him at 217, but Hendren played the innings of his life (to that date) and was strongly supported by Chapman, Tate and Larwood. It began to look as though England would bat longer than had been expected from the line-up. In this innings, they made 521, Hendren 169.

The Australian batsmen were clearly very tired when they went in with an hour to go, and they made the most terrible start. Chapman was able to set attacking fields, and Larwood slipped himself. Chapman took a stunning catch in the gully off Woodfull and Australia were 44 for 4 at the close. It was known that Gregory would take no further part in the match because of a knee injury (in fact, he never played again) and their position was desperate. Several players virtually gave themselves up on the third day and they were all out for 122.

Some Australians criticised Chapman for playing the game too hard when he now batted again, and it has even been suggested that this action left a permanent mark on Bradman, making him a tough and ruthless captain when his time came. I personally doubt this; it is difficult to see how Chapman could have acted otherwise. The only way he could possibly have lost the match would have been by enforcing the follow-on. If Australia had made 500 or so and rain had then fallen giving England a sticky wicket to bat on, anything might have happened. It is not very likely that the demoralised Australians would have managed a big score, but stranger things have happened. Chapman did the right thing.

England didn't hurry in their second innings and Hammond, coming in at 69 for 2, scored a rather casual 28 before being caught by F C Thompson, one of the substitutes. (Thompson, a prolific Queensland batsman, was one of the best Australian players never to appear officially in a Test.) Hendren had a good match, making a bright 45, and Mead and Jardine also batted well. Chapman declared at 342 for 8, not so much out of mercy as in a sensible desire to get the Australians in for another tricky final hour. Larwood got Ponsford again, but bad light then stopped play. On the last day, Australia, batting with nine men (Kelleway was ill) on a rain-ruined wicket, were all out for 66, Woodfull carrying his bat for 30. England had won by the record margin of 675 runs.

★ ★ ★ ★ ★

Both sides regrouped for the second Test at Sydney. England had got away with a three-bowler strategy once, but it would be risky to persevere with it over a whole series – sooner or later, a bowler would break down. Geary came in for Mead, a decision calculated to lighten the burden on Hammond. Australia had to replace Gregory and Kelleway, and brought in the medium-paced Nothling and Blackie, a 46-year-old off-spinner. Ironmonger was also 46, though at the time he was believed to be 'only' 41, and it is amazing today to think of two men of this age sustaining the attack in a timeless Test. Australia's other change seems yet more incomprehensible, for they dropped Bradman. He was at this time just one of their young hopefuls and by all accounts he had not batted very well at Brisbane, but it is still surprising that he was replaced by Vic Richardson, who had not over the years been much in favour with the selectors.

Ryder won the toss this time and again Australia did none too well. It was Larwood who shattered their morale (and Ponsford's hand, putting him out for the season) though Geary picked up the wickets, returning the excellent figures of 5 for 35. Australia were all out for 253 early on the second day and England now had the chance to make the rubber virtually safe. It would be surprising indeed if Australia could come back from two-nil down. No team had yet managed this, though Australia were to do so in 1936-37 – but then Bradman, in his prime, obeyed none of the natural laws. The light wasn't good and Hobbs and Sutcliffe were properly cautious until the latter, just after lunch, let fly most uncharacteristically, getting his left foot nowhere near the pitch of the ball, and was taken at cover.

Hammond walked in at 37 for 1 and we might perhaps pause to reflect that this was the very moment at which he ceased to be one of the supporting cast and became the star. He was about to play a big innings, to follow it with three more and establish himself as England's leading player for a generation. He played freely from the start, but the light got much worse and the players had to come off. There followed a very moving presentation to Jack Hobbs in recognition of his great performances in Australia over the years, and he may well have been emotionally affected. Be that as it may, he was out very soon after the resumption and there was a minor crisis, at 65 for 2. Some writers have argued that it was at this moment that Hammond transformed himself from a brilliant attacking player into a grim, disciplined international – that, from now on, he cut out the hook, ceased to dart down the wicket to the spinners, and generally began to play the percentages. I doubt whether it was this dramatic.

On this second afternoon the wicket was greasy, if not actually sticky, and the series was there for the taking if, and only if, Hammond and Jardine (who had joined him) could build an innings. Naturally they took things carefully, concentrating on keeping Grimmett out and taking what runs they could off the other bowlers. Equally naturally, having found that this policy paid, Hammond batted with similar care in the remaining matches. In two of the next three series against Australia, he was rather out of sorts and batted accordingly. The second of those series was the bodyline one, which was played pretty grimly anyway. Thereafter, Hammond was very much the senior man and ready to leave the antics to the youngsters.

I have already quoted Neville Cardus on Hammond's more responsible Test-match style, before he ever got to Australia, but this was certainly not a consistent feature of his batting against the other Test countries. I don't believe there was ever a conscious change of approach but, like other players, Hammond was affected by the atmosphere of a game as well as the tactical situation. In this match he and Jardine went quietly along to the close, when the score was 113 for 2, Hammond 33, and the innings well under way.

Overnight the scene had changed. The wicket had rolled out well and Hammond accordingly took the fight to the bowlers, scattering the attacking fields. He soon lost Jardine, run out by a fine piece of fielding with no blame attaching to either batsman, but Hendren was in fine form and scored run for run with him. Hammond went from 33 to 100 in 95 minutes, and scored a second 100 in some three hours. So much for the notion that he was playing the percentages. The simple arithmetic is impressive enough, but those who were lucky enough to be there rhapsodised about his stroke play, particularly his off-side hitting off the back foot. A chart of his whole innings shows that he hit 21 fours on the off-side, to nine on the on-side. He treated all the spinners roughly, and he was 201 at the close of the day, out of an England total of 420 for 5.

On the fourth day, Hammond went on as though there had never been a break, adding 50 more runs in an hour before suddenly losing confidence, or perhaps concentration, against Ironmonger and playing very timidly for 20 minutes before being bowled off the inside edge for 251. Nobody could understand it, and it seems that he couldn't explain it himself.

It didn't matter to anybody except Hammond, who would doubtless have liked to have passed Foster's record score of 287. The tail, led by Geary, added another 140 and England were all out for the record score in a Test of 636. Australia fought hard in the second innings in spite of Ponsford's absence; Woodfull and Hendry made centuries in their score of 397, but England needed only 15 to win and Chapman didn't trouble his senior batsmen to appear again, the tail-enders doing the job. England were well on top.

★　★　★　★　★

Naturally, England retained their winning team for the Melbourne Test. Australia made three changes. Bradman came in for Ponsford and this time he stayed – for 20 years! Two new bowlers, Oxenham and a'Beckett, replaced Hendry and Ironmonger. This gave the side the extraordinary number of four medium-pacers and only two spinners – and no fast bowler at all. The Australian cupboard was pretty bare at this time, although Tim Wall was beginning to make his mark in Shield cricket. There was a marginal improvement in the side's fielding and the batting was certainly longer, with Oxenham at No 9. Ryder won the toss, but they lost three quick wickets before he and Kippax pulled the game round, both scoring centuries. After that, only Bradman with a staunch 79, held things together and Australia were all out for 397, by no means a good score on a beautiful wicket. Hammond dismissed Bradman with a yorker, but he bowled only eight overs and it was apparent that Chapman was going to nurse his new-found batting hero.

This time it was England who had to face an hour at the wicket after fielding for almost two days, and Hobbs got out before the close, playing a rather tired stroke. It was by no means common to use a night watchman at that time, and Hammond went in at No 3 as usual and quietly played out time. Next day, he batted at his best. He was offered very little that was driveable, and took most of his runs from searing off-side hits off the back foot. He hit 17 fours in all, ten of them in the arc between cover and the bowler. He scored 157 in just under five hours on the third day, a rate which aroused no particular comment, though it would be considered pretty sensational today. In all, he made exactly 200 out of 336 made while he was in, and was out at 364 for 5. The Australians were quick to counter attack and England were all out for 417, only 20 ahead. Blackie, who had had Hammond caught, took 6 for 94 in 44 overs, a wonderful effort at the age of 46.

Most onlookers thought that the game was now veering towards Australia – it seemed unlikely that the wicket would last and there was rain about. Richardson and Hendry failed for the second time in the match, but Woodfull and Kippax restored the position and the score was 118 for 2 at the end of the fourth day. Next morning, England soon got rid of Kippax and Ryder, but the game continued its erratic course as Woodfull and Bradman took the score to 201. Tate took the new ball and at once had Woodfull caught at the wicket for a fine fighting 107, and White then took a hand, bowling Oldfield and a'Beckett for next to nothing. Now Australia reaped the benefit of that extended line-up, Bradman and Oxenham adding 93 for the eighth wicket before Bradman was out for 112, his first Test 100. Australia were 347 for 8 at the close, 327 ahead. Surely they had the match won, for 300-odd always take a deal of getting in the fourth innings.

It rained heavily in the night and this seemed to have made an Australian win certain, for the Melbourne wicket was one of the most difficult in the world when it was wet. Play began after an hour's delay and White took the last two wickets quickly. The Australian tail-enders were only too glad to get out – they wanted to be bowling on this Heaven-sent wicket. Nobody gave England any chance at all; the only speculation was whether they could reach three figures. The rest of the story belongs much more to Hobbs and Sutcliffe than to Hammond. On a really vile pitch, the two great batsmen made 105 in 138 minutes, essentially by allowing the good balls to hit them, and thumping the bad ones with all their strength. Against a rather undistinguished attack, this proved to be good enough.

An incident during this sixth day caused some discussion. Hobbs signalled for a new bat, but selected none of the array brought out to him. It was clear that he was sending a message to his captain and when he was out, that message was clear. Jardine, and not Hammond, replaced him. What is not quite clear is whether it fell to Chapman to make the change, for one account has it that he was absent from the dressing-room at the material time, but somebody took the decision to launch Jardine into the action. It was, and remains, uncertain whether Hobbs thought Hammond too impulsive to cope with the difficulties, or whether it was a matter of Jardine being the more expendable. It hardly matters, but the point is that Hammond was such an important part of the machine that his fate was the critical matter. The ploy worked. Sutcliffe and Jardine were still together at the end of the day. The score was 171 for 1, and the game half-won.

On the seventh day, the pitch was much improved, though it was never to be easy. Jardine was out after half an hour, and now at last Hammond did come in. He batted with the utmost confidence; there was no bowler fast enough to trouble him when the new ball was taken and it seemed that he and Sutcliffe might well knock off the runs. However, he was out, and in a rather bizarre way. He went down the wicket to Grimmett and came down hard on the ball, which screwed back to Oldfield who stumped him while he was still wondering where the ball had got to. Under the Laws as they stood at the time, this ranked as a run out which seemed hard on Grimmett who had beaten the batsman fairly, but the important thing was that Hammond was out for 32 and the score 257 for 3. Sutcliffe and Hendren took it on to 318, when there was a rather silly little collapse, including another run-out, a genuine one this time, but England won safely enough by three wickets and had retained the Ashes. The honours went to Sutcliffe who had made 135, but Hammond had laid the foundations in the first innings. It had been an enthralling Test match and there was another still to come.

★ ★ ★ ★ ★

In those days, it was very much the custom to treat each Test as an entity, and neither side relaxed at all. Hobbs made a tentative suggestion that he should stand down to enable the side to rebuild, but he was persuaded out of this after resting while the side visited Tasmania. (Hobbs was a very poor sailor and only visited Tasmania once, on his first tour). England made no changes for the Adelaide Test, and it is a little surprising that Australia made only one, replacing Richardson with the brilliant and graceful young Archie Jackson.

Chapman won the toss and England got away to an excellent start, Hobbs and Sutcliffe making 143 for the first wicket. It didn't last; both were out at the same score and Jardine failed, so that, at 149 for 3, Hammond was in the middle of a crisis. Hendren failed too, but Chapman now rose to the occasion, playing his best innings (39) since Brisbane, while Hammond played as solidly and composedly as in the two previous Tests. He was understandably slow. He was getting little support and he must have been very tired by now, for although he had had little to do in Tasmania, he had made the trip and he had worked very hard in the first three Tests. He took four hours to reach his 100, and the eleventh man, Jack White, was with him by that time. Hammond made 119 in all, out of a total of 334.

Australia made a terrible start, losing three men for 19, but in this series, somebody generally made runs in every innings and this time, it was Jackson, the newcomer. He batted soundly and elegantly, and found supporters in Ryder, Bradman and a'Beckett. It is odd to write of Bradman as a supporter to anybody, but the two were regarded at the time as rising stars of equal possibilities and did in fact score run for run in a partnership of 82. Jackson scored 164 and was sixth out at 287, but Tate and White did not allow the powerful Australian tail to capitalise on his efforts, and had them all out for 369, 35 ahead.

Hobbs and Sutcliffe both failed for once and were out before that small lead was wiped out, leaving Hammond who had made 602 in his last four Test innings, to take up his burden yet again. For a while, he batted as though conscious of the weight, taking two hours to reach 50, but the situation was a serious one. He and Jardine had already had two crucial partnerships in the series and this was their greatest joint effort. They scored only 185 from the time they came together just before lunch on the fourth day to the close, and they were even slower next day. Such a good judge as MA Noble was convinced that not only was this kind of batting killing Test cricket as a spectacle – what he would have said about some more recent exhibitions is better left unthought – but it was not in Jardine's own interest. Noble believed that Jardine was born to be a forcing batsman and would have been happier in that mode. This judgment appeared to have been vindicated when Jardine was caught – at silly-point – for 98 and a collapse followed.

Understandably, Hammond was too tired to take charge of both ends and although he looked safe enough, he was finally caught and bowled by Ryder when he had made 177. He had hit 17 fours, only one of them on the leg-side, which does rather suggest that he was playing the percentages this time. He was only the third batsman to score two centuries in an England-Australia Test, and only two more players have done so since. Bardsley, Sutcliffe, Compton and Morris are the successful players. In the course of this innings, Hammond overtook Sutcliffe's 734 runs in the 1924-25 series, till then the highest aggregate in a series.

Hammond had not yet won the game for his side, for England were 'only' 292 ahead on a good wicket with three wickets to fall. Tate played a typical forcing innings of 47, and the eventual lead was 348. The runs would take a lot of getting – but the wicket was still playing easily, Hammond would not be up to much bowling after batting for nearly 12 hours in all, Geary was carrying a leg injury and Tate and White had bowled 102 overs between them in the first innings – it was to be a test of stamina.

Woodfull and Jackson survived the last few overs of the fifth day and began serenely on the sixth, but White struck twice, having Woodfull and Hendry caught while Geary had Jackson caught at the wicket. Australia were 74 for 3 and struggling. However, in this absorbing series, there was always another twist to the plot and Kippax and Ryder now provided it by adding 137, Ryder being dropped off a relatively easy chance to the bowler. Jack White was severely criticised for his mistake, but it should not be forgotten that he was being worked very hard and was in his 38th year. He would have more to say in this match.

Kippax was caught off White at 211, but Bradman settled in and things looked good for Australia – but White now made amends for his dropped catch by holding a far more difficult return from Ryder. The game was beautifully balanced, however England must have been very aware that they were effectively a bowler short. Hammond came into the picture with a magnificent falling catch at slip to get rid of a'Beckett. The sixth day ended with Australia needing 89 to win and Bradman still in possession with some solid players to support him. Two years later, it would have been odds on Australia, but Bradman was not yet the power he was to become.

Next day, Oxenham and Bradman put on another 48, and Australia seemed to be almost home when Oxenham fell, again to White, who was bowling magnificently. Then, with only 29 needed, Bradman was run out. Oldfield called him for a single to Hobbs at cover, which may indicate how severe the pressure was. Hobbs was still deadly at short range, but Noble declares that Bradman would have got in if he had been backing up. We shall never know. The situation was now almost too tense for the players or the watchers, but Jack White was the coolest man on the field, and he had both Grimmett and Blackie caught. England had won by 12 runs, in one of the finest Tests ever played. White had bowled 749 balls and taken 13 wickets for 256, to share the honours with Hammond.

★ ★ ★ ★ ★

Geary was fit to play in the fifth Test at Melbourne, but England were forced to make two changes. Sutcliffe was injured and Chapman was said to be suffering from influenza. This may have been a tactical illness – he had been out of form – in any event, England were able to call on Leyland and Tyldesley, both strong replacements. Australia introduced three new caps – Fairfax, an all-rounder; Hornibrook, slow left-arm; and Tim Wall, a fast bowler whom they might perhaps have tried sooner. White, captaining England, won the toss and sent Jardine in with Hobbs. They were a little slow at the start and when Jardine got out, Hammond was strangely uncertain.

Once again, we have to remember how hard Hammond had been worked. He had made over 1,400 first-class runs in Australia and had done a good deal of bowling. Moreover, he fielded at slip and it can be argued that slip has to concentrate totally on every ball, and has to be virtually at the same pitch of readiness as the batsman each time the bowler's arm comes over. It must take more out of the fielder than fielding at, say, mid-off, where there is plenty of work but more relaxation. In matches such as the Fourth Test, where he batted for the major part of each innings, Hammond's concentration was at full stretch throughout, and may by now have been faltering. He was out for 38, excellently caught in the gully by Fairfax.

There is a suggestion that the Australians had observed by now that Hammond had eliminated the hook and, to some extent the cut, from his repertoire, and that they set out to test his cutting in this match. If so, they succeeded, for he was out trying to cut in each innings, but they had left it a little late, and it hardly mattered. There were others to do the batting job, and it was the bowling, if anything, that let England down in this last match. Hobbs, also very weary, batted for most of the first day for 142. Leyland scored 137 in his first Ashes Test and Hendren 95. England scored 519 in all, which should have guaranteed victory, but did not.

With the exception of Bradman, the Australians batted very deliberately. They scored overall at less than two runs an over and even Bradman needed 247 balls for his 123. The England bowling figures tell the story. Tate 62 overs, White 75.3 and Geary 81, and they bowled 84 maidens between them. Significantly, White used Hammond for only 16 overs, which may indicate that he *was* flagging a little. But Australia had the runs in the book and were only 28 behind.

For the first time since Brisbane, the English batting faltered – perhaps because Sutcliffe, the bedrock, was missing. Jardine was out first ball, and Larwood was sent in as night-watchman, a ploy which is seldom wholly successful, though Larwood himself was to prove an exception to the rule four years later. He got out early next day, and Hammond played a remarkably scratchy innings. Noble wrote that he was stale, his timing faulty and his strokes uncertain. He was out for 16 and the collapse continued, until England were 131 for 6. Leyland and Tate fought back, Tate collaring Grimmett and scoring off him at the rate of a run a ball, but the innings closed for 257 and Australia were set to make 286 in the fourth innings.

This would usually be reckoned a very tall order indeed, but this score had been comfortably exceeded in the preceding two Tests and the chances were reckoned to be even. Ryder took the very unusual step of sending in *two* night-watchmen, presumably to protect Woodfull, seen at the time as his trump card. Oldfield and Hornibrook did wonders, not only seeing out the day but going on until the last over before lunch on the next day. True, they were very slow and they were helped by some missed catches, but they took the edge off the bowling and Woodfull capitalised. He too was slow, but the pitch was standing up well and Larwood and Tate were very weary. Hammond was the only bowler to make any impression, taking the first three wickets, but by the time he bowled Woodfull, then regarded by Australians as 'the

34

Unbowlable', Australia were 129 for 3, with only one major batsman out. Jackson fell before the close, but Kippax and Ryder played out time. It was the first time that a Test had gone into the eighth day, although it was not a remarkably high-scoring game. Kippax was run out at 204 and immediately afterwards Ryder was given not out in the face of a very confident run-out appeal. This proved to be the last incident of what must have been a pretty dull match, as Ryder and Bradman knocked off the runs and saved Australia from a whitewash that they hardly deserved on the comparative merits.

Hammond returned to England, acknowledged as the world's best batsman. He had easily beaten the previous record aggregate for series and was the first man to average over 100. It is true that he didn't score very fast – he received 2,521 balls – but it must be remembered that the bowlers went on to the defensive against him very early and that Grimmett, Ironmonger and Blackie were three of the most accurate bowlers in history. None could deny the grace and force of his off-side strokes. He was never to dominate a series against Australia again, but he was, for now, on top of the world.

	Innings	N.O.	H.S.	Runs	Average
Series 1928/29	9	1	251	905	113.12
Career to date	21	2	251	1337	70.36

	Balls	Runs	Wickets	Average
Series 1928/9	714	287	5	57.40
Career to date	1916	789	23	34.30

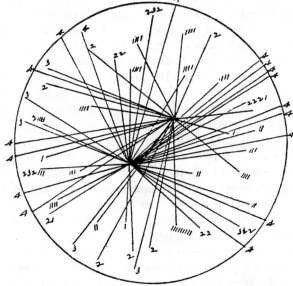

Diagram of Hammond's innings at Melbourne, 1928-29.

6   The hope of his side

Hammond returned to England established as the leading batsman in England and very generally seen as the best in the world, a title he was not to retain for long. Followers of any sport are apt to acclaim a new hero and then to expect him to live up to *their* expectations, and unsurprisingly many British sportsmen and sportswomen have wilted under the pressure. Hammond didn't wilt, but the plain fact is that he was never to have quite such a good season again. Nobody should have expected him to repeat his 1928-29 performance, of course; no batsmen, to that date, had ever had a whole run of successful Test series. Unfortunately for Hammond, a totally new phenomenon called Don Bradman had now arrived on the scene. Bradman did repeat his successes, over and over again, and Hammond was doomed to live out his Test career in the shadow of the terrible little man from Bowral. He never complained, but he must sometimes have thought that there was little justice.

In 1929, Gloucestershire's fortunes took a turn for the better. Beverley Lyon took over the captaincy and soon showed himself to be something of a genius at the black art. He was both ingenious and inspirational and his side responded, winning 15 matches and coming fourth in the championship, unlucky perhaps not to have done better still. It is doubtful if this was to Hammond's benefit – it put him under further pressure; he had to maintain his position as England's leading batsman and also score a lot of quick runs for his county. Gloucestershire were not a strong bowling side, they relied heavily on Parker, Goddard and Sinfield and didn't really have an opening attack at all. Apart from the three I have named, Charles Barnett, essentially a batsman who bowled a little, took 31 wickets and nobody else took as many as 20. Hammond missed a number of games through injury and was hardly fit to bowl all season, even if Lyon had not been desperately keen to save his strength for batting. Lyon, in fact, had to make bricks without straw, as did Percy Fender at the same period.

Hammond began the season as he had left off in Australia, scoring 365 runs before he got out. He went in at Edgbaston only six weeks after the end of a strenuous tour and scored 238 not out. It is fair to say that the long sea-voyages of those days fulfilled a real function in resting and relaxing the players, far more than a quick air-trip and a little business with one's agent, which would no doubt have been Hammond's programme today, after such a success on tour. The bank-manager and the wife might not agree, but the cricket-watchers got the benefit. Hammond made three centuries before the first Test, the only one he was to play at Edgbaston.

South Africa had virtually produced a new team for this tour. Only three of the party had been to England before, and several had yet to appear in a Test. In the longer term, the policy paid off. They lost the series, partly because they had some terrible luck in the way of illness and injuries, but they built a side for the next decade. Four men made their debut in the first Test, including 'Tuppy' Owen-Smith, who was to have his hour of glory later on, and Bruce Mitchell, who was to be their mainstay for 20 years. Chapman had not yet returned from Australia and Jack White captained England, who introduced Killick, a Cambridge undergraduate, to replace the injured Hobbs, and the brilliant Duleepsinhji. Percy Fender was in sparkling form that year, and he replaced Geary in the side that had lost at Melbourne.

England won the toss and batted pretty poorly on a good Edgbaston wicket. Killick made 31, neither success nor failure, but of the rest, only Hendren (70) and Tate (40) played up to their expected form. Hammond was out for 18, Neville Cardus describing the dismissal in rather helpless terms. 'He inexplicably played over a straight ball and was bowled.' Well, it happens to everybody sometimes, but of course Hammond was never to be allowed to fail henceforth, explicably or inexplicably. Fortunately, South Africa did no better. Catterall and Mitchell made 119 for the first wicket, but Larwood and Tate were rather too much for the others. They were all out for 250, a lead of 5 runs. Mitchell scored 88 in seven hours, giving the crowd a glimpse – a prolonged glimpse – of things to come.

England went much better in the second innings. Once again, Killick got out just when he was looking settled, on 23, but Sutcliffe and Hammond both made centuries. *Wisden,* puzzlingly, says that Hammond batted in a style similar to that of his centuries in Australia, but he batted in fact very much faster than in Australia, scoring his 138 in 200 minutes, a speed which we should consider positively breakneck today. He may have accelerated later, for Cardus comments that he 'vacillated between fine art and conscientious utility.' He and Sutcliffe put on 221 and White was able to declare at 308 for 4, leaving plenty of time for another instalment of conscientious utility from Mitchell, who made 61. The match ended in a tame draw.

★   ★   ★   ★   ★

The second Test at Lord's was one of Hammond's poor games, of which he had more than many great batsmen. England brought in O'Connor and Robins for Duleepsinhji and Fender. White won the toss again, and disaster struck. Killick was out for 3 and Hammond, after apparently starting very smoothly, was caught off a very good ball from the fast-medium Morkel. Cardus went right over the top: 'Seldom have I seen a cricketer in a Test match open an innings so easefully, so gracefully, yet so masterfully.' (Since Hammond scored only 8, Cardus was reading a lot into a little.) Then: 'The crowd were shocked when Hammond let fly at the pitch of a beautiful length ball from Morkel which was just beginning to swing away.'

Well, perhaps. O'Connor also failed, but Hendren, and then Leyland, helped Sutcliffe to right the ship, and England made 302. South Africa topped this by 20 and had England going in again in poor light soon after tea on the second day. Hammond had strained a muscle and left the field, after getting Mitchell stumped, the only stumping among his 83 Test wickets.

England got into trouble again in the second innings. White sensibly kept Hammond back until the next day, and the openers were out before a successful appeal against the light. It rained in the night and on the Tuesday morning, the lively Ochse got the ball to fly about a bit. Hendren and Leyland saw off his first assault, but Hendren and Hammond were both bowled by sharp breakbacks from Morkel. Hammond had made only 13 in the match.

England were 117 for 5, but Leyland in his typically uncomplicated style, and Tate, a genuine all-rounder at this stage of his career, made 129 in 70 minutes and White was able to declare at 312 for 8. The declaration gave little away, South Africa being asked to score 293 in three hours, and Robins, spinning the ball sharply, had them in trouble before bad light ended play. The match ended in near-tragedy when Larwood laid Cameron out with a frightful blow to the head which might well have killed him. Many of those present thought it had, but he made a good recovery.

The third Test at Leeds, was a splendid match. The England selectors continued to tinker, replacing Killick with Bowley of Sussex and ruthlessly ditching the two debutants from Lord's in favour of Woolley and Freeman, a poor reward for Robins' incisive bowling. Freeman quickly earned his keep, taking 7 for 115 as South Africa were put out for 236. Sutcliffe fell on the first evening, and Duckworth came in as night-watchman to join Hammond. Next day, some felt that the wicket-keeper outshone Hammond, and Cardus waxed sarcastic: 'Duckworth's strokes were free, Hammond's heavy with labour.'

With respect, Cardus was rather missing the point. Once he has survived the evening, and the opening overs next day, it is the night-watchman's business to get on or get out; nobody will thank him for sticking around and putting his side behind the clock, least of all in a three-day Test. In any event, the figures do not support the unkind judgment, for the two put on 55 for the third wicket, of which Duckworth scored 21. Hammond went on to a very correct 65, Woolley made 83, and England were all out for 328. Larwood was injured, but the other bowlers were irresistible and South Africa were 116 for 7 at the close. It seemed that the game was over, but Owen-Smith was still batting.

I seem to be going on rather a lot about Cardus and his idiosyncrasies in this chapter, but I cannot resist reminding the reader that this was the occasion on which the great man, assuming that there was nothing left in the match, played truant. He wrote in later life that he took off for the seaside with his girlfriend – he came to grief, as England nearly did. Owen-Smith played the innings of a lifetime, making 129 in 165 minutes, and he and Bell put on 103 for the last wicket. Cardus had to 'dismiss' the girlfriend and cobble a report together from the agency material. To do him justice, you'd never guess that he hadn't been there if he hadn't planted a few clues.

England had to make 184 to win, and they made a bit of a mess of it. Sutcliffe fell early and then Hammond made a duck, caught and bowled by Morkel, who had now had him out three times in four innings. Bowley and Woolley made a stand, but then three more wickets went down between 98 and 110, all to Vincent. Tate and Woolley retrieved the situation with some panache, adding 76 in 45 minutes – neither of those two ever adjusted his free style of play in a tense situation. England were one up, but South Africa were putting up a good fight.

★　　★　　★　　★　　★

Hammond had been carrying a leg injury ever since the Lord's Test, and although he played a full part in his next two games, bowling 24 overs for the Players at Lord's, his leg gave way at that point and he had to miss the fourth Test. Note this; he missed only two home Tests between 1928 and 1946, in each case through indisposition. Not many players have *always* been picked for England when fit and available.

Wyatt replaced him and scored an estimable 113, without dazzling anybody. Woolley made 154, and Carr, who had taken over the captaincy, was able to declare at 427 for 7. England had taken a chance by going into the Test with only three specialist bowlers, but a timely shower on the second morning gave Freeman his opportunity, and he took 12 for 171. The tourists were all out for 130 and 265, and England had won the rubber.

★   ★   ★   ★   ★

Hammond was fit again for the Oval, and England fielded their best batting side of the series. Hobbs, Sutcliffe, Hammond, Woolley, Wyatt, Leyland, Carr and Ames were the first eight. But there was a price. Hammond was still unfit to bowl and once again England had only three first-line bowlers. However it should be said that Wyatt was a much better bowler than most people thought – for example he got Hammond himself out eight times. Carr must have been relieved to win the toss, but Vincent and the others ran through the batting, in effect. In a rain-interrupted first-day, England scored 164 for 4, but they collapsed on the Monday and were all out for 258. Sutcliffe with 104, was the only success and Hammond was stumped off Vincent for 17.

South Africa made a dreadful start, losing 3 wickets for 20, but Taylor and Deane, with the best batting of the series, put on 214 at more than a run a minute. South Africa were 283 for 5 at the close and the Tuesday saw some of the brightest batting, over a whole day, ever seen in a Test. Cameron, Morkel and McMillan all made 50s and South Africa added 209 in two and a half hours. England had to go in against a deficit of 234, to save the match.

England had no idea of merely saving the game, but went for the bowling from the start with real style. Hobbs and Sutcliffe (mostly Hobbs) made 77 in 75 minutes, and Hammond then played at his finest. He scored 101 in just over two hours, and Sutcliffe made his second 100 of the match. He was the first man to do this twice in Tests. Altogether, 473 runs were scored on this final day, for only 4 wickets, and most of the runs came from the front-line bowlers. South Africa had emerged from the series with considerable credit.

Taking into account the fact that he had been injured for much of the summer, Hammond had had a pretty good series, but of course he was now being judged against the very high standard he had set himself in Australia, and it was Woolley, with an average of 126, and Sutcliffe, with four centuries, who took the eye. Nevertheless, Hammond ended the summer more firmly established than ever as the No 3 batsman in a strong team.

	Innings	N.O.	H.S.	Runs	Average	100	50
1929	8	2	138*	352	58.66	2	1
To date	29	4	251	1689	67.56	6	5

	Balls	Runs	Wickets	Average
1929	288	95	1	95.00
To date	2204	884	24	36.83

7 Conquistador

England actually went on two Test-playing tours in the winter of 1929-30, and still left the best players at home. Of Chapman's victorious team, only Hendren and Ames went to the West Indies, where Hendren was sensationally successful, and none of them went to New Zealand. Hobbs, Sutcliffe, Larwood, Tate, Jardine, Chapman, White, Duckworth – all were rested. So, of course, was Hammond, of whom much could be expected when the Australians came to England in 1930.

The two touring sides did well. A young team gathered around Frank Woolley, lost to Victoria and to Queensland, but was unbeaten in New Zealand. One would have liked to have seen the match against New South Wales, in which Bradman, Kippax and Jackson all made centuries and McCabe made 90, and Woolley responded with 219. A total of 1,607 runs were scored in four days. The other party drew 1-1 with the West Indies, the series ending with a 'Timeless Test' which had to end when the tourists had to leave to catch their boat, just as Hammond's team was to do nine years later in Durban. Hendren made 1,765 runs on this tour at an average of 135.76, and Sandham made 325 and 50 in that final match, and never played in another Test. Those selectors!

Notwithstanding all these feats, the public looked to the men who had beaten Australia in 1928-29 to repeat the dose in England. It was very soon apparent that it wasn't going to be easy. Bradman started his tour sensationally, scoring 236 at Worcester and carrying on from there. He made 1,000 runs before the end of May with a predictable inevitability. Meanwhile, Hammond was making a rather uncertain start. He scored 211 not out in an extraordinary game at Oxford in which Gloucestershire scored 627 for 2, but he didn't pass 50 in the Championship until his ninth innings, a score of 199 against Surrey, which he followed with an attractive 79 in the Test Trial. His place in the England side was secure, of course. England relied at Nottingham on their established players, eight of whom had been members of the 1928-29 party. Woolley, Robins and Richard Tyldesley came in for Jardine, who had played very little in 1929, Geary and White. The selection of two leg-spinners has an odd look today, but it was by no means unusual then, and it worked. Australia continued with the combination that had won the fifth Test in 1928-29, but brought back Ponsford and Richardson, and introduced McCabe.

★   ★   ★   ★   ★

England made a poor start. Hobbs and Sutcliffe got as far as 53, in an uncharacteristically shaky stand, before Sutcliffe was caught off Fairfax. Hammond was lbw to Grimmett when he had made only 8, the same bowler getting rid of Woolley and Hendren. With the score at 71 for 4, the Nottingham crowd must have thought they were back in 1921. However, Hobbs was still there, playing calmly and confidently, and Chapman who had been in very poor form so far, now played a typically breezy innings of 52 scored out of 82 while he was in. Larwood didn't stay long, but Hobbs stayed almost until the close before being out for 78. He had held the side together without ever taking the eye, and his unselfish work was rewarded next day.

Play was held up by overnight rain, and when the game started after lunch, England were soon all out for the relatively poor total of 270, but this soon looked a reasonable score as Australia struggled on a responsive pitch. All the England bowlers got wickets and only Kippax, the most correct and 'English' in method, showed up well. He scored 64 not out, in a total of 144, and England went in again with a comfortable lead, but not too much time if they were to force a win. Hobbs played brilliantly, starting soon after the opening of the third day and being out, stumped off Grimmett before lunch, having made 74. Hammond was lbw to Grimmett again, for 4, and he had had a poor match. When Sutcliffe had to retire hurt, England's strategy seemed to going awry, but Hendren with some good support, made sure that enough runs were made and Australia were set to make 429 to win.

Even this might not have been beyond them, for Larwood was taken ill overnight after dismissing Woodfull on the third evening. The weather was sticky and the pitch as easy as it had been at any time in the match. Hammond rose to the occasion – he took no wickets, but sent down 29 overs in long spells which enabled Chapman to preserve Robins for the attacking role which suited him. Bradman batted finely, making 131 in 260 minutes, but the innings had two climactic moments, the first when the unknown Copley, fielding substitute for Sutcliffe, took a blinding and historic catch to get rid of McCabe, and the second when Robins bowled Bradman with a googly which he left alone. There was no recovering from that and Australia were all out for 335. They had fought hard, but England were one up and their hopes were high.

★   ★   ★   ★   ★

Although Hammond had done nothing with the bat in this match and failed in his only county match before the Lord's Test, nobody expected him to be dropped, and he wasn't. Sutcliffe was still unfit and the selectors, surprisingly, moved Woolley up to open with Hobbs, to leave room for Duleepsinhji to come in after Hammond. Larwood was also still unfit and Allen replaced him, making his Test debut. White came in for Tydesley, to present a more balanced attack, for what it was worth.

Hobbs failed this time, but Woolley began in the most brilliant style, treating the attack with some disdain. Those who were there said after the event that they always knew it couldn't last, but it took a very fine catch by Wall in the gully, to dismiss him. He had made 41 out of 53, and Hammond was still only on 11. He now batted quietly and sensibly, but just as it seemed that he had dug himself in for a long innings, he made ground to play defensively against Grimmett, but missed and was bowled for 38. Things did not look well, either for Hammond or England.

Duleepsinhji was in good form, however, playing Grimmett mostly off the back foot at first, and at the other end Hendren supported him confidently. They added 104 before Hendren was caught soon after the new ball was taken. The game took another turn when Chapman and Allen failed, but Tate, never easily intimidated, joined Duleep in the next recovery. They took the score from 239 for 6 to 337, and when White came in at No10 and began to bat soundly, England's position began to look secure. It appears that at this stage Chapman, or somebody, sent out word to Duleep to have a hit. He did so with a will, and got out. England had not yet worked out that a four-day match was not quite like a three-day one. Established ideas were about to be overturned forever.

England were 405 for 9 at the end of the day. White and Duckworth added 20 with ominous ease in the morning, and Woodfull and Ponsford set off in pursuit. They began slowly and the crowd grew restive, but the batsmen knew very well what they were about and accelerated after lunch. Woodfull, remembered as the stodgiest of batsmen, scored 43 in 55 minutes, and it must have looked as if a wicket would never fall. Hereabouts, another legend was born – this was a good match for legends. King George V arrived at the ground for a brief visit. The teams were presented to him, and Ponsford was out immediately afterwards. It became fashionable to refer to His Majesty as England's best change bowler, but there is little evidence of other Royal wickets. Ponsford was out at 162.

Bradman came in, ran yards down the wicket to hit White's first ball for four, and dominated the bowling from that moment, hunting up and down the wicket to the slow bowlers and hooking and pulling Tate and Allen whenever they dropped short, and sometimes even when they didn't. Hammond, who was to bowl 35 overs in the innings, contained him as well as anyone; Bradman scored at over four an over throughout his innings, but at less than three an over off Hammond. This was to recur throughout the series. Dazzling as Bradman's speed was, he never scored with great freedom against Hammond. Woodfull was out just before the close, when the score was 404 for 2, with Bradman on 155, and the game in Australia's hands.

The slaughter continued on the third day. Bradman and Kippax began relatively slowly, taking care to wear Tate down before accelerating, but by lunchtime the total was 544. Bradman was most brilliantly caught by Chapman off White at about 2.50 pm; good judges asserted that it was the first ball he had lifted in the whole innings. Whether this is true or not, this is generally agreed to be the best of all his great innings. He had made 254 off 376 balls. At 585 for 3, Australia had nothing to lose and their sturdy middle order now hit at everything, McCabe and Richardson scoring a run a ball. Hammond picked up McCabe's wicket, but Woodfull was able to declare at tea, at 729 for 6.

Hobbs and Woolley were tired men when they went in, as, with a combined age of 90, they were entitled to be. They did their best to play out time, but might have done better to play their natural game. In his book on the series, Fender makes the interesting suggestion that Hammond might have been a better choice as opener than Woolley, but I think he forgets those 35 overs. In any event, both openers got out and Hammond and Duleep had to stay in to the close. They managed it, but Grimmett gave everybody some nasty moments.

Grimmett soon had Hammond in the morning, caught at short-leg off one which popped a little, for 32. Hendren and Duleep soon followed him and England were in terrible trouble at 147 for 5. They had their one stroke of luck when Chapman skied the first ball he received from Grimmett, and Ponsford and Richardson left it to each other. He went on to 121, alternating pad-play and mighty hits and was well supported by Allen. If Robins and White had not got into a muddle which caused White to be run out, England might just have saved the game, but they were all out for 375 and Australia needed only 72 to win.

There was a flurry of excitement when Robins took two quick wickets and Bradman was again miraculously caught by Chapman, but Australia got safely home with seven wickets and plenty of time to spare. Hammond had made 38 and 32 and bowled 39 relatively inexpensive overs. He could not be said to have failed, but he owed England some runs.

★　★　★　★　★

England made wholesale changes for the Leeds Test. Sutcliffe was fit again and he and Leyland came in for Woolley and Hendren. The bowlers, except for Tate, got the sack, Larwood, Geary and Tyldesley coming back. This was all very understandable, but the Bradman problem had not been solved. Woodfull won the toss this time. Jackson was out at once, and then Bradman went to work again. 105 before lunch, 220 by tea and 309 by the close are figures which tell their own story and it was lucky for England that the other batsmen were in less scintillating form. Australia were 'only' 458 for 3 at the close, but Bradman and McCabe were still together. Once again, Hammond was relatively inexpensive, taking 1 for 46 in 17 overs in the innings.

England got away with it, relatively speaking, on the Saturday. Three wickets, including Bradman's (334) fell quickly and they were all out for 566 when they must have been looking for another 700. 566 was always going to be enough, but things might have been worse. Hobbs and Sutcliffe stayed till after lunch and Hammond came in at 53 for 1. He started cautiously, but looked like playing a long innings. Fender suggests that he profited from observing Duleep's very positive treatment of Grimmett, and the figures rather bear this out, for Hammond scored 35 off 81 balls from the leg-spinner. Duleep himself didn't stay long, being bowled by Hornibrook, who seemed to have worked him out since that long innings at Lord's – he dismissed him in four of his last six innings at a cost of only 65 runs.

Two more wickets fell before the close. It was by no means the regular thing to use a night-watchman in those days, but when Leyland was out at 6.10 pm, Geary came in ahead of Chapman. He was immediately run out trying for a short run to Vic Richardson – a pretty felonious deed on two counts – and in came Duckworth. It was a dubious move tactically, but it proved successful. He and Hammond played out time, at which point Hammond had been in almost three hours for 61.

The next day, it rained heavily. The captains disagreed about the pitch as early in the day as 2.30, but the umpires did not order a start until 5.30 and Australia's chance of forcing a win looked slight. The sodden wicket was slow and took little spin. Neither Duckworth nor Hammond made any attempt to force the game and indeed they would have been rash to do so, given the state of game and pitch. They were still there when the umpires brought them off at 6.15 pm.

On the last day, Duckworth was finally out ten minutes past noon. He had scored 33, and used up much valuable time. Meanwhile Hammond had gone quietly along, content to keep the bowlers at bay and had reached his 100 just before Duckworth was out. It had taken him four and a half hours and was the first sizeable score he had made in the series. Although he must have been pleased enough to have saved the game, he may also have reflected on the mutability of cricket, hearing himself praised for a dogged match-saving effort when, only 18 months earlier, Australia had been at their wits' end to contain him and despaired of getting him out.

There was no getting away from the fact that the brilliant Bradman was now the world's best-known cricketer; indeed his face and history were becoming known to tens of thousands who had never before taken the slightest interest in sport, a phenomenon which would find no parallel until Denis Compton came along. All other cricketers, including Hammond, faded into insignificance beside him.

Hammond did not long survive Duckworth, being caught at the wicket off McCabe for 113. He had been slow, but had played the innings demanded of him. Chapman and Tate made a few, and England reached 391. England had to bat again, but looked safe enough until Hobbs was run out, which didn't happen often, but Bradman's throw was a fine one. So Hammond found himself back at the wicket not long after getting out and, when all interest had gone from the game, was caught at the wicket for 35 off the bowling of Grimmett, who was still giving him more trouble than any other Australian bowler. The light was very poor by now and the umpires took them off early, rather to the disgust of the Australian press. Australia were unlucky not to be one up. During his 100, Hammond passed his 1,000 runs against Australia, in his eighth Ashes Test, an English record.

★　　★　　★　　★　　★

The selectors were following the sensible policy of staying with their batsmen in the hope that they were learning how to cope with Grimmett, and switching their bowlers in the hope that they would hit upon somebody that Bradman couldn't cope with. For the second time, they retained Tate and jettisoned the rest of the attack, introducing Tom Goddard, a new cap, Nichols and Peebles. Ian Peebles was something of a gamble. He had done very well for Oxford earlier in the summer, but this has never been much of a guide to Test form when unsupported by county performance. It was worth trying though, and it nearly came off. Peebles was much less experienced than Robins, but *he* had been most cruelly exposed at Lord's; and Freeman seemed to have lost the confidence of the selectors, if he had ever had it.

Woodfull and Ponsford started very slowly on a Manchester wicket that took a little spin from the start – there had been some rain overnight – but not quickly enough to be really menacing. Peebles was the only man to beat the bat, though it was observed that Hammond was difficult to get away. The batsmen scored only 75 in 150 minutes before lunch, and Woodfull was out soon after. Bradman was at once in terrible trouble against Peebles. He was dropped by Hammond at first slip, to the general consternation, but Duleep caught him very soon after, for 14.

All England was in a ferment of excitement, wondering if the bogeyman had at last found his master. Kippax was equally troubled by Peebles; one story has it that the young man had been bowling all season at the new, larger stumps which were being experimentally used in domestic cricket and that every time he beat the bat, the ball was just a little too short and lifting over the bails. It may possibly have been so, but the effect of his beating the bat was that Chapman naturally kept him on too long and he was eventually collared by the later batsmen.

Hammond now demonstrated his great value to the side, for as Peebles tired, he came on for a new spell and bowled both Ponsford and Richardson. Peebles had McCabe lbw, bowling at the right set of stumps for once (one assumes) and Australia were 192 for 5 at tea. However, they had a long batting order on this tour, and Peebles was now 'gone'. They had reached 275 for 7 by the close and were getting out of the hole.

The wicket took spin more quickly next day, and it was not much to England's credit that Australia, with Grimmett in the lead, were able to add another 70. Hammond had bowled 21 overs for 24 runs and 2 wickets and had been the steadiest of the bowlers. Peebles, in the end, took 3 for 150, but he had been unlucky to be overbowled.

Hobbs and Sutcliffe made a splendid start. Wall beat the bat several times, but Sutcliffe took the game to him, and the great pair put up the 100 for the eleventh and last time against Australia. Hammond failed, playing on to Wall when he had made only 3. It was suggested by some that he had played back to a half-volley, which would have been uncharacteristic, but he was not having a good series. Sutcliffe was out soon afterwards and although Duleep again took good runs from Grimmett, he fell to McCabe, and England were 221 for 5 at the close, with the game well-balanced.

As it happened, that was virtually the end of the match. Only an hour's play was possible on the third day, during which England went to 251 for 8, and the last day was washed out altogether. With all to play for, the England selectors now did some curious things. The match was to be played to a finish and it was not too surprising that they dropped Chapman, although they were bitterly criticised. His strength as a batsman was his aggressive strokeplay, but he had been out of form ever since the Lord's Test, and he had taken some odd decisions as captain, particularly in his handling of Peebles. Wyatt, his replacement, was a brave batsman and a profound thinker. England supporters could only wish him luck in tackling the twin problems of Bradman, strongly supported, and Grimmett, less strongly supported, but a force to be reckoned with.

It seems strange that for a timeless match the selectors should have packed the batting, picking only three specialised bowlers; in a way, this was a compliment to Hammond the bowler, who would be filling the gap, but it was less of a compliment to Hammond the batsman, since one of the new men, Whysall was to bat at No3 to protect him. The other batsman were unchanged, Whysall replacing a bowler, Goddard. Larwood returned in place of Nichols.

★　★　★　★　★

Hammond had been in good batting form between the Tests with two not out centuries and must have been looking to re-assert himself on what would surely be the plumbest of Oval pitches. Hobbs and Sutcliffe made another cautious start, and Sutcliffe had still not come out of his shell when Hobbs hooked Wall for 4, tried to do the same to the next ball and was very well taken at short-leg. Wall had Whysall soon after lunch and, surprisingly, Duleep came in next. This was carrying the policy of protecting Hammond rather far but, initially, it worked. Duleep had played Grimmett more confidently than the other batsmen throughout the summer, and once again he sailed into him. Grimmett was taken off, and Hornibrook replaced him, but did no better. Grimmett came back and this time had Duleep at once, skying the ball to mid-off. Grimmett was never a man to take liberties with. Duleep had made 50 from only 78 balls, but 162 for 3 was not a good score in a timeless Test. Sutcliffe was still very much in possession, but Hammond had to come off if England were to make a really big score.

He didn't come off. He could make little of Grimmett, and even less of McCabe, off whom he scored just one run off 15 balls before playing on, again, to a ball which may have come back a little. He had scored only 13. Leyland also failed, and England were 197 for 5. Wyatt had been regarded as a poor replacement for the dashing Chapman, and his selection had been almost universally condemned – there had even been an anonymous letter threatening his assassination! He may well have felt pretty apprehensive, after all this, as he came in to face a considerable crisis. He got a most heartening reception. The crowd, reasoning no doubt that it wasn't his fault he had replaced Chapman, applauded him warmly all the way to the wicket, and applauded him again when he got off the mark. Wyatt responded with a typically brave innings. Sutcliffe had survived the earlier alarms in his usual imperturbable fashion, although he had batted very slowly. He now took charge and Wyatt dropped into the supporting role, and by the close they had taken the score to 316. It was by no means enough, but something had already been saved from the wreck.

They went on to 367 the next morning, before Sutcliffe was out for 161. It had been one of his greatest innings. Wyatt soon followed him, with 64, and nobody else did much, the innings closing for 405. Ponsford had been suffering from a chill, and seemed to decide to get his runs before his strength ran out. He reached 50 in only 65 minutes and carried on at the same excellent pace to score 110 in 159 minutes, with only one chance. (Duckworth was having a very poor match and put down several chances.) Bradman joined Woodfull and scored 27 in three short spells before the close. Play was interrupted on both the second and third days by recurrent showers. Woodfull was out on this second day, for 54.

Only three and a half hours play was possible on the Monday, and Bradman and Jackson were at the wicket for most of it. Australia were 403 for 3 at the end and the Lord's match was repeating itself with a deadly sameness. However there was an interesting variation on the Tuesday, which was to have dire consequences. The ball was flying about after the rain, and it was observed that Bradman backed away from one or two of Larwood's kickers. Many people see in this the genesis of bodyline; it was certainly the only chink that had been discerned in Bradman's armour, apart from that uncertainty against Peebles at Old Trafford. Victory, of course, has a thousand fathers, and there are many theories about the origin of bodyline, but the flinching was recorded at the time by Fender. Bradman was out at last for 232, caught by Duckworth off Larwood, though many people on the ground thought he hadn't touched the ball, and, as the wicket eased, McCabe, Fairfax and Oldfield took Australia out of reach. England had to go in again, 290 behind.

It was far too many. Hobbs failed again, not surprisingly after such a long stint in the field, and his wonderful Test career thus ended sadly. What would have been the fifth day was completely washed out and that only prolonged the agony. Whysall and Sutcliffe were out early on the sixth morning and Hammond came in at 118 for 3. Now, when it was too late, he batted finely, defying the spinners while the rest of the batting folded about him. He scored 60 and was last out, England lost by an innings and 39 runs.

If one looks at Hammond as an all-rounder, he really didn't have a bad series in 1930. He scored 306 at an average of 34 and although he only took five wickets, they were all front line batsmen, McCabe (twice), Ponsford, Woodfull and Richardson, and he conceded only two

50

runs an over. He and Tate were the only bowlers to contain the batsmen at all effectively. But judged by the high standard he had set himself in the previous series, he had failed, and the comparison with Bradman made this all the more apparent. It may seem unfair to judge him against the master-spirit of the age, but the fact is that he did live in Bradman's shadow for the rest of his career, right to the ironic end. From time to time, Bradman would start a series badly, but he generally finished on top, the bodyline series always excepted. Still, Hammond had more than justified his selection and certainly had no clear English rival, though the selectors must have had high hopes of Duleepsinhji, hopes doomed to be disappointed. Hammond's figures were:

	Innings	N.O.	H.S.	Runs	Average	100	50
1930	9	–	113	306	34.00	1	1
To date	38	4	251	1995	58.67	7	6

	Balls	Runs	Wickets	Average
1930	890	302	5	60.40
To date	3094	1186	29	40.89

Immediately following the fifth Test, Gloucestershire met the Australians in a remarkable match which it would be a shame to ignore. Woodfull, Wall and Oldfield rested, but the Australian side was still a strong one and when Gloucestershire were whisked out for 72 on a drying wicket, the usual big Australian win over a county was expected. The Australians may have batted a little carelessly but, if so, Parker and Goddard took full advantage. Ponsford and Bradman, who never gave anything away, made runs, but nobody else did and they were all out for 157 before tea on the second day. Hammond batted quite superbly in the second innings, scoring 50 in under an hour and being undefeated at the close, with 76 out of a total of 147 for 3.

Hammond was out early on the third morning, and Hornibrook bowled the rest out cheaply. The county made 202, leaving Australia needing only 118 to win. Lyon had no runs to spare, and he opened with Goddard and Parker. The latter, scurvily treated by the England selectors since 1921 when he had played his only Test, had a point to prove, and he believed that the match could still be won. He may have tried too hard at the start, for he certainly bowled less accurately than usual. McCabe and Jackson scored 59 for the first wicket. The match was more than half won, and it is said that several players went into the town for haircuts they hadn't had time for in London. Scouts were soon out searching for them, three quick wickets having fallen. At lunch, Australia were 67 for 3, and people were beginning to wonder.

51

The Australians must still have been confident. After all, Bradman was still in, and had he not scored 2,564 runs on tour already, only 6 runs short of Trumper's record with four matches still to come? But Charlie Parker was now well in the groove; he dismissed Kippax and, after Ponsford had been brilliantly run out by Sinfield, he bowled Bradman. Australia were 81 for 6 now, and 86 for 7 when a'Beckett lashed out at Parker and was caught.

Grimmett and Hurwood put their heads down and grafted their way towards the target, but when only ten runs were wanted, Parker had Hurwood lbw on about the twentieth confident shout. Hornibrook, no batsman, joined Grimmett, who now had to farm the bowling and do what he could to win it on his own. Hornibrook was dropped at the wicket, and then, with only three runs to be got, Grimmett holed out at cover after batting for an hour for 12. Hornibrook and Walker, the reserve keeper, batted for four overs, the fielders appealing at every other ball; a leg-bye came and then an edged single from Hornibrook. Finally, with all Bristol holding its breath, a Goddard appeal won the verdict, and a thrilling match ended in a tie. It may have been some slight consolation to Hammond, but the Ashes had still been lost.

8   Jack of all trades?

The side that went to South Africa in 1930-31 was much stronger than the 1927-28 combination. The intention was to send more or less the best possible team, although the omission of Sutcliffe was severely criticised and with hindsight, it can be seen that Geary would have been very valuable on the matting wickets. Larwood was also left out, but this was less surprising, for he had been totally unsuccessful against Australia and anyway the wickets wouldn't offer him much.

The batting was strong. Chapman had been restored to the captaincy and Wyatt played under him. The side had been picked before the Oval Test, and Wyatt was not the sort of man to worry unduly about status. Hendren, Hammond and Leyland were the experienced professional core and were joined by Sandham and Turnbull. It seems a little odd to class Sandham among those of less experience – he had scored 375 runs in his last Test match – but he had been consistently neglected by the selectors and had played in only 14 Tests. He was to play in no more. The bowling was in the hands of Tate, White, Goddard and Peebles, who had played against Australia, and Allom and Voce, who had not. Hammond would be expected to do his share and, on the evidence of 1927-28, would do it well. The wicket-keepers were both from Lancashire – Duckworth and Farrimond – a rare occasion when a man who didn't often play for his county was thought good enough for England.

There were only two specialist opening batsmen in the side, and Hammond after making exactly 100 against Western Province in the first match, was asked to go in first against Griqualand West. It was no secret that he didn't care for the job, but he scored 53. Sandham was injured in a motor accident after the third match and played no more on the tour. Happily, he made a complete recovery and was playing again in 1931. Chapman was reluctant to persevere with the experiment with Hammond – or perhaps Hammond was reluctant – and he tried first Leyland and then Jack White as partners for Wyatt, but he was probably going to have to come back to Hammond at some stage.

The pressure on him to do so was increased by events in the first Test, at Johannesburg. South Africa made a poor start, being reduced to 81 for 9 by Tate, Voce and Peebles. At this point a very easy catch was put down off Peebles, and this proved to be the turning-point. McMillan and Newson added 45 for the last wicket, and then Nupen got the openers, Wyatt and Leyland, out cheaply. Hammond made the top score of 49, but *Wisden* criticises him for his excessive caution on the second day. It *was* Boxing Day, and his eye may not have been at its keenest, nor his legs at their swiftest. England finished only 67 ahead and the South Africans, batting consistently, retrieved the postion, scoring 306. Voce and Hammond were distinctly the best bowlers, Hammond taking 4 for 63 in 25 overs, still on Boxing Day.

England needed 240 to win, and this time Catterall, an excellent batsman but quite an ordinary medium-pace bowler, got the openers out and when Nupen had Hendren caught, the score was 30 for 3. Hammond was again the batsman most likely to succeed and he made 63 before being stumped off Vincent. The score was now 131 for 4, and with Turnbull well set, England had a real chance, but it wasn't to be. Nupen was both accurate and sharp, and he took 6 for 87 and bowled South Africa to a 28-run win. As it turned out, this was the only match to be finished, and it decided the series, but it certainly wasn't Hammond's fault.

★　　★　　★　　★　　★

In a way, both Nupen and Hammond were poorly rewarded. Before the Tests began there had been considerable dissension in the South African camp, and a strong body of opinion in favour of bringing back 'Nummy' Deane who had led the side in 1929. This lobby was now successful and Deane took over for the Capetown Test. The veteran batsman Herby Taylor was also recalled at the age of 41. Hammond, for his part, was now persuaded to open the batting. It was a risk – if he had been played out of form by the shift, there was a rather shaky middle order, with Turnbull and Chapman at five and six, but it was a high compliment to Hammond's powers that the risk was taken. For some reason he, rather than Voce, opened the bowling too.

This was the first Test in South Africa to be played on turf and the tour management may have been looking for an under-prepared pitch and early movement off the seam. If so, they were disappointed for it turned out to be a belter and Hammond was no more successful than anybody else as Mitchell and Siedle scored 260 for the first wicket, which was then the South African record for any wicket, and remains the record opening stand to this day, and therefore, possibly, for ever. Hammond was in fact troubled by a septic foot and was probably not really fit to bowl.

On the second day, Duckworth was unfit to take the field; he had strained a ligament in his hand. In a predicament, Chapman turned logically enough, to Hammond, who was the best all-round fielder in the side and well capable of keeping wicket although not up to much running about. By all accounts, he kept very well, and looked as though he had been at it all his life. (Much the same was said of Bradman, when he kept all day in a Shield match some eight years later.) Hammond's proficiency was taken pretty much for granted, but consider the circumstances. It was a hot day; he was in pain from his foot and his concentration must have suffered; and England's bowlers were not the easiest hand in the world to take, with a fast left-arm man and Leyland, a very occasional slow left-arm bowler, bowling 30 overs. Nevertheless, he did keep well, allowing only eight byes in a total of 513, and apparently missing no chances. He was indeed a useful member of any team, as all his captains acknowledged.

Once South Africa had declared, Hammond had still to open the batting. We have already seen that he didn't much care for this and now he was footsore, his head probably aching from the unaccustomed strain of keeping wicket, and he had to bat with a runner, never helpful to a batsman's concentration. He started slowly, for him, and Wyatt led the way in their opening stand of 75. Hammond was able to do without a runner on the third day. He got out for 57, made out of 120 for 2, and could tell himself that he had given his side a pretty fair start.

Leyland and Hendren added another 82, but that middle order wilted and it took a hard-fought 93 from Hendren to take the score to 350. England had just failed to avoid the follow-on. Hammond went in again, without a runner, and he and Wyatt saw the day out. Wyatt went early on the last day but Hendren, with 86, and Hammond (65) were largely responsible for England's saving the match. All out for 252, they were only 89 ahead, but there was no time for South Africa to go in. Hammond had had a good, if painful, match and had been the architect of the successful rearguard action.

★　　★　　★　　★　　★

The South Africans continued their erratic course of selection when they left out Nupen and Balaskas for the next Test, which was back on the mat at Durban. As it turned out, the match was ruined by rain, although England came quite close to what would have been a sensational win. South Africa batted first, lost 4 men for 51 and must then have been pretty happy to watch the raindrops trickling down the windowpanes for the next day and a half. On the third day, they were all out for 177, Voce being the chief destroyer, and then Hammond led the way in a fine opening stand.

Wyatt was out for 54 on the fourth and last morning, but by then Hammond was already past his century and he and Leyland were still there when Chapman declared at lunch at 223 for 1, Hammond 136. South Africa fell into unexpected trouble and were 47 for 3, but Taylor dug them out with 64 not out. Hammond took the valuable wickets of Catterall and Cameron in a fine spell of 11-6-9-2, but South Africa escaped with a draw. Hammond had now played five innings for 370 runs, and his lowest score was 49. He must be due for a bad match soon, it seemed.

★ ★ ★ ★ ★

The England management now embarked on another experiment. Hammond had done splendidly as an opener, but he may have been making his feelings known. Alternatively, they may have decided that the middle order could no longer be left as it was; at all events, they recruited Harry Lee, the very experienced Middlesex opener, who was coaching in South Africa. He was not sensational, scoring 139 in five innings in provincial matches, but it was decided that this was good enough to justify risking him in a Test and so he got his only England cap. (Lee says in his memoirs that there was some little dispute and that he never received the cap itself, but that's not a part of the Hammond story.) He replaced White, which meant that England were packing their batting and relying on Hammond for a full bowling contribution. There was no rest for him on this tour; he was certainly earning his pay.

Chapman won the toss and batted. Lee was out for 18, but the other batsmen all did well, and they were 338 for 6 at the end of the day. Hammond made an uncharacteristically slow 75 in three hours, but Hendren and Leyland were batting briskly enough at the other end. Deane had withdrawn again and Cameron, leading South Africa for the first time, was probably not enjoying the experience. England lost quick wickets on the second day, but a bright little last-wicket stand of 57 by Tate and Voce saw them to 442. Curnow got out early, but Siedle and Mitchell were in form again, and South Africa, 166 for 2 at the close, looked pretty safe.

On the third day, Peebles bowled particularly well and once again it took all Herbie Taylor's skill and experience to save the situation, but it *was* saved and the follow-on narrowly averted, South Africa finishing 147 behind.

England made rather a mess of their second innings. When they went in, hoping to force the pace, the light was very bad and play was interrupted by showers. Nupen, back in the side, was not the man to allow easy runs, and he took 6 for 46. Hammond fell cheaply at last

56

(15), to Catterall, who was having a memorable season with the ball – he only took seven Test wickets in his career, all in the three matches of this series. Hendren and Leyland pulled England round from 23 for 3, but Chapman was obliged to declare at 169 for 9, leaving four hours for South Africa to make 317 or for his bowlers to force a win. With only three front-line bowlers, it was asking too much, and Mitchell and Cameron made sure of the draw. 153 for 5 at one time, South Africa finished at 280 for 7. They were only 37 short, but there were a few cheap runs towards the end when everybody relaxed.

★   ★   ★   ★   ★

England now needed to win the last Test back again at Durban to share the series. There was no help for it, they had to recall a bowler, which meant dropping Lee and moving Hammond to open. There seemed to be just a chance of a win when Chapman won the toss in uncertain weather and after overnight rain. Eagerly, he put South Africa in, but there followed a farcical incident which in these cynical and degenerate days would have led to furious allegations of bad faith.

The Tests that season were being played with the new, larger stumps and it was only as the match was about to begin that it was discovered that the ground didn't possess a set of bails to fit them. Minor cricket was still being played with the smaller stumps and no set could be borrowed. The sports shops of Durban were scoured without success, forcing the umpires to make a set before the game could start. It was a ludicrous situation and Chapman's feelings as he watched them toiling away with hammer and chisel must have been agitated to say the least, knowing how rapidly the wicket was drying out. In fact, he grew tired of watching and *Wisden* records that he led his players on to the field while the umpires completed their task. They had probably implored him to leave them to it. One can imagine, too, what Jardine would have said in such a situation, but then *he* would have had two spare sets of bails in his bag!

Not much time was actually lost, but the moral effect may have been considerable. In any event, rain cut down play to 70 minutes on this day and South Africa didn't lose a wicket.

Next day, South Africa batted quietly and reasonably successfully, taking all day to score 220. In the context of the series it was all they needed, for it was never going to be possible for England to force a win in two days. Hammond had bowled well, dismissing Mitchell the top-scorer, and Dalton, but he failed to give England the big start they needed, being out for 29. None of the batsmen found it easy to force the pace until Farrimond and Tate made 62 for the seventh wicket, and by then the game was up.

South Africa batted for most of the last day, in a relaxed way, and Cameron was able to make a token declaration in time for Hammond to get out for 28 and for Siedle to have his only bowl in a Test, getting Turnbull out. South Africa had achieved the series win they had fought hard for, but they may have been a bit lucky. Hammond had had a fine series with 517 runs, 109 inexpensive overs and 9 catches. More to the point, he had met his captain's every demand and was more firmly established than ever as the linchpin of the side.

	Innings	N.O.	H.S.	Runs	Average	100	50
1930/31	9	1	136*	517	64.62	1	4
To date	47	5	251	2512	59.80	8	10

	Balls	Runs	Wickets	Average
1930/31	654	240	9	26.66
To date	3748	1426	38	37.52

9 Lucifer, Son of the Morning

1931 was the wettest summer between the wars in England and the appalling conditions were reflected in the figures of nearly all the major batsmen. Herbert Sutcliffe was the remarkable exception, scoring 3,006 runs at an average of 96.96, and Jardine and the Nawab of Pataudi also did very well. Hammond did no better than most of the others, scoring less than 2,000 runs for the only time between his 1926 illness and the war, but he had his good moments, one of them in a Test. He started the season well with a 100 and two 50s in his first five innings, but a lean patch followed. He probably felt somewhat stale after a hard tour, but he was an obvious choice for what was arranged as the only Test of the summer, against New Zealand.

England had a new captain, both Chapman and Wyatt being passed over in favour of Jardine who, although he couldn't play throughout the season, was clearly the Establishment's pick for the next tour of Australia. It is rather fashionable to look upon Jardine as the villain of the Bodyline series and to forget that he was a very fine batsman and a captain who would had distinguished himself in any era, irrespective of the stern tactics he saw fit to adopt. The tragedy was that he was a logical thinker who carried his logic to the point where it went beyond common sense or sensitivity. Hence the title of this chapter – Lucifer was a fallen angel.

Facing the unblooded New Zealand team, England felt able to experiment with a new opening pair. Sutcliffe had strained a thigh muscle and was deemed not to be fit, although he was in fact in the middle of a rich vein of form for Yorkshire and actually scored 230 at Folkestone on the first day of the Test. (He did eventually succumb to the strain and take a couple of matches off.)

Arnold and Bakewell opened for England, and this is a good moment to take stock of the openers who paved the way for Hammond, though not always successfully. Between Hobbs' retirement in 1930 and the outbreak of war, 35 men opened for England in 60 Tests, and in the matches in which Hammond played, the average opening partnership was just 35, something of a contrast with the days of Hobbs and Sutcliffe. In other words, he frequently found himself coming in to a slightly fraught situation, to face bowlers with their tails up.

In the Lord's Test, Lowry won the toss for New Zealand and batted on a pitch that must have been doing a bit. Dempster and Mills made a solid start, but once they had been parted at 58, Peebles and Robins took a grip and they were all out for 224. Hammond bowled 10.3 overs for 8 runs and 1 wicket, a fairly typical piece of tight bowling. England made a shocking start, losing both openers and Hammond to the medium-paced Cromb with only 31 on the board. Hammond was now so highly regarded by the critics that they looked for every reason but the obvious for each dismissal, and Cardus said that he got out to:

'A ball that did not swing, but went through straight at a killing speed from the earth.'

It seemed that the mantle of Hobbs had descended on him and he could only be defeated by an unplayable ball. No doubt Hammond himself knew better. Duleepsinhji was also out cheaply and England were 62 for 4. Jardine was playing a dour but necessary innings and Woolley looked in form from the start. Jardine left at 129 and when Woolley was out at 188, having scored 80 in even time, New Zealand may have had visions of a win. Peebles came in ahead of Allen but was stumped at once and an eventful day ended with the score 190 for 7.

On the Monday the match was transformed by a stand by Ames and Allen which remains the Test record for the eighth wicket. They added 246 in well under three hours, driving freely and taking full advantage of some loose bowling towards the end. It must be recorded to New Zealand's great credit that they bowled more than 22 overs an hour throughout.

When New Zealand went in again, 230 behind, they lost Mills at once, but Dempster was at his very best and they were 161 for 2 at the close. A draw seemed the only possible result when, after Hammond had bowled Dempster for 120, Page and Blunt made another long stand. The fourth wicket fell at 360, with New Zealand 130 ahead, but a collapse followed, Peebles and Robins reducing them to 406 for 8. Lowry and Allcott saved the situation with a bright little stand and Lowry was able to make a token declaration.

Arnold and Bakewell batted better this time, and Hammond batted brightly for 46 before being run out. England were 146 for 5 at the end, still needing 94. No doubt, if they had had plenty of time, they would have got the runs safely enough, but New Zealand had, after all, declared, and could feel pretty pleased with themselves. What could not be denied was that it had been a cracking game; in three days, 1,293 runs were scored off 421 overs. New Zealand were at once offered two more Tests which they accepted.

★　　★　　★　　★　　★

England made three interesting changes for the second Test at the Oval. Sutcliffe was fit again and the unlucky Arnold was dropped after scoring 0 and 34 in what was to be his only Test. FR Brown, who had had a great season for Cambridge, replaced Robins in the all-round slot, and the selectors decided to introduce a bowler for a batsman, to go for a win in three days. They played Hedley Verity in only his second season, in place of Woolley, who is generally supposed to have fallen out with his autocratic captain at Lord's. More prosaically, one may observe that Woolley had now virtually given up bowling and could no longer be seen as an all-rounder. The strategy was successful.

New Zealand had two pieces of bad luck. Stewart Dempster, far and away their best bat and one of the best in New Zealand history, was injured; and Tom Lowry lost the toss. The match was played in showery weather and after the first day the pitch was never really reliable. Sutcliffe and Bakewell began with a stand of 84, and Duleepsinhji then batted quite magnificently, scoring 109 in 135 minutes and putting on 178 with Sutcliffe. At this stage of the season, people were beginning to see Duleep as the great hope of 'English' batting. He had led the way against Grimmett the year before and he was in the middle of a really excellent season for Sussex. Now he was showing the way again. Hammond responded to the challenge to his authority by scoring 100 in as many minutes before Jardine declared at 416 for 4. He gave a difficult stumping chance, but otherwise batted faultlessly, with 14 fours.

Allen took his chance now. The ball was skidding through on the greasy pitch and he had the first four men out with only 53 on the board. Lowry, always a battler, led a minor recovery, but Allen came again to break his partnership with Kerr and the innings ended at 193, half-an-hour before the end of the second day. Jardine put them in again and Peebles bowled Weir before the close. Next day, several batsmen got a start, but Vivian's 51 was the highest score and they were all out for 197, losing by an innings.

★   ★   ★   ★   ★

The third Test was substantially ruined by rain, play being delayed until the third afternoon, when Sutcliffe made 109 and Hammond 16. Sutcliffe had emerged at the top of the batting with the freakish average of 226, for once out, which Hammond was to improve on in due course. Hammond had maintained his reputation as a batsman, but there had been little need for him to bowl. Duleep had played in his last Test, though nobody could know this at the time. He was, naturally, omitted against India the following year and before the 1932 season was over, had succumbed to the tuberculosis which was to end his career.

	Innnings	N.O.	H.S.	Runs	Average
1931	4	1	100*	169	56.33
To date	51	6	251	2681	59.57

	Balls	Runs	Wickets	Average
1931	195	68	2	34.00
To date	3943	1494	40	37.35

★　　★　　★　　★　　★

England were not touring in 1931-32, and there have been few winters since without a tour of any sort, more's the pity. India were the visitors in 1932. Like the New Zealanders, they were making their first Test-playing visit and had been granted only one Test, at Lord's. The team was saddled with a captain and vice-captain who were in no sense up to Test standard, which cannot have been good for morale or management. Nevertheless when they came to the Test they could look back on a pretty good season in which they had only lost once, to Hampshire on a wet wicket. They had had the better of a draw with a medium-strength MCC side, and had given Lancashire plenty to think about with CK Nayudu, who was to lead them in the Test, and Amar Singh scoring fine centuries in a total of 493.

England made an odd choice of opener, in a sense, when they picked Percy Holmes to partner Sutcliffe. Holmes was in the form of his life – he and Sutcliffe had just made their 555 for the first wicket against Essex – but he was 45 years old and hadn't played for England since 1927-28. Perhaps the selectors might have gone for a younger man, but maybe they were unwilling to seem to be patronising the Indians. Otherwise, the most interesting choice was that of Bowes, playing in his first Test and due for a good match.

Jardine won the toss and batted, but both Holmes and Sutcliffe were whistled out immediately by Mahomed Nissar, a big bustling attacker whom some people still rate as India's best-ever fast bowler. Certainly he and Amar Singh, who opened with him in this match, are strong contenders for selection as the best pair ever to open for India. Woolley was run out at 19 – opinions differed about whether it was his fault or Hammond's, but Woolley was always a somewhat casual runner – and England were in a spot. As usual Jardine was unperturbed, and he and Hammond took the score to 101 before Hammond was bowled by Amar Singh for 35. After this, only Jardine and Ames did much and England were all out for 259, round about five o'clock. India lost no wicket that night, but didn't make much of Bowes and Voce next day. Hampered by injuries to Nayudu and Nazir Ali, they were out for 189, 70 behind.

62

For a long time, England seemed to have thrown away their advantage. The openers failed again and so did Woolley and Hammond, who only scored 12. Once again, Jardine came to the rescue – one does wonder what he said in the dressing-room – and this time, Paynter, Brown and Robins supported him strongly. Jardine declared at 275 for 8 with plenty of time to get India out. All the England bowlers took wickets and Hammond finished the innings off with a fine spell in which he took 3 for 9 off 33 balls.

★   ★   ★   ★   ★

Hammond now embarked a very fine spell of batting in domestic cricket. He made 100s off Nottinghamshire with Larwood and Voce, and Yorkshire, on course for the Championship. He wasn't always successful in Gentlemen-Players matches, but he made a great 110 in 125 minutes this year, against five Test bowlers. It was a fine match, containing big scores from Hobbs, Duleep and the Nawab of Pataudi, as well as Hammond. Finally, he had two great matches against Lancashire, scoring 164 and 48 at Cheltenham, and then in a tremendous exhibition of stamina at Liverpool, scoring 264 and bowling 77 overs to take 7 for 106, the performance of a young man in his prime.

	Innings	N.O.	H.S.	Runs	Average	100	50
1932	2	–	35	47	23.50	–	–
To date	53	6	251	2728	58.04	9	11

	Balls	Runs	Wickets	Average
1932	57	24	3	8.00
To date	4000	1518	43	35.30

10 Lucifer – Continued

It is not a part of the purpose of this book to discuss the tactics and morality of the Bodyline dispute. Many books have been written on this subject alone, and I have listed the most useful in the bibliography at the end of this book if anyone wants to do some further reading. My objective is to describe Hammond's part in the drama. It was a considerable part, too; all things considered, he probably contributed as much as anyone other than Larwood to England's four to one win.

The team was picked piecemeal during the 1932 season, and thinking Australians probably realised what was in the wind when Bowes was added to the side at the very end of the summer. Bowes had been freely criticised for some robust short-pitched bowling, notably in Yorkshire's match with Surrey, and he was at the time seen as a bowler whose main weapon was the bouncer. Later of course, he blossomed as a fast-medium bowler with all the skills. One of the sternest critics was Sir Pelham Warner, who was also one of the selectors who picked him as a strategic move and then, as one of the managers of the team, was very critical of the tactics employed. It was an odd, piquant situation, but then it was an odd, piquant series. The other three fast bowlers were Larwood and Voce, the leading purveyors of bodyline, and Allen, who consistently refused to join in. As an amateur, of course, he could afford to.

Verity was the only finger-spinner and two leg-spinners, Brown and Robins, were originally selected. When Robins had to decline, Mitchell of Derbyshire, another leg-spinner who had yet to play in a Test, replaced him. Tate, by now something of a veteran, was also picked, and most people thought he would keep one end going while two fast bowlers took turns at the other. In the event, Jardine picked three fast bowlers whenever he could, and even four on one occasion, and Tate's role fell to Hammond. It was an important task, which he discharged successfully.

The batting was powerful, only lacking an experienced and reliable opening partner for Sutcliffe. Wyatt and Jardine alternated in the role and did well enough, averaging 30.8 between them when opening. Besides these three and Hammond, there were also Pataudi, Leyland

and Paynter. Of the two wicket-keepers, Ames was preferred to Duckworth in the Tests, as being much the better batsman and a pretty good keeper anyway.

Hammond began the tour well, scoring 77 in his first match against a Combined Australian XI at Perth. He was out for 27 against South Australia. In a score of 634, this mattered little, but it was disquieting that he got out to Grimmett, reviving memories of 1930. In the Tests, Grimmett only got him out once, and was to dismiss him only once more in his career.

When the MCC reached Melbourne, they encountered a mystery bowler about whom they had heard a good deal. Fleetwood-Smith was a left-arm wrist spinner, then as now a rarity. Hammond was deputed to knock him out of consideration for the Tests and did so, scoring 203 in quick time. Fleetwood-Smith took 2 for 124 in 25 overs, and wasn't picked, but he may perhaps have felt that he had the last laugh four years later. Hammond scored 20 against New South Wales, again in the midst of plenty, and was ready for the Tests.

Meanwhile Australia were in some disarray. When the bodyline attack (yet to be so christened) was launched, the batsmen, one and all, faltered. Bradman was embroiled in a ridiculous argument with the Board of Control about whether he could both comment on the Tests and play in them and this argument resulted in a kind of nervous breakdown, so that he missed the first Test at Sydney. Jardine picked three of his fast men, omitting Bowes, and challenged Australia to meet the new weapon.

Drama abounded. Australia lost 4 wickets for 87, nobody facing the bowling with confidence, but McCabe and Richardson, fearless players chancing their arms, made a brave recovery, taking the score to 216 before Richardson was out, caught by Hammond. This was Hammond's first impact on the match and the catch was made at short-leg. When bodyline was in full swing, there was no demand for a slip and Hammond fielded either at short-leg or deep square-leg, distinguishing himself in either position, as he did wherever he was put. McCabe was playing the innings of a lifetime, or so it appeared, though he was to play two more innings which were epic by any standards. He made 187 but none of the later batsmen made much of the bowling till Wall joined McCabe in a fighting last-wicket stand, broken at last by Hammond, who had put in some fine economical bowling.

England were in well before lunch on the second day and Sutcliffe and Wyatt made an excellent start. Australia had picked Nagel, an inexperienced fast-medium bowler who had taken 8 for 32 for an Australian XI against MCC, but he was finding this pitch more difficult to cope with. Wall was steady but no more, and O'Reilly looked distinctly the likeliest bowler to succeed. Hammond came in at 112 for 1 and batted aggressively from the start. He reached 50 in 57 minutes and had made 87 in 130 minutes when play ended with the score 252 for 1, Sutcliffe 116. The match was half won already.

Hammond went on for another hour on the third day before being caught at cover for 112. He had hit 16 fours, nine of them on the off-side. A diagram of his strokes suggests that the Australian attack was directed quite as much at the leg-stump as at the off, and this is borne out by Sutcliffe's stroke distribution, for he hit four fours on the off-side, only one in front of the wicket, and nine on the leg-side. Just for comparison, McCabe hit 25 fours, only four of them in front of the wicket on the off-side, and the diagram of his innings tells most graphically where the English attack was directed.

England didn't quite capitalise as they should have on their start of 300 for 2. Sutcliffe was tired and slowing down, and Pataudi was distinctly tedious. He seemed to have set his sights on scoring a 100 in his first Test and he managed it, but it was hard going and he rather handed the initiative to Australia. His last 41 took 173 minutes and put a certain amount of pressure on his partners, who didn't achieve much. England were all out for 524 and Australia were still in the game if they could make a good start.

They didn't. Larwood and Voce had the openers, Woodfull and Ponsford, out for 10, and there was no recovery. Fingleton and McCabe each made a few, but Australia were 164 for 9 and the scores were level at the close. Hammond had had a long bowl in the heat of the day (while Larwood had a real rest) and picked up two good wickets – McCabe and Richardson – for 37. The tactic was successful, as Larwood came back to devastate the lower order, and Jardine is properly appreciative of Hammond's great effort in his very readable (if polemical) account of the tour.

There followed a farcical last day, Australia's last wicket falling to the ninth ball bowled, with no run scored, and England scoring a single off the first ball. England were one up, and Australia had never been in the match.

★   ★   ★   ★   ★

Jardine rested his key men, Larwood and Hammond, when the team went to Tasmania before the second Test in Melbourne. England would dearly have liked to win this one and go two up, and they looked to be odds-on, but it turned out otherwise. The fast attack had been so successful in Sydney that Jardine decided to bank on it in the second match, omitting Verity and playing all four fast bowlers. If things got at all out of hand, Hammond would have some work to do.

Bradman was fit again and his difficulties with the Board resolved. His confrontation with Larwood and the others might well decide both the match and the series. He and Leo O'Brien replaced Kippax and Ponsford, who had looked uneasy against the fast men; significantly, it seemed that O'Brien, in his first Test, would bat at No 3 to shield Bradman, the only time that it was ever acknowledged that he needed protection, sticky wickets always excepted. The other change was also significant. Nagel was replaced by Ironmonger, a third spinner for a seamer – was this a clue as to the wicket to be provided?

It was a clue. Australia batted first and it was soon apparent that the game was being played on an English wicket and where the ball would move about off the seam and in response to spin, but at no great pace. Allen made the first break, bowling Woodfull off his legs, and O'Brien duly appeared. He and Fingleton were still there at lunch with the score only 42, but Larwood had been having boot trouble and it seemed that he would play little part in the day.

Because of this trouble of Larwood's, Bowes was on soon after lunch, and was bowling when O'Brien was foolishly run out. Bradman entered to tumultuous applause, only to play the first ball into his stumps. It was the most famous duck in Test history – the world's greatest batsman destroyed by a long-hop from the opposition's least-considered bowler – but it is difficult not to believe that the great man was affected by the pressure and the novel threat now being posed.

Fingleton and McCabe made a stand, the most remarkable incident of which was that Hammond dropped a catch from Fingleton. It didn't happen often. The outcome was that McCabe was dismissed, for the batsmen took a single when the ball went down, and McCabe was out at once. There was no real recovery, Australia being 194 for 7 at the close and 228 all out next day. Hammond had bowled 10 overs for 21 runs and all the fast bowlers had taken wickets. It all looked very much like the first Test and the crowd sat back to await the big England score that was on the cards.

But England had had no spinners with which to exploit the wicket and it was now seen that a bowler who really spun the ball would be rewarded. O'Reilly probably got more work on the ball than any bowler of the period, and he soon had everybody in trouble. He had Wyatt lbw with the score at 30 and then, to the universal surprise, Hammond played back to Wall and was bowled by one that may have come back a little for 8. This was a crisis; Pataudi could be a very pawky player when the going was rough and Leyland had not at this stage worked O'Reilly out, as he was to do in 1934. Sutcliffe ran into a sticky patch and failed to hit his way out of it and in no time at all England were 110 for 6. It was not the sort of wicket where a lower-order batsman would succeed when the stars had failed and England subsided to 169 all out. O'Reilly had bowled magnificently with 5 for 63 in 34.3 overs.

Larwood had a new pair of boots by now, and he and Allen attacked with a will to restrict Australia's lead. Fingleton and O'Brien went cheaply, but Bradman for the first time in the season against the English bowlers, looked comfortable. (He had already taken two big 100s off Victoria). Although nobody stayed with him for very long, he was making a total which in this low-scoring match would be enough to win. There was a stiffish breeze blowing straight down the ground and none of the fast men cared to bowl into it for long; it was the situation that England must have feared most when they left Verity out. Hammond rose, as ever, to the occasion and plugged away into the wind for 10.5 overs, taking 3 for 21, and once again Jardine pays him a generous tribute:

> 'What we should have done without Hammond I really do not know.'

Bradman was on 98 when Ironmonger, at that time reckoned to be comfortably the worst Test batsman in the world, came in, but the veteran didn't let him down, surviving two balls from Voce. Bradman completed a three-hour 100, rapturously received, and then saw Ironmonger run out.

England had managed to stay in the match, but 251 would take a deal of getting on that wicket, particularly against O'Reilly and the others. Sutcliffe and Wyatt made a good start and were 43 at the end of the third day, but O'Reilly got them both in the morning, with the score still only 53. Hammond faced a huge task. Pataudi never began to cope and was out at 70, and Jardine has given a vivid description of the three balls he had from Ironmonger, all of which turned sharply, the degree of turn varying each time. He was caught off the third. Once Ames had failed and the score was 77 for 5, Hammond had no choice but to have a hit. It might have come off, but it did not, and he was caught at mid-off, off O'Reilly for 23. England were all out for 139, and well beaten. O'Reilly again took five wickets, and he and Bradman were the match-winners. The England batsmen cannot be blamed too much – they faced three high-class spinners on a very helpful wicket – but they might perhaps have made a few more runs.

★　★　★　★　★

The series was now tied at 1–1, and, for the moment, the bodyline threat had receded. It was England who had to regroup, but they kept the changes to the minimum for the third Test at Adelaide. Pataudi was dropped, which seems hard on a player who had made a 100 in his first

Test, but he had been very slow at Sydney and had looked completely out of touch at Melbourne. Furthermore, Jardine had concluded that it was essential to play another left-hander as a counter to O'Reilly, and Paynter was waiting in the wings.

There is an alternative theory about this change. It is said that Pataudi was a conscientious objector to bodyline and had refused duty in the leg-trap and was omitted for this reason. I'm not so sure about this. I can believe in the objection, but Jardine was tough enough to send even a Nawab home, and I believe he would have done it. Verity returned, of course. Jardine was ready enough to admit to a *tactical* error, and he brought him back for Bowes. Australia brought Ponsford back in place of O'Brien, who could consider himself rather unlucky, if that is, he fancied more of the same. Many people would think he was well out of it.

England made a dreadful start giving them cause to congratulate themselves that they had included Paynter and hadn't dropped Wyatt, who may have been a candidate for exclusion if they had decided to stay with Pataudi. Four men were out with the score of 30, including Hammond, out caught at the wicket for 2 as he fanned at Wall. The pitch was lively to start with, and Hobbs remarks that Hammond had had trouble with some rising balls before he was out. One of the game's little ironies; it was supposed to be Bradman who would be upset by fliers, but there would be plenty of that before the game was over.

Leyland and Wyatt, tough characters both, righted the ship and took the score to 186 as the wicket dried into a typical Adelaide shirt-front. They were both out to the spinners within ten runs of each other, and Paynter then played another fine fighting innings. England were 236 for 7 at the close, and it didn't really look enough. Much depended on Paynter, and he and Verity did wonderfully well on the second day, taking the score on to 324 before they were separated. Verity was particularly at ease against Ironmonger and surprised everybody by his ability and confidence. The final total was 341, not a great score but far, far more than had seemed likely. Then the trouble started.

Fingleton was out to Allen without scoring and Bradman came in to join Woodfull. With the last ball of his second over, and while still bowling with an orthodox field, Larwood hit Woodfull over the heart and almost laid him out. Accounts of what was said and by whom vary considerably, but there is little doubt that Jardine tried to turn the screw on Bradman by making encouraging noises to the bowler within his hearing. After Allen's next over, received by Bradman, Jardine switched Larwood's field to the now familiar bodyline formation, and this provoked an uproar, the crowd seeing it as a blatant intimidation. Jardine always claimed that it was a purely tactical switch, the ball having lost a little of its shine, but it is difficult indeed to believe that such an astute tactician as the England captain was unaware of the psychological pressure he was exerting, on Woodfull as well as on Bradman.

Jardine writes, innocently, that Woodfull had only to ask his permission to leave the field if he didn't feel up to continuing, but surely that was just what Jardine would have wanted? He would have got at McCabe, the next batsman, while Larwood was still fresh and when Woodfull returned, he would have had to play himself in all over again. Anyway, Woodfull stayed on amidst the rumpus, played the first ball of that third over for a single which was almost a chance and, to his horror, saw Bradman caught off the next ball. Jardine had hooked the bigger fish, and he soon had McCabe and Woodfull too. Australia were 51 for 4, and there followed the famous and unedifying scene in the dressing-room, when Woodfull administered his stinging rebuke to manager Warner. Meanwhile, the crowd were roaring in anger and there was a real risk of a riot. All this must have disturbed the batsmen more than the fielding side and Ponsford and Richardson did well to survive to the close.

Voce had had to leave the field with an injury on this second day, and Jardine nursed him carefully on the third, turning again to Hammond in the minor crisis. Hammond responded with a tight, accurate spell – he bowled 17.4 overs in the innings for only 30 runs. He had Oldfield missed at the wicket, which itself had its effect on the match, for soon afterwards Larwood hit Oldfield on the head, which further inflamed the crowd, who might well have invaded the pitch. Oldfield was not as badly hurt as had at first appeared – although he did have to miss the next Test – and he freely admitted that the mishap was his own fault, as he had mis-hooked a not-too-short ball on to his head. Amidst renewed uproar, Australia were all out for 222 and England seemed to have the game in their hands.

Sutcliffe fell early and Jardine was joined by Wyatt, promoted in the order, possibly because Jardine thought that Hammond would make quicker progress once the bowling was worn down, possibly because Hammond was tired after bowling 17 overs in great heat. England were 85 for 1 at the end of the day and Jardine was going well for the first time in the series. It was typical of him to bat particularly well when under frenzied attack from the crowd. Wyatt was the more aggressive partner and continued in the same vein next day, scoring 49 out of 84 before getting out to O'Reilly. Still Hammond didn't come in, Allen preceding him.

Allen didn't stay long, and Hammond joined Jardine and injected some life into the batting. He soon lost Jardine, but he played Grimmett with a new confidence and was soon picking out the slow-footed

70

Ironmonger in the field and taking easy singles, mostly off the back foot. Leyland was also in good fettle, and when he got out the score was 245 for 5 and the match as good as won. England were not so sure of this, and Hammond and Ames looked for yet more runs.

There followed one of the more amusing dismissals of Hammond's career, amusing because it had no effect on the match. Bradman, a very occasional bowler, came on and Hammond, properly and wisely, gave the junior partner some advice.

'Don't take things lightly, just because it's Bradman,' he said. 'We need to be not out at the close.' Whereupon he walked back to his crease, played all round a full toss and was bowled for 85. He was not pleased. Bradman took only two Test wickets in all, the other being Ivan Barrow of the West Indies, and the wicket must have given him some quiet pleasure. As I say, it mattered little. England were 296 for 6 at the close, and the next day Ames and Verity batted well to see England to 412 all out. Vic Richardson had kept wicket in Oldfield's absence, and had done pretty well, but it can't have helped the out-cricket.

Australia now had to try to make the huge score of 532 to win, and would bat ten men. Woodfull had recovered from his knock – he had fielded throughout – and he would open.

He batted throughout, too. The scorecard reads oddly. Fingleton was out for a pair, bowled by a glorious ball from Larwood that pitched middle-and-leg and hit the top of the off-stump. Ponsford batted third and was caught off Larwood at 12 so that Bradman came in to a crisis. He batted brilliantly, but, some thought, irresponsibly. He played fine forcing strokes off Larwood and Allen, but was too cavalier by half with Verity and paid the penalty after scoring 66 off just 71 balls.

That was that. Richardson made 21, Woodfull carried his bat for 73, and nobody else got double figures. Australia, all out for 193 and lost by 338 runs. Voce could bowl only four overs, but Larwood and Allen were too much for the batsmen and Hammond needed to bowl only nine overs. England now looked to be odds-on to win the series, if they ever got on the field again.

For the next three weeks there was more action in the committee-rooms than in the middle. This is not the place to analyse the discussion or the drafting of the cablegrams; it suffices to say that the players did take the field at Brisbane, doubtless in wary mood. Voce was still unfit and Mitchell came in, the selectors gambling that in the heat of Brisbane a mixed attack would last longer than a trio of pacemen, but it meant that Larwood would be the only man to bowl bodyline. Australia, curiously, went for a longer batting line-up, replacing Fingleton and Grimmett with two young and promising batsmen, Darling and Bromley. Bromley could bowl a little, but it was an odd decision for a side that was 1-2 down. Love replaced Oldfield.

Although Grimmett had been dropped, England were still worrying about the Australian spinners and decided to appoint two batsmen to take all reasonable risks to knock O'Reilly and Ironmonger off their length. The obvious choices were Leyland, an aggressive left-hander, and Hammond, who had already seen Fleetwood-Smith out of contention. The plan didn't come off, but its conception throws a light on Jardine's approach which may startle any who think of him as a dour and unimaginative Scot and no more.

Australia batted first in searing heat and early on had the luck they needed. Richardson, a brave and dogged player, opened with Woodfull, and a number of streaky shots failed to go to hand. No actual chances were recorded but there were some near things and when lunch came without a wicket, Australia could feel that they were ahead on points. The wicket could only get better and some of the steam had been taken out of Larwood and Allen. Jardine was already making extensive use of Hammond, saving Verity for later in the day.

The batsmen accelerated after lunch, still looking safe, but Hammond made a break. Before lunch, Richardson had played forward to him and been beaten outside the leg-stump. Hammond waited patiently to beat him again and when he did, Ames made no mistake with the stumping.

England were relieved to have got a wicket, but with the score already 133, the ground had for once on this tour been well prepared for Bradman. He might have been expected to set out his stall for a high score, but all observers agreed that he went about hs work in a somewhat panicky way. Strokes in the air, inside edges, a scoop over the head of mid-on followed each other in a bewildering sequence. But he bore a charmed life and survived to the end of the day, having seen Woodfull bowled by a full-toss and McCabe most brilliantly caught in the gully by Jardine. It had been an odd sort of day – Bradman batting carelessly and getting away with it and Larwood failing to take a wicket – but Australia were beginning to get on top.

On the second day, England showed what a great side they were, bodyline or no bodyline. Larwood bowled Bradman right at the start, a wicket that could be credited to the bodyline strategy, for he was trying to cut a ball off his leg-stump – and this began a collapse from which there was no recovery. Ponsford was bowled round his legs by Larwood, Darling was taken at the wicket, and Bromley, after a brave attempt to collar the bowling, well caught at short-leg. Ironmonger made 8, his highest score against England, before Hammond had him stumped to finish off the innings. Hammond only had four stumpings made off him in Tests and two were in this innings. Ames' keeping is often underrated, as is often the fate of those keepers who are also class batsmen, but it says a great deal for his skill that he could stand up to a bowler of Hammond's pace and make stumpings. It also speaks volumes for Hammond's accuracy. He had bowled 23 overs in the enervating heat and taken 2 for 61.

Australia were all out for 340, and England were back in the game, but with two factors against them. They were all very tired after that day and a half's fielding in very hot weather, and Paynter had left the field with tonsilitis and was unlikely to be fit to bat. In the circumstances, Jardine postponed until the Monday his plan for knocking the spinners out of action, and he and Sutcliffe batted quietly in fading light, for two hours. Quietly is of course a relative term – they scored 99, which would be thought good enough today, but the over-rate with only one fast bowler in the side, was pretty high. Jardine complains in his book that the over-rate was slow on the Monday morning, only 18 overs being bowled in the first hour; we would be happy enough with that in 1990.

This third day went anything but well for England. Jardine was caught at the wicket, early on, off the back of his bat. (There is a suspicion that this was a poor decision; Jardine refers to three doubtful decisions on the day, without being more specific, but Hobbs hints clearly that Jardine was unlucky). Hammond now came in to attempt to blow the spinners away, but failed to do so. They were so accurate that he made only 20 in 90 minutes, including a six, and he was then bowled by a full-toss from McCabe. This was the second time in the series that he had fallen to a full-toss and it is – it must be – possible that the extra pressure of the bodyline dispute, or the specific orders he had in this innings, distracted him.

Sutcliffe and Leyland were out soon after, and Leyland in turn failed in his new task, being caught at square-leg off O'Reilly after making 12 off 48 balls. Looking back, it is difficult to see why Jardine ordered this unusual ploy; his batsmen had taken plenty of runs off the spinners in Adelaide without extravagance, and had indeed taken Grimmett out of the firing line for the summer. Perhaps the answer lies in Jardine's superiority complex; simply winning wasn't enough, but he needed to impose his authority on the other side, with bat *and* ball.

Allen didn't stay long and then, at 216 for 6, to universal surprise, a wan-looking Paynter appeared, sporting an enormous Panama hat. Warner writes in glowing terms of Paynter's heroic evasion of the hospital authorities, but the Revised Standard Version makes it pretty clear that Jardine, furious at Paynter's failure to report sick before the match, had told him he was to bat if it killed him. Paynter batted very quietly until the close, losing both Ames and Larwood, and England were 271 for 8. The match was turning into a classic encounter but, on the face of it, Australia were forging ahead.

Paynter evidently felt a little better in the morning and batted more positively and without error. Verity, who was in really good batting form at this stage of the tour, stayed with him, though not without a few adventures, and Paynter wasn't out till after lunch, when he had scored 83. England finished 16 ahead.

It was noticeable throughout the series that, even when Australia did well in the first innings, they failed in the second, forced into error by the bombardment. (The same phenomenon has been observed in recent Tests involving the West Indies fast attack.) Richardson put up a fight, scoring 32 out of 46 before being finely caught by Verity. Bradman batted at first wicket down and Jardine, sensing perhaps that this was the climatic moment of the series, threw Larwood at him. Woodfull tried to keep Bradman at the other end, but in vain. Bradman made two or three brilliant, but uppish cuts and then holed out at backward point for 24. It was apparent that Larwood had 'got to him'. Larwood now took one of the finest catches of a series that had seen some very good ones, to get rid of Ponsford, and it was all over. Australia had made only 175, and England needed 160 to win the Ashes.

It should have been easy, but the Australian spinners made England work for it. Sutcliffe fell to Wall, and Jardine used Leyland next to try again to annihilate the spinners. He batted perfectly safely, but certainly made no great impact on either O'Reilly or Ironmonger, and it may be that his heart wasn't in the policy. He was nevertheless going better than his captain, who was tedious indeed. It may have been on this occasion that Jardine apologised for batting like an old spinster defending her honour and, if so, the jest was appropriate, for he made only 24 off 112 balls. He was out before the end of the fifth day, and Hammond came in.

Hammond was no more successful in going for the bowling than he had been in the first innings. There was good reason for having a hit this time, for it had begun to rain and it was sound policy to get some runs on the board before the wicket could be affected. Hammond went for a big hit off Ironmonger and sliced to cover, when he had made 14. Leyland was out, too, but Ames and Paynter knocked off the last few runs. Paynter finishing it off with a six. The Ashes had been won, but the arguments continued and still continue to this day.

Voce was fit again for the final Test at Sydney and replaced Mitchell to restore the normal balance, or imbalance, of the side. Australia made four changes, Oldfield, also fit again, replacing Love, and Alexander, a tearaway but inexperienced fast bowler, replacing the injured Wall. The three-bowler experiment was abandoned and Lee, a spinning all-rounder, and O'Brien replaced Ponsford and Bromley.

Australia batted first and England – relaxing perhaps – gave a dismal fielding display. Jardine estimates that 12 chances went down in the first innings, but observers put it at about six. There is no record of Hammond dropping anything. The chances apart, Australia batted consistently and fast – very fast. Richardson was out for none and then Bradman scored 48 off 56 balls – it was a little too rich to last. He was hitting through the covers, wherever the ball was pitched and without moving his feet. Larwood was taken off for a brief rest and Bradman scored 40 in the half an hour while he was away, but as soon as he came back, Larwood bowled Bradman round his legs for 48. Woodfull was already out and Australia was now 64 for 3, but when O'Brien and McCabe came together, the catches began to go down. They added 99 in quick time, and by the close the score was 296 for 5. Larwood had been limping and it was initially thought that he was having more boot-trouble, but the word from the dressing-room at the close was that he was suffering from skinned toes. Just as well, thought the England partisans, that the series was already won.

On the second day, the pace of the batting accelerated – not so the pace of the bowlers. Larwood now looked distinctly lame and Allen was manifestly stale, after a hard series. Darling and Oldfield scored fast, the catches still going down, and when Darling was bowled, Lee came in and hit everything, scoring 42 in 35 minutes. Hammond bowled very little while all this was going on, which is surprising, because he had been much used by Jardine in the earlier games whenever the scoring had to be damped down. Jardine had evidently concluded that he would need a long innings from him. Australia finished with 435 off 108 six-ball overs, a remarkable rate of scoring, but England had only themselves to blame.

Jardine fell early in the England innings, but Hammond made a brisk start, scoring 26 in his first half-hour and 72 in 134 minutes before the close of the second day. The score was then 159 for 2. Sutcliffe had been out shortly before the end, and Larwood had come in as the night-watchman. This was a curious decision. England didn't invariably use the ploy at this time and Leyland, the next on the card, was the last batsman on earth to need protection. What is more to the point, Larwood was not an obvious choice, being a bit of a dasher, who was seldom encouraged to bat very long for his county. Jardine says that the idea was to give Larwood a good rest after he batted, to bring him up fresh for the Australian second innings, but he seems to have forgotten to mention this to Larwood, who consequently batted in something of a paddy. He survived that night, and batted splendidly the next day.

Australia had been almost as fallible in the field as England and poor Alexander, in his first Test, must have been wondering what Test cricket was all about. Larwood may have decided that nobody would catch the ball if he did lift it, or he may, as I have suggested, still have been in a rage at this form of compulsory overtime. What is certain is that he batted quite brilliantly, completely outshining Hammond. (Larwood scored 98 off 148 balls, Hammond 101 off 205, itself a highly commendable rate of scoring).

Hammond was the first to get out; he had hit 12 fours and played some beautiful strokes, but he *had* been dropped three times. Larwood was exceedingly unlucky to get out when he did, because he was caught by 'Dainty' Ironmonger, generally agreed at that time to be the worst fielder in Test cricket. This brought England to 310 for 4 and with plenty of batting to come, a big score was in prospect, but nobody really cashed in on the good start and they were all out for 454, only 19 ahead. Lee was the most successful bowler and there were two run-outs, Ames being considered, on photographic evidence, to have had a rough decision against him. However as he was trying to take a second run to Bradman, he probably deserved all he got.

Yet again, Australia got off to a bad start, Allen making a juggling catch to dismiss Richardson, who thus made a pair, and to give Larwood his last wicket of the series and, as it turned out, of his Test career. He went lame again after another hour or so, though not before he had 'pinked' Bradman for the first time in the series. Bradman had batted as though expecting this; he was even more frenetic than in the earlier Tests, backing away to slash through the covers, walking across his wicket to hook, and generally deploying the whole of his strange new repertoire. Larwood finally had to abandon the attempt to bowl, but Jardine wouldn't let him leave the field till Bradman was yorked by Verity. Then Jardine let Larwood go and the two protagonists left the field together, saying not a word to each other.

Woodfull had watched Bradman's fireworks unemotionally, himself scoring at three an over off the fast men; he generally scored faster than he appeared to. He now had to endure a sorry collapse at the other end. The Australians probably ought to have made more of Larwood's absence, but once again they seemed to have been worn down in the first innings, and this time England were holding their catches. After seeing all his batsmen fall for single-figure scores, the weary – and surely heartbroken – Woodfull played on to Allen and Australia were all out for 182, Verity having taken 5 for 33. England needed 164 to win.

Jardine made another surprising switch, going in first with Wyatt and keeping Sutcliffe back in case, he explained, Ironmonger was able to exploit the spot Verity had found, when an experienced head might be needed. He had nothing to worry about; he and Wyatt batted out time and went on to 43 the next day. Ironmonger did then account for both Jardine and Leyland with sharply-turning balls, and this brought Hammond in for his last innings of the series. It was one of his best; he started slowly, taking the measure of Ironmonger, but as the veteran tired, he played him with increasing fluency, once on-driving him for four. He hit O'Reilly for a lofted four and a six and seemed relaxed and ready to end this unhappy series on a positive note. Wyatt was solidity itself and the end came quickly, Hammond ending the match with a magnificent straight-drive for six, his third of the series. Wyatt had scored 61, Hammond 75.

So ended the most controversial series of all; the arguments are endlessly being renewed. Hammond had played a crucial role. He had been distinctly the most forceful and consistent of England's batsmen, actually having figures identical to Sutcliffe's though he had scored rather faster. (Bradman had a better average than either, and *he* was generally supposed to have failed.) Hammond had also bowled some invaluable spells into the wind and at awkward moments, and his captain fully appreciated that this had been a vital factor in the success of the fast men. He had fielded well in unfamiliar positions and, like the rest of the team, had loyally supported Jardine in a policy which he seems not to have approved. (As a major batsman who would be a prime target for any imitators, he is unlikely to have been a fervent supporter of bodyline, and in later writings, he made it clear that he thought it against the spirit of the game.) The entertaining part of the trip was still to come, but his Test figures were now:

	Innings	N.O.	H.S.	Runs	Average	100	50
1932/33 (A)	9	1	112	440	55.00	2	2
To date	62	7	251	3168	57.60	11	13

	Balls	Runs	Wickets	Average
1932/33 (A)	725	291	9	32.33
To date	4725	1809	52	34.78

11 Average, five hundred and sixty-three

The Englishmen played two matches in Australia after the final Test – the first, against Victoria, was drawn very much in the home team's favour, though it was reckoned as a tie under the system then in force, the scores being level, though Victoria had seven wickets in hand. The final match, from which Hammond was rested, was drawn. The team then moved on to New Zealand.

This was the first time an English team which had played an Australian Test series had gone on to New Zealand. It seemed rather a burdensome addition, but the visit was a great success and the trip was repeated on subsequent tours until the structure of Test cricket changed in the 1970s, to reflect New Zealand's growing strength.

In 1933, New Zealand were anything but strong and their team for the first Test at Christchurch contained two young bowlers making their first appearance in a Test. Both were Australian-born. One, Horace Smith, opened the bowling with the slow-medium FT Badcock. Badcock bowled the first over and had Sutcliffe caught off the very first ball and Hammond dropped at slip later in the over. At the other end, Smith bowled Paynter with *his* first ball and thus joined the short list of bowlers who have opened their Test career with a first-ball wicket. Oddly, only two of these – Tate and Intikhab Alam – have gone on to great things in their later career.

Hammond settled down and was soon pushing a rather so-so attack all round the field. He lost Wyatt run out at 46, and Jardine at 133, and then he and Ames cut loose. At this stage of his career, Ames was a powerful and consistent batsman who, on his day, looked not unlike Hammond himself at the wicket. This was his day and they added 242 in 145 minutes, of which Ames made 103. They were particularly hard on the second Australian-born newcomer, Doug Freeman, at 18 the youngest man to play for New Zealand. He had taken 9 for 187 in his first first-class match against Auckland and had been picked on the strength of this. Hammond and Ames took his measure and scored freely off him. England were 418 for 5 at the end of the first day, Hammond 223 not out.

He was out almost at once on the second day for 227 and was then able to watch Brown and Voce rub it in, scoring 108 in 45 minutes. Brown had not been seriously considered for the Tests in Australia, his leg-breaks not fitting into Jardine's master-plan, and this was some small consolation for him. Jardine declared at 560 for 8. New Zealand made a brave reply in the circumstances and were 153 for 3 at the end of the day. In a three-day game, a draw was always likely, and it was made certain by a dust storm and heavy rain on the final day. Hammond bowled only two overs, and took two catches.

★   ★   ★   ★   ★

The next Test at Auckland followed only four days later. The unlucky Smith had taken no more wickets after Paynter's, and was dropped. Freeman may have thought himself even more unlucky *not* to be dropped, as the match unfolded. The new opening bowler was Dunning, a medium-pacer with a reportedly unlovely action. England appear to have taken the match fairly lightly. Jardine declared himself unavailable, leaving Wyatt to captain the side. Duckworth came in to keep wicket, Ames being played for his batting, so that every member of the team had had at least one Test. Bowes came in for Voce and had a very good match.

This time Page won the toss and batted, and Bowes took two wickets before a run was on the board. He continued to trouble everyone except Dempster who, coming in at 0 for 2, was 83 not out in a score of 158, and deserved a century if ever a man did. Sutcliffe and Wyatt made a sound start, scoring 56, and then Hammond played the most spectacular innings seen in Test cricket to that date, Jessop and Bradman not excepted. His 100 came up in less than two and a quarter hours, and then he accelerated. *Wisden* says that the third 50 took him only 38 minutes and although he then took a bit of a breather, he went completely dotty after reaching 200 and went on to 336 in little more than an hour.

He gave only one chance, and *that* put Dempster off the field – an incident that was to be repeated in his great 240 at Lord's in 1938. He hit ten sixes, which still remains the Test record in 1990, in spite of the advent of heavier bats and charismatic all-rounders, and 33 fours. At one point, he hit the unfortunate Newman, a medium-paced left-arm bowler, for three sixes off consecutive balls. All this with no very conspicuous support from his colleagues; Wyatt made 60, but nobody else got 40, and Hammond made his 336 out of 492 scored while he was in. He had beaten Bradman's record, but nobody was very excited about that. In those days, England-Australia matches were very much

79

more important than any other Tests and certainly when Hutton made his 364, it was the beating of Bradman's 334 that was seen as the significant achievement.

Once again, the last day was virtually washed out and the match drawn. Hammond had the slightly ridiculous series average of 563.00, but we might perhaps spare a thought for poor Doug Freeman, whose Test career was over before his nineteenth birthday. He had taken one wicket for 169 – the wicket was that of Sutcliffe, which may have been some consolation – but imagine the feelings of so young a bowler, encountering Hammond at his very best, not once but twice.

	Innings	N.O.	H.S.	Runs	Average	100	50
1932/33 (NZ)	2	1	336*	563	563.00	2	–
To date	64	8	336*	3731	66.64	13	13

	Balls	Run	Wickets	Average
1932/33 (NZ)	42	19	–	–
To date	4767	1828	52	35.15

Hammond had now overtaken Hendren's Test aggregate and was third only to Hobbs and Sutcliffe.

12 'We had it coming to us'

Hammond had a sensationally successful 1933. He might have been expected to suffer some reaction after a hard and emotional tour, but there was no sign of this. Within six weeks of his spectacular innings at Auckland, he was playing against Kent at Bristol, scoring 55 and 51 and bowling 52 overs as Gloucester won a thrilling game by eight runs. A week later, he took 178 off Middlesex, and so his summer continued. He scored 3,323 runs in the season at an average of 67.81 and this is still the seventh highest aggregate ever recorded. At this stage of his career he was more and more able to produce really massive scores and he made four double-centuries during the season. Together with his two triumphs in New Zealand, he had made six scores over 200 in six months, equalling anything Bradman ever did.

Hammond's torrent of runs was not carried through into his Test performance, though this was not regarded very seriously. The West Indies came to England in 1933, and they were not seen as dangerous opponents. Over the three three-day Tests, it was felt that somebody would get the runs against them and that England was, at the worst, safe against defeat. The relative failure of one batsman was not a critical matter. Jardine, not yet in disgrace with the Establishment, was the only possible captain.

Of the batsmen who had played in Australia, Sutcliffe, Hammond and Leyland were available and selected for the first Test at Lord's. CF Walters, who had recently moved from Glamorgan to Worcestershire and had been making a lot of runs, came in as an opener, and Turnbull, the captain of Glamorgan, at No 6. Larwood was unfit, and Macaulay partnered Allen as opening bowlers, while Robins, who had not been able to go to Australia, came back into the side. Oddly to modern eyes, the West Indies were short of bowlers. Constantine was playing for Nelson in the Lancashire League and the tour management hoped to secure him for the Tests, but Nelson could not at first see their way to releasing Constantine, and the West Indies had to settle for Francis, another League player, to partner Martindale, a full member of the side and a formidably fast bowler.

Jardine won the toss, and Walters and Sutcliffe began rather deliberately. It may well have been that when Hammond succeeded Sutcliffe, he felt that he should push the score along, and perhaps he took the bowling rather lightly. Cardus commented that he pulled two short balls from Achong, the slow left-arm bowler, for 'quite contemptuous fours' and that the stroke which got him out caught in the gully, was of the kind which 'nowadays a county batsman makes only under strong pressure'. Whose was the pressure? Whatever the reason, Hammond did play a rare uncontrolled stroke, and was out for 29.

Leyland failed and when Walters was out, England were 106 for 4 and in difficulties. Jardine and Turnbull each got a start but without consolidating and the score was 155 for 6. However, the England side of that era generally batted long and Ames, strongly supported, pulled the game round. He made 83 not out, and England finished on 296, Martindale being the best bowler with four wickets.

296 proved to be more than enough. The West Indies made a disastrous start, Allen dismissing Roach and Headley, the batting stars, cheaply and Robins making hay of the middle order. They were all out for 97 and, although Headley batted well in the second innings, the side was out again for 172 and England had won by tea-time on the third day. The West Indies had looked somewhat overawed. Cardus made a remark of some prescience:

'Humour would sprout and blossom at Lord's if the fast bowlers of the West Indies would indulge themselves, ever so politely, in bodyline methods.'

Was Cardus simply being mischievous? It has been suggested that when the West Indies *did* 'indulge themselves' at Old Trafford, they had been encouraged to do so by the powers-that-were, who wanted to see what all the fuss was about. Possibly Cardus had heard a whisper of this. If the visitors had been thinking about a little mayhem at Lord's they would have thought again, once Constantine was unavailable, but the pitch would probably have suited the new bowling better than the one at Manchester.

★   ★   ★   ★   ★

Both sides made changes for Old Trafford. Constantine was now available and replaced Francis; Wiles and Valentine took over from Merry and Griffith. On the face of it, it seems strange that they should have left Griffith out, if they were going to experiment with bodyline, but although he had been fast enough in his time, he was in his fortieth year, and had lost much of his pace. Allen had not been fully fit at

Lord's and he gave way to Clark, another potential exponent of bodyline, being, like Voce, a quick left-arm bowler whose natural line brought the ball in to the right-handed batsman. Leyland, unfit, and the unlucky Turnbull gave way to Wyatt and James Langridge.

This time the West Indies made an altogether better start. Roach went early, but Headley and Barrow played splendidly and put on 200 at a run a minute. Headley had already hit four centuries on the tour and was by now seen as the best batsman in the world outside England and Australia or, putting it another way, third only to Bradman and Hammond. It was fitting that he should play a great innings in a Test and once Barrow was out, he carried the flag almost alone, making 169 not out in a total of 375 which insured against defeat in a three-day match.

Some West Indian accounts of this innings assert very clearly that Clark bowled bodyline, or something very like it, and that what followed was by way of retaliation, but Constantine's own version is that the team decided, before the Test, to experiment with a bodyline attack. Certainly Sutcliffe and Walters faced a barrage of short balls and a bodyline field was set. When Sutcliffe was run out, Hammond became the prime target. He had his chin cut open by one ball, though the newspaper accounts suggest that this particular ball was 'not a bodyliner' which rather suggests that he may have played it into his face as Oldfield had done at Adelaide. Hammond's reaction was much as Bradman's had been; he attacked the other bowlers, looking to get some runs while he could and driving Headley for two huge sixes. When he was out, caught in the leg-trap for 34, he made the interesting comment, in private, that 'we started this, and we had it coming to us' but he clearly thought it was not a legitimate part of the game.

What followed is part of the folklore of bodyline. Wyatt and Walters were soon out and England were in some danger of having to follow on, but Jardine played the short stuff with immense skill and courage. He and Ames took the score from 134 for 4 to 217, and then Robins joined him in a great stand of 140 in two hours. It may have been significant that it was the amateur batsmen who faced the direct attack better; after all, the very livelihood of the pros was at stake. Jardine scored 127, playing for the most part with a straight bat, drawing himself up to his full height – he was a tall man – and playing the ball down to his feet. Old-fashioned observers were quick to announce that he had shown the Australians how to go about it, and that all the trouble could have been avoided if they had played 'properly' but this was nonsense. The Old Trafford wicket was slow and predictable, the worst possible proving-ground. Jardine would not have survived long if he had tried to play Larwood in the orthodox style on Australian pitches.

England finished one run behind and when the West Indians batted again, Clark certainly did launch a full-scale bodyline attack, but he was on his own and they were able to wait him out. After that, Langridge troubled them with spin and at 132 for 7, they seemed to have let England back into the game, but Constantine, who seldom shone with the bat in Tests as he did in other matches, saved the situation, adding 59 with Achong for the eighth wicket. There was never a moment when a sensible declaration could be made, and a lively match petered out in a draw. *Wisden's* comment on the tactics is a classic – it must be remembered that at this time the Establishment hadn't made up its collective mind about the morality of bodyline:

> '. . . most of those who were watching it for the first time must have come to the conclusion that, while strictly within the law, it was not nice'

Constantine had dismissed Hammond once again, in the only innings in which he bowled to him in 1933, but it is very pleasing to record that Hammond approached his great rival after the match and suggested that it was time they buried the hatchet. Thereafter, they were still trying all they knew to get the better of each other, and indeed Constantine troubled Hammond more than any other West Indian bowler to the end of their careers – but the needle had gone out of the encounters.

★　　★　　★　　★　　★

England made wholesale changes for the Oval Test. Jardine was injured, and Wyatt resumed the captaincy. Sutcliffe, suffering from some slight eye-trouble, gave way to Bakewell, and Turnbull came back. Nichols and Charles Barnett replaced Macaulay and Verity, the selectors deciding that Langridge, who had bowled well at Manchester, was the only finger-spinner they needed. Finally, 'Father' Marriott, a schoolmaster who only played for Kent in the holidays, took over from Robins as the leg-spinner. He was to be highly successful, but he was 37 years old, and it wasn't a constructive selection. Constantine was unavailable for the West Indies, and it seemed unlikely that their flirtation with bodyline would be repeated – they had made their point.

Once again, England made a poor start. Walters failed and Hammond was missed before he had scored. He never got going, and was well caught by the wicket-keeper down the leg-side off the fast-medium Valentine who thus took his only Test wicket. England were 68 for 4 at one moment, and it was well for them that Bakewell was playing soundly. Langridge was out of touch, but stayed for a long time, and after Bakewell had got out for 107, the only century of his Test career, Ames, Barnett and Nichols, powerful players to be coming in at seven, eight and nine saw the score to an acceptable 312.

Bakewell was an interesting and tragic figure. He was the most 'two-eyed' batsman on view in an era where many such players flourished, but emerged from his ugly stance to play scintillating strokes. He overcame the handicap of carrying a sensationally weak Northamptonshire side and more than once forced his way into a strong England batting side. Just as it seemed possible that he would achieve a permanent Test place, he was badly injured in a motor accident and played no more.

The selectors' decision to pack the batting had been justified, and their choice of Marriott was now justified also in the short term, for he went through the West Indies in no time at all, taking 5 for 37 in 71 balls. Wyatt put them in again and this time Roach attacked the fast men in his most aggressive style, putting on 77 in 40 minutes with Barrow. Once they were parted, Marriott did it again, this time taking 6 for 59. Headley's concentration was affected by two sharp knocks, but the others were simply unable to construe Marriott at all. It is one of cricket's oddities that he never played for England again, but he played so little that he could only force his way into the side for the final Test of any series, and there wasn't always a vacancy.

For once Hammond played no significant part in a Test series. He never got going with the bat, bowled only five overs and took four catches. It was very odd in the context of a marvellous county season – immediately after the third Test, he scored 231 against a formidable Derbyshire attack and 264 in six hours for Gloucester against the West Indies. He took another century off them at Folkestone and on the same ground scored 184 against the MCC. This lack of Test form was seen as a natural reaction after his heavy work in Australia. He was rested from the tour of India, in sensible anticipation of the task before him in 1934 when the Australians were coming, if cricket's diplomats could agree on the terms of reference.

Batting

	Innings	N.O.	H.S.	Runs	Average	100	50
1933	3	0	34	74	24.66	–	–
To date	67	8	336*	3805	64.49	13	13

Bowling

	Balls	Runs	Wickets	Average
1933	30	27	–	–
To date	4797	1855	52	35.67

13   A paradox, a paradox

For Hammond, 1934 was in a sense a re-run of 1933. He was senationally successful in county cricket but a total failure in the Tests. This was a more serious matter than in 1933, the Australians being the visitors, and the Tests closely enough contested for it to be arguable that Hammond's failure was the primary reason why the Ashes changed hands. My own first introduction to cricket history came when, one day in 1944, I picked up in Wimbledon Library a copy of Neville Cardus's brilliant *Good Days*. The book contains his daily reports on the Tests of 1934 and, as well as being bemused by all the talk about direct attack and sundry characters who weren't even there, I was at least half-way to being convinced that Hammond was a fine batsmen who sometimes – too often – failed on the big occasion. That was totally unfair, but such was the power of Cardus's writing.

Hammond started the year unluckily. He was suffering from a strained back and missed Gloucestershire's first match. He turned out against Middlesex at Lord's and scored 72, but his back went again and he had to drop out of cricket for nearly a month. Such was his reputation that nobody contemplated leaving him out of the England team for the first Test at Trent Bridge, even after he had failed in the Test Trial.

The season had been a pretty fraught one, so far. Jardine had declared before it started that he had 'neither the intention nor the desire' to play in the Tests. He undoubtedly realised that he would not be allowed to set the fields he wanted if he were captain and he would not have wished to captain a losing side using what he regarded as outmoded and ineffective tactics. (There were some pretty complex behind-the-scenes discussions, but this is not a history of backstairs diplomacy and the curious reader is referred to any one of several excellent modern histories of the whole miserable business.)

The MCC were clearly relieved by Jardine's decision to stand down but were probably less happy about Larwood's apparent reluctance to play using orthodox tactics. He declared himself unfit for this Test, possibly to allow the authorities time to change their minds about tactics if the Test were lost; it will be convenient to close this part of the story by saying that, following the first Test, both he and Voce declared themselves unavailable for the rest of the series. England would have to manage without them and without bodyline.

Wyatt was the obvious choice as captain and he was duly appointed, but he suffered nearly all season from the effects of a fractured thumb – he was one of the most brittle cricketers of all time – and he was in fact unfit for the first Test. At that time, it was unthinkable that England should be captained by a professional and the selectors turned to the senior of the three amateurs playing, CF Walters. This was the first Test against Australia and it would be an ordeal for him to lead the side, but there was a wealth of experience there, and nobody who would be likely to make life difficult for a new captain.

It was a pretty good side, the batting, apart from Walters himself, being Sutcliffe, Hammond, Leyland, Pataudi and Hendren, who was having a remarkable Indian summer and had scored 100s against the Australians for both MCC and Middlesex. Ames was in excellent form with the bat and headed the averages for a good part of the summer. Geary was the all-rounder and the other bowlers were Farnes, Verity and Mitchell.

Australia had made a good start to the tour, never once looking in danger of defeat. As ever the batsmen had made a lot of runs. Bradman had gone through a bad patch, judged by his own very high standards, but had emerged from it with a scintillating 160 against Middlesex, and six other Australian batsmen had made 100s. The bowling had looked much less impressive and it was evident that the result of the series would depend on how well the England batsmen coped with Grimmett and O'Reilly. Hammond's performance here would be crucial.

Woodfull won the toss and he and Ponsford started slowly and, on the whole, safely. Farnes bowled with fire and life but with a totally orthodox field. It was he who made the break at last, getting Ponsford caught at the wicket at 77 (it seems to have been a doubtful decision) and then he had Woodfull brilliantly caught in the gully by Verity just before lunch. Bradman came in and began to play rather wildly, as indeed he did in his first four innings in the series. He made a rapid 29, memorably described by Cardus as his 'great ride to the everlasting bonfire' and was caught by Hammond off the wicket-keeper's glove. Two wickets then fell quickly and it was left to Chipperfield, playing in his first Test, to put things right. He did so with the utmost aplomb, first supporting McCabe and then taking charge in partnerships with Oldfield and with Grimmett. But, poor Chipperfield, he reached 99 just before lunch on the second day and, after what must have seemed an intolerably long break, was out immediately afterwards, passing into the record books as the first man to make 99 on his Test debut.

Australia were all out for 374, no bad score in the circumstances,

Farnes being the most effective bowler with 5 for 102 in this first Test. Walters and Sutcliffe began uncertainly, but got to 45 before Walters was out to Grimmett. Hammond was very aware that England looked to him for a lead, and he began in defensive vein, looking safe but handing the initiative to the spinners. All at once, the game took its decisive turn. Sutcliffe, who had been going well was caught, and then Hammond, trying to open out, played too soon at O'Reilly and was caught at mid-on. Leyland was out before the close and Australia were well on top.

Pataudi had been extremely shaky from the moment he came in and he was out to Wall early on the third day, the only batsman not to be out to either Grimmett or O'Reilly. When Ames fell, the score was a horrific 165 for 6, but Hendren and Geary, the two oldest men in the side, added 101 to keep England in the match – but only just. They were all out for 268, 106 behind and it was now a matter of Woodfull's timing of his declaration.

Farnes and Hammond shot the openers out, and Bradman was again uncertain and flashy, getting out to Farnes when he had made 25, but Brown and McCabe took charge, and Australia were 159 for 3 at the close. Woodfull played it very safe on the last day, batting on till 12.30pm and leaving England to make 380 or more realistically, to bat for 285 minutes to save the game. He was cutting it rather fine, but Test captains seldom take the slightest risk with a declaration, certainly not in the first game of a series. As usual when England were trying to keep the game quiet, Hammond had had a long bowl, sending down 12 overs for just 25 runs.

Sutcliffe and Walters started confidently, making a chanceless 27 in 45 minutes before lunch, but of course the trouble would start when the shine was off and Grimmett and O'Reilly came on together. Grimmett struck the first blow at 2.50pm when he had Sutcliffe caught at slip. England must have thought they had every chance of saving the game, particularly as Hammond looked good from the outset. He was defensive but sound, and when O'Reilly overpitched, he thumped him for two good fours. Woodfull now switched his two spinners to the opposite ends and this proved to be the decisive move. Hammond was stumped, which might suggest that he was playing irresponsibly, but in fact he was beaten by Grimmett on the forward stroke and simply overbalanced. He had batted for 45 minutes for 16. Walters, Pataudi and Hendren were all out before tea – Pataudi *was* somewhat irresponsible, skying an attempted off-drive – and England were 115 for 5.

After tea, Leyland and Ames, who were to be England's heroes during the whole series, batted doggedly if scratchily for almost an hour. The Australians must have been thinking that they had lost their chance when Ames was bowled by O'Reilly with 46 minutes to go. Geary fell at once and although Leyland and Verity fought it out like good Yorkshiremen, the great pair of spinners got through at last, bowling England out for 141 with ten minutes to spare. Woodfull's cautious judgement had been vindicated, although he must have had some nasty moments. Grimmett had taken 8 for 120, O'Reilly 11 for 129, and it was clearer than ever that they were the key men – they and the England batsmen who had to face them.

★　　★　　★　　★　　★

It was generally thought that England would make a number of changes for the Lord's Test, but in fact there were only two. Wyatt was just about fit enough to play, though his thumb was in a splint and bothered him for the rest of the season. He replaced Pataudi, who never played again for England though he returned as captain of the Indian touring team in 1946.

The selectors decided to play two fast bowlers; it is strange, today, to read the critics' comments on 'the artillery of England – the barrage of fast bowling' (Cardus), but it was distinctly unusual, before bodyline, to open with two outright fast men – of course the selection, like everything else that summer, had diplomatic overtones. Ironically, the match was decided by a top-class spinner, aided by the weather, and neither Farnes nor Geary, now relegated to first change, played much part. Hammond, indeed, bowled one over more than Farnes, which is not to say that anybody thought him a better bowler. Australia made one enforced change – Ponsford was ill, and Bromley replaced him.

Sutcliffe and Walters began well. Sutcliffe was very subdued, but this hardly seemed to matter when Walters was in such good form, playing all the bowlers well and looking distinctly sounder against Grimmett than he had at Nottingham. Grimmett, in fact, was unusually expensive and Woodfull brought Chipperfield on to replace him at one o'clock. Chipperfield was very much the third-string spinner, and it was a complete surprise when he had Sutcliffe lbw. Worse followed, for Hammond played forward to him, hard but rather carelessly, and was caught and bowled for 2. England were in trouble again, and if they failed, Hammond would be the one to take the blame.

Things continued to go badly. Hendren was caught off Wall, and then Walters, deceived by O'Reilly's slower ball, was caught at short-leg. Wyatt was clearly troubled by his injury and it all looked very bleak, but Leyland at this stage of his career had just about solved the riddle of O'Reilly – he was at all events playing him as well as anybody ever did – and Grimmett was having one of his rare off-days. Wyatt, out of touch, struggled along until Chipperfield came back and had him caught, at 182 for 5. Ames rightly took no risks at all, concentrating on defence while Leyland undramatically established his dominance. It was one of those days when the initiative changes slowly but surely until the underdog is in total command. As Cardus put it: 'Leyland hit a no-ball for six. . . and 20,000 people woke up and discovered that Australia had lost grip on the match'. Reading about it, that's exactly how it seems. 182 had become 293, with Leyland and Ames still together, and nobody quite knew how it had happened.

The Saturday was an odd day. On the face of it, Australia established a strong position, possibly a winning one. It looked very like the stage reached half-way through the same Test four years earlier, though Australia had further to go. However, a decision of Wyatt's had already settled the outcome, though nobody could possibly have guessed it. At the start, Leyland and Ames went on where they had left off. Leyland completed a 100 entirely typical of him, unspectacular but dutiful, and then Ames took over the leading role with sterling support from Geary and Verity. Ames was out before lunch and at the interval the score was 410 for 9.

Now Wyatt took his crucial decision. He was no doubt mindful of the disastrous forcing of the game four years earlier, when England sacrificed a chance of making 500 and then found that 425 was by no means enough. He allowed Verity and Bowes to bat on after lunch, and they batted very soundly to take the score to 440. It might not be enough, but it was a good score after the catastrophic start.

Woodfull and Brown dealt with the so-called artillery in the most authoritative way. It was suggested by Fender that Farnes might not have been fully fit, and he certainly showed less fire than at Nottingham. Bowes seemed unsure about his tactics; he tried to bump a few at the batsmen, but certainly didn't launch anything like an all-out physical attack. Each batsman had a narrow escape or two against him, and finally he bowled Woodfull with the score at 68.

Bradman followed and, much as at Nottingham, he went for everything. At this point in the season, he seemed to be saying to opposing captains and bowlers 'See, here I am, prepared to play strokes and give you a chance – no need for fancy theories.' It has to be remembered that he was far from well throughout the season, but there was some psychological damage, too. Whatever the cause, he tore into Farnes and Verity, scoring 36 off 37 balls, but was then caught and bowled by Verity, in much the same way as Hammond got out; one wonders whether this was an early manifestation of the ridge we heard so much about in the '60s and thereafter. Australia were now 141 for 2,

90

and needed to consolidate. Consolidate they did, and Brown and McCabe were still there at the end of the day, the score being 192. Brown had made a fine century on his first appearance in a Lord's Test.

When the play was analysed in the Sunday papers, most people expected a long Australian score, maybe 600, and an uphill fight by England to save the game. True, Bradman was out, but there was plenty of batting to come, and the bowlers had all been played with confidence. However, it rained for much of the Sunday, and this changed everything. In those days, pitches were of course left uncovered and England had one of the best wet-wicket bowlers in the world in Verity. The follow-on could then be enforced, even in a four-day match, by a side with a lead of 150, so that the Australians' first target was 291.

It was faintly surprising that Wyatt put Verity on at the Pavilion End, where he would have to turn the ball up the very considerable slope. Wyatt was a very thoughtful captain who missed very little and he must have had a reason. He may well have thought that Verity would turn the ball so much that, with the slope, he would beat everything whereas, from the other end, he would be able to get his arm-ball to move with the slope. Or he may have reasoned that it would be lift rather than turn which would do the business. In any event, such was his decision; he could always switch Verity if he needed to.

England had an early success when Bowes had Brown caught behind, but Verity soon came into the action, taking three quick wickets. At 218 for 6, Australia were in terrible trouble, but they had some real fighters in the team and Chipperfield and Oldfield were not to be brushed aside. Oldfield was very experienced in English conditions – he was on his fifth tour, including the AIF tour of 1919 – and Chipperfield was a very English-type player with a very straight bat. They had put on 40, and Australia needed only 33 more to put England in again, when Verity had Oldfield caught.

Grimmett, another veteran, succeeded him and he too looked sound and safe. Wyatt baffled observers by changing Verity over to the Nursery End; perhaps he should have been there all along, but the change unsettled him, and Wyatt promptly put him back at the Pavilion end. Things were getting very tight when Bowes forced Grimmett to play on; the players took lunch, if they could eat any, with Australia needing just 18. This was a really critical point, for if England had had to bat again, they would have been hard put to it to score quickly, and Wyatt would have had a tricky declaration decision to make, as Woodfull had had at Nottingham. Furthermore, it might rain again.

However, all turned out well for England. Verity got O'Reilly and Wall out after lunch and Australia had fallen short by seven runs. The wisdom of Wyatt's safety-first decision on the Saturday was now plain to see. Had he declared at 410, the follow-on would have been saved without doubt. Bowes made the first break in the second innings, getting Brown caught at long-leg off a bouncer. By an extraordinary irony, this was the first wicket to fall to the bouncer in the series, and there were to be only three more. Times had indeed changed.

McCabe came in ahead of Bradman – Woodfull must have been hoping against hope for an interruption and a better wicket on the fourth day – but he was out at once and Bradman had to face the music. He opened with two rather desperate-looking strokes, then settled into defence. However, Verity played upon his patience till when he was on 13 he got him to hit all across a good-length ball which he skied heavens high. Any one of four men could have got to it, but Wyatt called firmly for Ames and he held it. This was the mortal blow. Woodfull fought on, as he always did, but Verity bowled him at 94, and the last rites were mercifully brief. Hammond, who had a long bowl and got a good deal out of the pitch, bowled Darling, and took two catches. England could count themselves rather lucky to have won, but Verity had bowled magnificently, to take 15 for 104.

★　★　★　★　★

So far, Hammond had done very little with the bat in the Tests, but as in 1933, he was doing wonders in the county matches. He had made 134 and 164 in the two games played between the first and second Tests, and he now played a tremendous innings of 290 against Kent in just 315 minutes, the highest score he had made in England. There was no question of leaving him out for Old Trafford, and indeed the selectors stayed with the first seven in the batting order, but omitted all the bowlers except Verity and brought in Allen, Clark and Hopwood, the Lancashire all-rounder. This seems to have been a little hard on Bowes, who had bowled well at Lord's on a pitch that wasn't giving him much help, but the selectors were looking to extend the batting and improve the fielding. Ponsford was fit again, and came back for Bromley.

Unusually Manchester was enjoying a heat-wave and the whole match was played out in warm, enervating weather. Several of the Australians were suffering from a form of tonsillitis which also affected a number of players at the All-England tennis championships and was dubbed 'Wimbledon throat' by the newspapers. In his generally run-down state, Bradman was one of the worst affected, but he played in the Test.

Wyatt won the toss again, and Sutcliffe and Walters opened on a beautiful batting wicket. Walters went off like a train, scoring 52 out of 68 in the first hour and handling all the bowlers with confidence. Sutcliffe was quieter, but equally at ease. Drinks were taken after this first hour and the ball was changed. This was by no means so regular a ploy as it has now become and contemporary accounts are silent about whose idea it was, but it worked. O'Reilly instantly deceived Walters with his slower ball, which came in to him and had him edging to short-leg. Wyatt came next, possibly because he felt the need to consolidate before turning Hammond loose, possibly because of Hammond's shaky Test performances to date. His decision turned out be an academic one, for he was bowled first ball and Hammond, after glancing his first ball for four, was bowled by the next. O'Reilly had taken three wickets in four balls, still a rare feat in a Test, and England were 72 for 3.

Sutcliffe now took charge, making a bee-line for O'Reilly's end, and under his protection, Hendren was able to settle. Runs continued to flow and at lunch the score was 126, made in two hours. It has a pleasantly old-fashioned look – a run a minute despite the collapse, but the over-rate was a generous one, with only one fast bowler on view. Sutcliffe was caught off O'Reilly soon after lunch, but he had done good service in settling things down after that one bad over, and England were now able to capitalise. Leyland was in excellent form throughout the series and he and Hendren, playing his last big innings for England, took the score to 340 before Hendren was out, yet again to O'Reilly, who bowled splendidly all day, the only dangerous bowler.

Leyland went on to another 100 next day, well supported by Ames, and when they were out the exhausted attack was roughly handled by Allen and Verity, who put on 95 in no time at all. On this occasion, Wyatt did think it safe to declare at 627 for 9, and curiously enough it wasn't – he lost himself a very faint chance of winning by doing so. Both Bradman and Chipperfield had been off the field with this throat infection during much of the England innings, and one or two others were distinctly under the weather, but England didn't bowl very well, and Australia managed to save the follow-on.

Clearly if Wyatt had gone on to, say, 675 (there is evidence that Allen and Verity were instructed to have a dip), it would have been that much more difficult for Australia to save the follow on. Even as it was, England should have had them out for under 400, but McCabe batted splendidly, as he often did in a crisis, Woodfull fought hard and long for 73, and the invalids batted and did valiantly, Bradman being noticeably more correct for being more subdued, a relative term, since he scored 30 off 52 balls. The England bowling and fielding was lackadaisical, but Hammond was excepted from the general criticism. He bowled 28.3 overs during which he dismissed Bradman, Ponsford and McCabe, a distinguished bag. He also ran Woodfull out with a fine pick-up on the turn and accurate throw, but it was all to no avail, as Chipperfield,

O'Reilly and Wall added 72 for the last two wickets and Australia finished only 136 behind.

It probably didn't matter very much. On a perfect wicket, Australia would no doubt have saved the game if they had followed on. As it was, the last day was pretty pointless. Sutcliffe and Walters made 123 perfunctory runs, before Wyatt made a token declaration. Hammond had time to make a slip catch before the game petered out with Hendren bowling a rare over and probably getting a laugh or two at the same time.

★   ★   ★   ★   ★

After all the furore about fast bowling, it was odd that England now opted to go into the Leeds Test with three spinners, plus Bowes and Hammond. As compared with the Old Trafford side, Bowes and Mitchell replaced Clark and Allen, who had not distinguished themselves. Hammond would have a lot of bowling to do; this was a compliment to him, but also perhaps, a recognition that he was not yet pulling his weight with the bat, though once again he had been in great county form between the Tests, scoring 217 against Notts and 114 against Leicestershire. The inexplicable pattern of his season was being maintained.

England batted first on a damp, but not difficult, pitch. Sutcliffe was injured and Keeton of Notts had come in. He started a little tentatively, while Walters again batted well, but once O'Reilly and Grimmett came on the scoring slowed right down. O'Reilly eventually trapped Keeton with his faster ball, which was always distinctly quick and, if he dropped it in the right place, good enough for anybody. Hammond batted at No 3, the experiment of batting Wyatt above him having been abandoned, but he and Walters were both very tentative.

The ball was turning a good deal, if slowly, and once again it was Chipperfield who made a vital break, getting Walters to give him a return catch. Chipperfield had an odd Test career as a bowler; he played in four series, but all of his five wickets were taken in 1934, and all of them were highly-rated batsmen. Hendren now joined Hammond and they seemed for a while to be mastering the conditions, Hammond at last showing glimpses of his county form, but Wall came back and bowled him with a sizeable breakback. It had been his best Test innings this season, but he had got as far as 37, and many observers thought he should have been able to build on that. Hendren was out at once and at 135 for 4, England were struggling.

This time there was no recovery. For once Leyland failed, and Wyatt was stumped forward in defence. The pavilion critics must have been

94

crying out for someone to take the attack by the scruff of the neck – Ames tried this and was caught at the wicket. England were all out for 200, a poor score on a slow wicket. However the day's sensations were not over. Brown and Ponsford opened, and Bowes now produced a breakback to defeat Brown. Woodfull didn't always use a night-watchman in these situations, but he did so this time, sending in Oldfield. He failed to stay the course, being caught by Ames in Bowes' next over. This put Woodfull in a real dilemma. He would not have been anxious to use another night-watchman, which would possibly have left a good player high and dry at the end of the innings, but this was no moment to risk Bradman. He did the brave thing and went in himself, but he was ill-rewarded, being bowled round his legs, second ball. There was no time for anyone else to bat and stumps were drawn at 39 for 3.

On the Saturday Bradman came in with two balls of Bowes' over to come. Each ball was bowled just short of a length and round about the leg-stump. 99 batsmen out of a 100 would have played them defensively, but Bradman was the hundredth, and he hit both balls whistling back past the bowler for four. This set the tone for the day. From that moment, he carried the game to England, offering only one fiendishly difficult chance which went to Hopwood's wrong hand and was dropped. Ponsford, too, was dropped once, off a very hard hit, but otherwise Australia accelerated remorselessly.

Hammond was the most economical of the bowlers, Ponsford scoring at only two runs an over from him, but nobody else could even contain them and it came as an enormous relief when Ponsford, in hitting Verity to the boundary contrived to tread on his wicket. By then the score was 427, and England had nothing to hope for but rain. Ponsford had made 181 and Bradman was looking as though no target was beyond him, but on the third day, Bowes produced a very fine spell as Australia looked for quick runs and 517 for 4 at one stage became 584 all out – it was surely enough, but it might have been a lot more. Bradman had made 304 in 430 minutes, batting almost as well as he had four years earlier, and had given his bowlers plenty of time to win.

Keeton fell early and he was accounted to be unlucky in having to bat on a slightly unusual wicket in his first Test innings and in an impossible situation in his second. It was to be a long time before he got another chance, and then he was to be unlucky again. Hammond came in at 28 for 1, and it was still only lunchtime on the third day. He made a shaky start. The peculiar ups and downs of his season seemed to be affecting his confidence, but he got over his early difficulties and was beginning to shape well when disaster struck. He played a ball to mid-wicket, both batsmen hesitated, then went for the run. Wall made a brillant pick-up and throw and Hammond was out by a wide margin. It was significant that, poor as Hammond's Test form had been, his dismissal for only 20 was seen by the critics as a stunning blow and although there was plenty of batting to come, most England supporters abandoned hope at this moment. Walters seemed to be affected by the mishap and was bowled before he could settle, but Hendren was calm. He and Wyatt took the score to 152, and then Leyland stayed with him to the close, which came at 188 for 4, with some very ominous storm clouds to disturb Woodfull's repose.

On the final day, Cardus was obliged to acknowledge that 'Providence is a good Englishman, as most of us have long suspected.' Hendren and Ames were soon out, and Hopwood was in terrible trouble, looking as though he would get out to O'Reilly at any moment, when the heavens opened and five minutes of torrential rain brought the match to an end. England had got away with it, though no observer believed they deserved to.

The England selectors were now in a lot of trouble. Both batting and bowling had been terribly exposed at Leeds and there seemed a distinct shortage of talented young players to fill the gaps. In four years' time there was to be a whole new generation, but for the moment there was nobody, as a glance at the 1934 first-class averages will show. The final Test at the Oval was to be played to a finish now and there was just nowhere for England to hide. The selectors named four fast bowlers – Allen, Bowes, Clark and Gover – leaving the final choice to the day of the match. Verity was an automatic choice, and Peebles of Middlesex was, rather bafflingly, named as a possible. He had played hardly any cricket in 1934, and it all savoured of panic. In the event he was injured in a county match on the day the selection was announced and we shall never know whether he would have played, or what would have happened to him if he had. He himself said he thought he was well out of it.

Sutcliffe was fit again and the selectors hoped to return to the Old Trafford line-up which had done so well, but Hendren injured his elbow and couldn't play. The selectors took an odd decision and picked Frank Woolley, as a response to the leg-spinners – but Woolley was now 47 and had never played against O'Reilly. Good judges thought he would be vulnerable to the googly, and so it proved. What of Hammond? He continued in amazing county form, hitting three centuries between the fourth and fifth Tests, including 302 not out against Glamorgan. It was inconceivable that he would fail yet again in a Test, and he was in everybody's team.

Hammond got no chance to show what he could do for the first two days, for Bradman and Ponsford repeated, indeed surpassed, their Leeds effort by making 451 for the second wicket, Bradman making 244 without a chance in 316 minutes. Ponsford enjoyed more luck, being dropped six times, mostly close to the wicket. There after, the other batsmen had only to consolidate and the final score was 701, achieved by tea-time on the second day. Walters and Sutcliffe, though they must have been very weary, did a wonderful job for England by batting out the day and scoring 90, with only one half-chance. England were still likely to lose, and by a very large margin, but given that Australia had at one point been 472 for 1, they had recovered some ground.

The third day, however, was a sorry one. Both the openers were out very early on and Woolley was out to O'Reilly just as predicted, caught at short-leg off one which lifted a little. Hammond was now bearing a huge burden of expectation and of personal anxiety too, no doubt. He failed to surmount his problems. After seeing Wyatt bowled, he himself was caught at the wicket off Ebeling, playing in his only Test in place of Wall, who was injured. Hammond had made only 15, and with him went, realistically, England's last chance of making the big score they needed.

Yet again, Leyland and Ames batted with skill and resolution and added 85 but then, apparently, Providence decided that he wasn't a good Englishman, whatever Mr Cardus thought. Ames, turning sharply at the end of a run, was stricken with lumbago – the occupational disease of cricketers – and had to leave the field. This was of course a double blow. It meant that the England innings was effectively in decline and also that, if Woodfull decided to bat again, a substitute wicket-keeper would have to be found.

Undaunted, Leyland battled on, exhibiting his usual sound defence and relishing his mastery of O'Reilly. Mr Fender's admirable analytical work tells us that he scored 36 runs off 46 balls from the great leg-spinner, pretty nearly five an over.

Allen and Verity gave useful support, but when Clark came in at 311 for 7, he brought the unwelcome news first that Ames would not be returning and second that Bowes wouldn't bat either. He was suffering from a fistula, a type of ulcer, last in the news when King Henry VIII had it. King Henry and Bill Bowes could scarcely be more contrasted characters, but their presence or absence was of equal significance to England (in the appropriate context, of course.) Bowes' batting was not of great significance but his bowling was, and his loss seemed to be the final blow to England's hopes of escaping total annihilation. Leyland lashed out once he heard the news and was bowled for a splendid 110. He was the first man to score three centuries for England in an Ashes series at home, and the feat was not equalled until David Gower did it in 1985.

Woodfull did bat again, 380 in front, and indeed he really had no choice in a timeless match. Wyatt asked Woolley to keep wicket and although he made a most brave attempt at it, many were saddened to see him in so undignified a role in what was clearly going to be his last Test. Hammond would very possibly have taken on the job if Bowes had not been unwell, but as it was, his bowling would be needed.

Clark, perhaps disgruntled at having to bowl again in an impossible situation, placed a full leg-theory field and let himself go. There is no evidence that he hit any of the batsmen, but he certainly got to Ponsford, and had him caught by Hammond in the leg-trap, having previously had Brown caught close in. Bradman and McCabe had a little luck in coping with this onslaught, but with Bowes away, it could not be sustained for long and they were soon doing much as they pleased. By the close, they were 186 for 2, helped by quite a few extras, the leg-stump attack having presented Woolley with problems – although he was seen to be enjoying himself most of the time.

Australia were thus 566 on going into the fourth day and it seemed that there was almost no limit to the score they might make. England could well be asked to make 1,000. Luckily it didn't turn out to be quite as bad as that.

Bowes had had a minor operation the day before and was fit to bowl and he bowled Bradman at once. The Australian had been 76 overnight and most people would have bet on his being the first to score a 200 and a century in the same Test, but it wasn't to be, and the statisticians had to wait until 1969 for Doug Walters to perform the feat. Bowes now bowled Woodfull and Clark had Kippax and McCabe caught. Australia were 236 for 6, and England were dying hard. The score hardly mattered, but the crowd were delighted by the fighting spirit. Hammond held two final catches – he took 11 in the series – and the whole England performance was marred only by their inability to separate Ebeling and O'Reilly, who added 55 for the last wicket. England had to make 708 to win, a ludicrous target, it appeared. The epic of Durban 1939 was undreamed of, but the situation was in any event quite different. The wicket was beginning to wear, and two great spinners lay in wait.

Two wickets fell before the spinners even got into action. McCabe bowled Walters and had Woolley caught at mid-off. Woolley must have been very tired after keeping and it was a sad moment. Hammond, as at Leeds, shaped well when all seemed lost, but he tried to drive O'Reilly and was caught and bowled for 43. It had been a miserably unsuccessful series for him and he had now to watch the rest of the side get out, batting in rather dispirited fashion. Ames was still absent and

98

England were all out for 145, losing by 562. Grimmett and O'Reilly had taken 53 wickets between them in the series and had destroyed England without a lot help from the pitches. They were probably the finest *pair* of spinners ever to take the field in England.

Hammond's figures make melancholy reading and the contrast with his figures in county matches, in which he averaged 126, is inexplicable:

	Innings	N.O.	H.S.	Runs	Average	100	50
1934	8	–	43	162	20.25	–	–
To date	75	8	336*	3967	59.20	13	13

	Balls	Runs	Wickets	Average
1934	723	364	5	72.80
To date	5520	2219	57	38.92

14   The strangest Test ever?

Hammond was of course selected for the MCC tour of the West Indies in 1934-35. Although the home side had done very well in the 1929-30 series, they had been well beaten in 1933, and it was not thought necessary to send the very strongest side – nevertheless Hammond's all-round skills would be needed. It seems odd today, to talk of taking chances with a selection for the West Indies but England still sent a second eleven in 1947-48. Slow learners, one might say.

Only six of the tourists had played in the Tests of 1934: Wyatt the captain, Hammond, Hendren, Leyland, Farnes and Ames. They were joined by only one other Test player, Farrimond, the second wicket-keeper. Then there were three amateurs – Holmes, who had had a reasonably good season for Surrey, DCH Townsend, who had had a middling sort of season for Oxford and was never in fact to play for a first-class county, and one WE Harbord, who played 16 matches for Yorkshire over a period of six years and was not, by any stretch of the imagination, a likely Test player. There were four uncapped professionals, Paine of Warwickshire, a left-arm spinner, Iddon the Lancashire all-rounder, Hollies, a leg-spinner of great promise, and Jim Smith of Middlesex, a fast-medium bowler and enormously powerful hitter. With hindsight, it doesn't look a powerful side and although some notable cricket was played by both sides, it wasn't successful.

For some years England sides visiting the West Indies had started in Barbados, and they usually got a rude shock. The 1925-26 side had been well beaten in the opening match and in the next four tours which began there, the MCC were either beaten or had the worst of a draw. This time, Barbados batted first and made 382 on a rain-affected pitch on which only Hollies looked at all threatening. MCC replied with only 170 (Hammond 2) and had to work hard to save the game. It was an inauspicious start, but Hammond restored English morale with a marvellous 281 not out in the return. He batted for six hours and gave no chance.

The climax of the innings sounds like something out of a boys' adventure book. Hammond and Jim Smith added 122 for the last wicket in 45 minutes, Smith making 83 of them with five sixes and nine fours.

100

Hammond was content to give him his head, though it will be noticed that he himself was going at about a run a minute at the time. Barbados had to follow on, but were saved by rain.

As I have suggested, the team for the first Test pretty well picked itself, Townsend, Harbord and Farrimond being left out. The West Indies were without Constantine and look to have been a bowler short, though as the match went that didn't matter. It was one of the strangest, most sensational matches in history.

There had been some rain before the match, and the wicket was likely to help the faster bowlers. Wyatt, knowing that a West Indian wicket can roll out fast and true on the second day, even when it has been a bed of pain for the batsmen on the first, put them in and got a quick wicket when Carew had a hook at Farnes, top-edged and was caught by Hendren. Carew didn't bat in the second innings, was dropped and for many years seemed likely to go down to posterity with the unhappy record of Innings 1 Runs 0 Average 0.00, but, surprisingly, he was picked again 13 years later against Allen's side, scored a century and played in two more Tests. One of the more bizarre Test careers, but no more bizarre than this Test, where only the great George Headley could do anything at all with the bowling. Farnes, Hollies and Paine all looked deadly, and the West Indies were all out for 102, Headley run out for 44. Hammond didn't bowl – though he did make one brilliant slip-catch to dismiss Rolph Grant.

When England batted the wicket was no better, and Wyatt and Leyland, two tried bad-wicket batsmen, were out with the score only 14. It seemed that nobody could cope with the West Indian fast bowlers on a pitch where the ball might do absolutely anything, but Hammond, by all accounts, batted serenely and immaculately, as if he were on a shirt-front at the Oval. By the close of play he had made 43, driving anything well pitched up and hooking Martindale off his eyebrows. Nobody else had been able to cope, and England were 81 for 5.

It rained again next day and the players didn't get on the field until after tea. Before he could gauge any change in the pace of the pitch, Hammond played a dead-bat stroke to a kicker and was caught at short-leg. Holmes also pushed out and was caught. Wyatt instantly declared, reasoning that his tail-enders wouldn't make many on the pitch (he had already used Jim Smith, who had been caught off a tremendous skier) and that he was better off bowling on such a pig of a wicket. He needed wickets before the rain returned, and he got them. Jack Grant shuffled his batsmen, hoping that his tail-enders would use up valuable time, but three wickets went down for four runs. Hylton and Christiani played out time, though not without some luck, and the close came at 33 for 3. West Indies were 54 ahead which might even be enough if the weather didn't improve.

Once again there was rain in the night and it continued all morning. They were able to make a start at three o'clock. Hylton and Christiani soon fell to Smith and then Headley, determined to seize the initiative, took a tremendous swipe at Farnes, but skied the ball to be caught by Paine for a duck. Tea was taken at 51 for 6 and to the general amazement Grant declared. It looked suicidal – he was only 72 ahead – but one can understand his thinking. The wicket would get no better that day which should help them to pick up a few wickets, but if he batted on, getting only a few more runs, the wicket could well roll out an easy one. Surely it couldn't rain for ever. He was of course gambling that acknowledged bad-wicket technicians such as Leyland, Hendren and, above all, Hammond, would fail.

From our distance, this match resembles a game of blindfold chess between the two captains, one daring gambit following another. Wyatt responded to Grant's challenge by sending in his opening bowlers to start the batting. Farnes and Smith thus became one of the very few pairs to open both the batting and the bowling in the same Test. This ploy, designed to gain time for the recognised batsmen, failed, the two players making two runs between them. Wyatt didn't persevere with the tactic, but followed with Holmes and Hendren; he was clearly saving Hammond for the *coup de grace*.

When Hendren pulled Hylton for a huge six, England seemed to be getting on top, but this was a game where a single wicket, or a single big hit, could sway the whole outcome, and when Holmes and Leyland were out, it was 29 for 4 and West Indian hopes were high. Now, at last, Hammond stalked to the wicket and once again he batted calmly and powerfully. This match was an example if one were needed of a truism that a really bad pitch reveals the true batting genius. Nobody would quarrel with the proposition that Hammond and Headley were by some distance the best two batsmen on view in this series, and on this pitch they looked to be not merely in a different class, but of a different species. In the end, the match was decided when Hammond came off twice and Headley only once.

Hendren stayed for a while, but compared with Hammond, he looked frenetic, using his feet well but incapable of ordinary stroke-play. He was out at 43 when Wyatt, still trying to preserve his remaining batsmen, sent in Paine. He made only 2, and then came Wyatt himself. He seemed unable to get the ball away, but his defence was as sound as Hammond's own and, with Hammond scoring with comparative ease, defence at the other end was all that was needed.

Hammond was now stepping back and playing the bouncers through

102

the gaps on the off-side and the runs were coming almost without a false stroke or a miscue. Some onlookers were deceived into thinking that the wicket was easing but it was really a matter of two masters of technique getting in and staying in. The whole episode didn't last very long, the 75 runs coming from 99 balls and Hammond finished the match with a glorious drive for six.

Grant was condemned for his bold declaration, but it had really represented his best chance and he had been thwarted by Hammond's wonderful batting. He was to have the last laugh, but for the moment he was the villain, Wyatt and Hammond the heroes. Some of the press comment makes one wonder about the sophistication and expertise of the writers; one local paper said that 'Hammond was never confident' – well, he had reason not to be – and the *Barbados Advocate* said that he was 'not the Hammond of last week'!

★   ★   ★   ★   ★

The team went on to Trinidad where they had rather the worst of two drawn matches with the island team, and then suffered a serious blow when Farnes strained his neck and dropped out of the team for the Test. The party was in any case short of bowlers and the attack for this Test looks a weak one with only two specialist bowlers in Smith and Paine. Wyatt and Hammond were going to have to do a lot of bowling.

For the home team, Constantine was now available and he, Martindale and Hylton were a fearsome attack. It may have been the thought of this that induced Wyatt to put the West Indies in but the move, ultimately, failed. He did capture early wickets, but Constantine scored 90, the highest innings of his Test career and only got out when going for runs off every ball with the last man in. The West Indies made 302, neither good nor bad, but it looked a lot better when England were 23 for 5. Hammond had made only 1 when he was very well caught by Rolph Grant as he fended at a riser from Hylton. There was more than a suspicion of intimidation about the work of the three fast bowlers in these Tests, an aftermath perhaps of the Bodyline Test in 1933, and Hammond didn't care for it. The later England batsmen recovered well, and they made 258, just 44 behind. The West Indies, Headley leading the way with 93, batted steadily until Grant declared at 280 for 6, leaving England to make 325 in four hours, an impossible task.

Once again, the fast men turned on a frightening display, comparable in the context of the time, with the bowling of the great West Indian teams of the 1980s. Constantine was warned by the umpire for intimidatory bowling. Hammond's distaste was again manifest, though he himself was bowled for 9 by a breakback from Constantine.

Wyatt repeated his device of shuffling the batting order, this time with the idea that the hitters would upset the fast bowlers' rhythm, but it was a failure, and a policy that nominated batsmen of the calibre of Leyland, Iddon and Holmes as nine, ten, jack deserved to fail. The West Indies won in the last over, and the England batsmen had had a bad match. Hammond had made only 10 runs, and although he had bowled 24 steady overs, had not taken a wicket. The outlook for him and England was uncertain.

★　★　★　★　★

Before the third Test, MCC won another of those extraordinary matches on an impossible wicket. Going in against a British Guiana score of 188 for 8 declared, they were 41 for 5 when Wyatt declared. He and Paine then put British Guiana out for 57, taking four wickets apiece. MCC got the 205 they needed with some ease, Hammond scoring 106 not out. This was further proof of Wyatt's theory that West Indian pitches rolled out better than any in the world once the rain was out of them, but it did encourage him to go on experimenting, with disastrous results.

The Test, again interrupted by rain, was a hard-fought draw, but Wyatt was never able to set a realistic target, the West Indies scoring 104 for 5 after being set 203 in something like two hours. Hammond was run out for 47 in the first innings. It seems to have been nobody's fault, but he was in with George Paine at the time, and they seldom batted together. Paine was essentially a bowler, but he was one of those whom Wyatt used a good deal to shield the recognised batsmen, in this case with better results for Paine himself – he made 49 – than for the 'proper' batsmen, none of whom scored more.

Hollies got the West Indies out for 184, 42 behind, and then Constantine bowled a tremendous spell. Now that Larwood was in decline, he was possibly the most formidable fast bowler in the world and his figures in this innings were 26-11-32-3, a really prodigious effort. One of the three was Hammond, bowled for 1, and for the moment it rather looked as though Constantine had got his number. They may have made their peace after the 1933 series, but there was always a little edge to their battles.

★　★　★　★　★

The result, then, would hinge on the last Test in Jamaica. It appears that Hammond was carrying a minor injury at this time – he didn't bowl in his last three matches on the tour – and this slightly disturbed the

Hammond's relaxed stance, the face of the bat closed.

The Player's team of 1932; most of the great players of the age; standing: Eddie Paynter, George Duckworth, Bill Voce, Frank Woolley, Maurice Tate, Harold Larwood; seated: Herbert Sutcliffe, Patsy Hendren, Jack Hobbs (captain), Walter Hammond, Tich Freeman.

The classic illustration of the cover-drive; Hammond at Sydney in 1928.

Past cover's left hand; Hammond in 1932/33 at Sydney.

Hammond could and did, hit to leg; a very effective sweep.

This picture shows Hammond in the ideal slip-fielding position, relaxed and ready.

Misfortune followed Hammond at every turn in 1934: for once at Leeds, he seemed to be mastering the bowling, but was run out.

Hammond driving Toshack for 6 on the sticky wicket at Brisbane, 1946,

A magnificent lofted drive; batting against the Dominion's in 1945, Hammond hit the ball into the Lord's Pavilion.

The impregnable defence of Len Hutton, who scored 364 for Hammond at the Oval, 1938.

The 200th run of his 240 at Lord's, 1938.

Hammond bowled by McCormick after making 240 at Lord's.

Hammond was frequently in trouble against Colin McCool in 1946/47, but reluctant to use his feet, in his old style.

The England team of 1946/47 to Australia, Hammond's last tour.
Back: *Langridge, Compton, Evans, Hutton.* Centre: *Wright, Washbrook, Ikin, A. Bedser, Pollard, Smith, R. Howard (Manager).* Front: *Voce, Gibb, Yardley, Hammond, Edrich, Fishlock, Hardstaff.*

'Tiger' O'Reilly, who got Hammond out ten times in Tests – determination written in every line of his face.

Constantine, one of Hammond's most formidable opponents, fast, and cunning with it.

balance of the attack. Farnes was fit at last, but the attack was still not a strong one and once Grant had won the toss, it was always going to be a hard match to win.

Headley had been promising a big innings from the start – he had made 44, 0, 25, 93 and 53 – and he now played at his very best. He batted over eight hours and scored 270 not out, and if Grant had not declared, he might have gone on to beat Hammond's record score. Grant himself had still to come in and he would have been able to keep an end going for Headley. However, Grant had a match to win and he declared. At once, Martindale struck a critical blow, hitting Wyatt in the face and inflicting a compound fracture of the jaw. Hammond had therefore to come in at the start of the innings, and Constantine got him again, this time for 11. Ames led a late recovery and scored 126, but England were all out for 271 and followed on.

Wyatt was of course unable to bat, and much depended on Hammond. He fought it out, making 34 before Martindale beat him for sheer pace and bowled him. England were all out for 103, a pretty inglorious end to a tour which had begun so excitingly. As I have suggested, it wasn't a very strong team and didn't have much luck, but Wyatt's captaincy, imaginative though it was, was not faultless. Only one player, Townsend, stayed in the same place in the batting order, thoughout, and Hammond, at different times, batted third, fourth, fifth and sixth. It had been a clever move to vary the order in that first, rain-ruined Test, but there was a hint of 'too clever by half' about some of the later manoeuvres.

Hammond had had an ordinary series. He had been responsible for England's win at Bridgetown, but he had been rather at Constantine's mercy later. Incredibly, he had now batted 19 times, in 12 Tests, since his record 336, without once passing 50. The figures are misleading and it was certainly much too soon to think of replacing him. He was making thousands of runs in other matches, and would no doubt do so in Tests before long, but simply on the figures, he was leaving a hole in the middle order.

	Innings	N.O.	H.S.	Runs	Average	100	50
1934/35	8	1	47	175	25.00	–	–
To date	83	9	336*	4142	55.97	13	13

	Balls	Runs	Wickets	Average
1934/5	150	48	–	–
To date	5670	2265	57	39.73

15   Back at the Top

Hammond, like the rest of the party, came back from the West Indies a little demoralised. He had batted so well in that first Test that it was difficult to come to terms with the failures in the succeeding matches. England now faced a good-looking South African side, and they didn't seem to have much reserve talent to draw upon.

Six of the 1929 South Africans came again: this was about the number to be expected, given the essentially amateur nature of the South African game, but each of the six had a good deal to recommend him. Bell was a tough and enduring fast bowler, who had had his moment of glory when he took 6 for 99 on his debut in 1929, and had bowled magnificently for a beaten side in Australia in 1931/32. Siedle, the opening bat, had had a poor series in 1929 but the selectors had kept faith with him, and Mitchell, his partner, had made a fine start then and was embarked on a long career as the sheet-anchor. Dalton, an all-rounder was another who had been out of form in 1929, but he had shown better form towards the end of that summer and had batted well since.

Vincent I have already mentioned. He is one of the underrated Test players of history, seldom mentioned when all-time sides are picked, but often returning good figures. Hammond was seldom at ease against him. In 1935, *The Times* correspondent described him as 'every bit as good as Verity'. This may be seen as slightly overdoing it – English critics are sometimes inclined to overrate visiting spinners – but it gives some idea of contemporary opinion. Finally, there was Jock Cameron, one of the finest wicketkeeper-batsmen of all time. He had taken England by storm in 1929, had lost some batting form when made the captain in Australia but, relieved of the leadership, was now back at his best.

Cameron's successor as captain was the team's greatest asset. Herby Wade, 29 years old, had yet to play in a Test, but he had batted consistently for Natal for some years, and had gained English experience in Yorkshire club cricket. He was a born leader, one of the great ones, and his players would go through fire and water for him. Other prominent newcomers were Eric Rowan, a confident attacking batsman, Dudley Nourse and Ken Viljoen, who would sustain the middle order for years to come, and Chud Langton, a medium-pacer who could achieve a lot of turn on the right wicket, and was accurate and persevering on any wicket. There was also Xenophon Balaskas – more of him presently.

The South Africans made a great start, overwhelming their opponents in true Australian style. Worcestershire, Leicestershire, Cambridge and Surrey were all easily defeated though Oxford managed to draw with them on an easy wicket. South Africa then had the better of a draw with a moderate MCC side, before returning to their winning ways, beating four more counties before the Nottingham Test. All the players, except Dalton and Balaskas, were fit, but they surprised many by leaving out Bell, which meant that Langton would double as opener and stock bowler.

Meanwhile, Hammond had had a rather indifferent start. This was the year in which the lbw law was changed, experimentally to begin with, to allow an appeal if the batsman obstructed, even if the ball had pitched outside the off-stump. The law was eventually adopted and we are still arguing about the merits. It was intended to discourage pad-play and it certainly did that, but it has brought about a great increase in the bowling of in-swingers and a reduction in the off-side play which is one of cricket's chief delights. At the time a number of leading batsmen felt that the change would be very difficult for them to cope with, but most of them did so in time.

Hammond was one of the pessimists about the law changes, and he certainly had a poor start to the season. In 18 innings, until 11 June, he passed 50 only three times, but he was also under a different pressure. He had now scored 99 centuries, and he was not the first player the find the hundredth 100 elusive. It came against Somerset on 13 June and the last 19 runs took 70 minutes, one of the slowest passages of his whole career.

The same weekend his selection for the first Test was announced although it had never been in much doubt. His reputation stood so high that he would have had to have had a prolonged spell of really poor form to be dropped; and, as I have suggested, other batsmen were having their troubles. England were in a time of transition. Woolley had clearly played his last Test and so, probably, had Hendren. Sutcliffe was nearing the end of a marvellous Test career, and with Hammond in a bad patch, that left only Wyatt who was sure to be captain, Walters and Leyland of the 1934 batsmen. There was a clear need for new blood, but there didn't seem to be a new generation forcing its way in.

Sutcliffe was proclaiming the talent of the young Hutton, but he had done nothing remarkable and neither Edrich nor Compton had yet appeared in county cricket. The bowling was equally thin. Larwood and Voce were out of favour for political reasons, and the other fast bowlers had done little against Australia. Verity stood alone.

The matches were to be played over three days, and four bowlers might well be enough. The selectors decided to open with Wyatt and Sutcliffe, and to play Hammond and Leyland. Iddon would be the all-rounder and would bat after Ames at No 7, and they went boldly for Mandy Mitchell-Innes, a second-year undergraduate who had made 168 for Oxford against the tourists. Nichols and Bowes would open the bowling, and Robins came back to share the spinning duties with Verity. It was the best they could have done and the best side that played that year. Some of the later selections were much harder to understand and the selectors would have done well to tinker as little as possible with a fair combination – but that's often the case in England.

When England batted, Wyatt and Sutcliffe made a very good start. Today, one would even call it dashing, since they had made 118 before Sutcliffe was out, still before lunch, but standards of enterprise were different then, and nobody complimented them on their speed.

Hammond started well, *The Times* man writing of his many noble strokes, but not for the first time, he had a certain amount of trouble with Vincent bowling over the wicket. Critics wondered about this line of attack, but they got their answer when Vincent had Hammond lbw, which rather suggests that he played for turn which didn't happen. Cardus thought that Hammond was trying to turn the ball to leg when it came on with the arm. Whatever the details, Hammond was out for 28 and England were 170 for 2.

Mitchell-Innes was out for 5 and then Wyatt, playing the innings of his life, added 139 with Leyland. *Wisden* is curiously muted about Wyatt's batting; it describes his innings as 'carefully played' and says that after an early escape he was 'laborious at times', but 149 in five hours would satisfy most people. *Wisden* also describes Leyland as providing 'the one piece of forcing batting', but Leyland made 69 out of 146 scored while he was in, and unless he was getting much less than his share of the strike, the comment lacks logic. The explanation is possibly that Leyland usually *looked* as though he were forcing the pace, while Wyatt was more of a persuader and deflector, finding the gaps in the field. The main thing was that England were 384 for 7, and Wyatt could declare with a good chance of forcing a win.

It rained on the Sunday giving England a real opportunity. The pitch was greasy rather than sticky, and although Wyatt brought Verity on early and kept him on, it was Nichols who did the major damage. He bowled Mitchell early, was tight and accurate all the afternoon, while the spinners nibbled their way through the middle order, and swept the tail away after tea, finishing with the excellent figures of 23.5-9-35-6. Cardus described it as 'honest fast bowling with no nonsense about outswerve, just quick sudden assaults on the stumps.' Wyatt might well have used Hammond and Nichols, rather similar in type, together, but he would have been hoping that his talented spinners would also get something from the turf, and indeed Verity bowled one to Nourse which jumped and hit either the shoulder of the bat or the batsman's thumb, and skied to Hammond at slip. Cardus described it as a 'nice feminine catch' which I take to mean that it was one which Auntie could have caught on the beach, and not that Hammond took it in any sort of unmasculine pose.

South Africa, all out 220, followed on, and Nichols completed his day's work by having Siedle caught. England were in a very strong position, but the weather now turned against them, the third day being washed out altogether. It seemed that it was only a matter of time before England took the lead.

★   ★   ★   ★   ★

The critics however were not entirely happy. Cardus wrote that Robins would no doubt get another chance at Lord's but could be regarded as England's googly bowler only for want of a better – an odd remark, considering that there were half-a-dozen googly bowlers on the county scene and that Freeman, for one, had taken 503 wickets in the previous two seasons. True, Freeman was 46, but I think the Australians would have picked him. It was certain that a googly bowler would be picked for the Lord's Test, for this was the year of the leather-jacket. In 1935 there was a plague of these creatures – the larvae of the crane-fly – and they, or the chemicals used to shift them, had left the Lord's pitches very bare and responsive to spin.

England were clearly going to go for a spinning attack, but they picked a very odd one. To begin with, they played two slow left-handers, Verity and Langridge. Lord's is one ground on which this is anything but a good idea, the slope being such that only one end is suitable for the spinner who leaves the bat. The selectors had then to pick the third spinner. Sir Pelham Warner, chairman of the selectors at the time, has a rather equivocal passage in his *Cricket Between Two Wars*. He makes it very plain that he and the other non-playing selectors, wanted to retain Robins, while Wyatt wanted Tommy Mitchell of Derbyshire, and that they gave way to Wyatt only reluctantly. Warner acknowledges that it was a Committee decision, but, by revealing the dissension, he dissociates himself from the outcome and the morality of such a disclosure is doubtful. The evidence about the merits of the two players is inconclusive. Robins finished higher in the seasonal averages, but Mitchell took more wickets and at a better striking-rate. Wyatt had now to handle three spinners, all turning away from the right-hander.

The selectors made another odd decision, playing Ames simply as a batsman and picking Farrimond, who spent most of the summer in Lancashire's second team, to keep wicket. There seems to have been an idea floating about that year that Ames wasn't keeping as well as he had been, but it still looks like a place wasted. At the last minute, Mitchell-Innes had to cry off – he was a martyr to hay-fever – and Holmes replaced him. The unlucky Mitchell-Innes never played in another Test.

Dalton and Balaskas were both fit and both played. Balaskas had taken only four wickets in the first four Tests of his career, but much was expected of him on the bare pitch. Cardus, perceptively, wrote that there was no reason why England should not fare as badly against him as ever they did against Grimmett, and that's just what happened.

This was the only toss Wade won in the series, but it proved the important one. South Africa were very shaky to begin with. Tommy Mitchell came on very early and turned the ball so much that Wyatt gave him three slips before lunch on the first day. Hammond was described as lurking close in at slip, anticipating and picking up in a marvellous manner, so perhaps he had a kind of roving commission. Siedle was bowled by Mitchell, and Verity dismissed Rowan and Nourse. Cameron came in at 98 for 4, and turned the match round with an innings of 'terribly cool and calculated ferocity' (Cardus). He made 90 in 105 minutes, with three sixes and six fours, before Nichols bowled him. Hammond wound up the innings, getting Langton and Bell out in the course of 5.3 inexpensive overs. South Africa were 228 all out, a good score on the pitch – it is worth noting that only three centuries were scored in county games at Lord's in the whole of the season – but England must still have hoped to better it.

They never really looked like doing so. The South African replacements were the most successful bowlers. Bell having Sutcliffe lbw playing no stroke and Balaskas bowling Leyland on the first evening. The final score was 75 for 2, which was about the best position reached by England in the match. Leyland had gone in above Hammond, possibly as a counter to Balaskas, but when he got out, Hammond went in, it being less fashionable then to employ a night-watchman. He made a good start, playing in the form of his best years.

In the morning, Balaskas opened at one end and Dalton soon relieved Crisp at the other. The batsmen looked comfortable enough, until Dalton bowled Hammond for 27 with an almost unplayable ball

110

described as 'running like a mouse to the base of the stumps'. JM Kilburn, less fanciful than Cardus, felt that Hammond's stroke, halfway between a back-stroke and a cut, was careless. At once, Wyatt tried to hook, got the ball too high and was caught for 53. After that, Balaskas took charge, spinning like a top and very accurately too. Nobody could cope with him, and when England were all out for 198, his figures were 32-8-49-5.

South Africa were only 30 ahead, but that was a lot in such a low-scoring game. Bruce Mitchell was in unusually assertive mood, and the wise men felt that he was trying to get a few before the spinners, Tommy Mitchell and Verity, came on. They were on after 15 minutes, but the score was already 27 for 0, and although Siedle was soon out, Mitchell and Rowan joined in the decisive stand, in the course of which it was apparent that England's Mitchell was bowling pretty poorly.

Wyatt was accused of over-bowling Mitchell, but there was little else he could do. Wrist-spin was the best ticket on such a pitch, and Wyatt could only hope that Mitchell would pick up a wicket or two and gain confidence. For the time being, he was finding the middle of the bat unerringly, and Bruce Mitchell and Rowan made the most of it. They added 104 in two hours and England seemed to have nothing to hope for but a draw. However Nichols and Verity engineered a collapse, causing the score to go from 136 for 1 to 177 for 6, and suddenly there was a glimmer of hope, but Bruce Mitchell was still there, now past his 100, and he was joined by Langton, a very competent bat, in the decisive stand of the match and the series. They saw out the day and on the Tuesday went on to 278 before Hammond caught Langton off his own bowling.

England needed 309 to win or, more realistically, they had to survive for some four and three-quarter hours. Sutcliffe and Ames were injured and, though both would bat, each would do so with a runner. Balaskas opened and had Wyatt out, rather unluckily, playing the ball on to his foot and thence to his wicket. It was the sort of thing that happens to a team once it is on the slide. Leyland again batted third and fell at once to Crisp, and Hammond came in.

As in the first innings, he began very well. Crisp made a couple rise quite sharply at his breastbone and he got up on his toes to thrust them down; then he drove Crisp to long-on, quite in his best style. He lay back and hammered Balaskas on the off-side, where Wade made a brilliant stop. Sutcliffe, hampered by his injury, was nevertheless in command, and it seemed briefly, that they were to save, possibly win, the match by historic batsmanship. But Langton found an outswinger for Hammond, who tried to force it and was taken at the wicket, again for 27.

Sutcliffe was lbw to the same bowler, for 38. It was the last innings of his wonderful Test career and he had made the top score, on one leg, in characteristic style, but it was all over now. Nobody else could cope with Balaskas and Langton on a wicket now taking a lot of spin, and England went from 90 for 4 to 151 all out, losing by 157 runs. Balaskas had taken 9 for 103 in the match and, although he was unfit for the remaining Tests, he had won the rubber, though one must not overlook the contributions of Langton who had taken six wickets and batted valuably, and of Mitchell who had played the innings of his life.

★　　★　　★　　★　　★

The England selectors may have thought about dropping Hammond for the third Test at Leeds. He had batted excitingly at Lord's, but had still not made enough runs, and it was now over two years since he had scored 50 in a Test. The fact was, though, that there were few likely-looking replacements and, with Sutcliffe unfit, the selectors had to retain experience and build around it. England were unlucky with injuries, Clark and Hollies both of whom had been selected, reporting sick, though South Africa could also claim to have been unlucky with injuries to Balaskas and Bell.

The England team, as originally picked, looked better balanced than at Lord's. Ames was restored to the post of wicket-keeper, which made a place available for a batsman or a bowler, and Hardstaff, the best so far of the new generation, came in. Denis Smith replaced Sutcliffe, and Barber of Yorkshire came in for Errol Holmes. In the absence of Hollies and Clark, Sims, the fourth leg-spinner to be selected, and Bowes were picked, so that England had four new caps. Then on the morning of the match, Leyland went down with lumbago. No reserve batsman was in attendance and there was a bit of a panic.

A board was carried round the ground, directing Arthur Mitchell of Yorkshire, if he happened to be present, to report to the pavilion. This recalls a vanished age; no PA system, no BBC team of commentators to put out a call, just a board carried round the ground. Happy days. Mitchell wasn't in fact present; he was at home catching up on the weeding. Brian Sellers dashed there in his car, managed to persuade Mitchell that he wasn't pulling his leg, and brought him back in triumph. In the very best story-book tradition, Mitchell had an excellent game.

Wyatt won the toss. He went in himself with Smith, to give Mitchell a chance to get his breath back, but he was out at once, and Barber was put in next, which suggests that Wyatt was very anxious to give Hammond every chance to make a score, for Barber was by no means the regular No 3 for Yorkshire. Barber and Smith batted well, making

112

52 in quick time, before Barber was out to Langton, who was beginning to look like England's bogeyman.

Hammond began very well indeed, according to *The Times* correspondent, who was particularly impressed by the way he played anything short. He lost Smith at 78, but Mitchell, recovered from the shocks of the morning, played with the utmost steadiness. Hammond was serenity itself, but after making that elusive 50, he was out rather unexpectedly when he got to 63. He followed one from Vincent till he decided it would beat the off-stump, left it alone at the last moment, only to find that it came straight on and had him lbw, rather in the same way as he had been out in the first Test. Cardus asked indignantly:

'Why is Hammond always getting out in Tests, inexplicably, even while he is riding the wave's crest?'

Hammond might have replied that he wasn't getting out on purpose; nevertheless it was a fact that as England's senior batsman, in the absence of Sutcliffe, he ought to have been going on to make 100 once in a while.

For the time being, England's fortunes were in the hands of Arthur Mitchell, and he fought nobly for three hours and 58 runs, before falling to Langton. Nobody else made runs, and England were all out for 216, Langton and Vincent taking four wickets each. It was a dangerous moment, although there was a suggestion that the wicket had been over-watered and that the opposition would have their troubles.

South Africa lost Bruce Mitchell on the first evening, lbw to Hammond. It may be said that whatever effect the new law was having on Hammond's batting, it was doing his bowling no harm at all; he took 60 wickets at 27.26 in 1935, as against 21 at 50.42 in 1934, and 13 of them were lbw, including nine present or future Test players. On the second day, all the England bowlers except Sims shared in the wickets as South Africa tumbled to 171 all out. This was largely due to some briliant fielding. Mitchell began in the deep, but managed to work his way into his accustomed place at silly mid-on, where he made a fine catch to dismiss Wade. Wyatt came on when South Africa were pulling the game round and had Viljoen caught, but the outstanding feat was a catch by Hammond to get rid of Rowan, the top scorer with 62. For once, Hammond dived for a catch, and he got both hands to a low chance 'while falling forward like loveliness and music incarnate' (Cardus – who else?)

Arthur Mitchell was promoted to open the second innings. Quick runs were needed and there were those who doubted if the dour Mitchell was the man for the moment. They needn't have worried, for he scored

54 in an hour, leading Smith in an excellent partnership of 128. The stage was set for Hammond, but Barber again batted third, which was a little surprising. Hammond finally got to the wicket late on the second day, and on the third morning he gave a brilliant display. For once he got right on top of Vincent and took the fight to him till he scarcely knew where to pitch the ball. At one point, Hammond hit him for three consecutive fours, a wristy flick to the on-side, a huge drive and a cut.

Before long it was simply a question of timing the declaration and, as so often, there were as many opinions as observers. A brief shower disturbed Wyatt's calculations; Cardus though he should have declared *during* the shower, which would have set a target of 322 in about five hours. Wyatt was possibly hoping for a dry ball and he batted on another 20 minutes, till the target was the impossible one of 340 in 275 minutes. Hammond was left not out with 87 made in 105 minutes, his highest and best score since his 336 at Auckland.

South Africa didn't go for the runs and being one up with what was on paper the weaker side, it isn't likely that they would have gone for any target. Siedle and Mitchell started well enough, but three quick wickets fell and England may have entertained hopes of a win. Mitchell and Wade hung on till the umpires took them off for bad light. The stoppage was a brief one, and then Hammond bowled Mitchell, a shrewd blow. Cameron was next and Hammond hit his stumps without dislodging a bail, but it is probable that South Africa would have survived even if he had got out.

The batsmen slowed down, not wanting the new ball to be taken, and at the very end Wilf Barber came on and had Cameron stumped with his second ball in Test cricket. It was also his last ball, so that his Test record stands for all time at 1 for 0. England had been rather unlucky not to force a win – they had had all the best of the game – but South Africa were hard to get out twice in three days.

★ ★ ★ ★ ★

Hammond was an obvious choice once more for the fourth Test at Old Trafford. The selectors continued to have bad luck and they also continued to panic a bit. Arthur Mitchell was of course retained in the chosen team, but this time he was unfit. He was replaced as an opener by Fred Bakewell of Northamptonshire, a beautiful player who tended to be picked only when others were injured. Leyland, fit again, and Robins, restored at last to favour, came in for Hardstaff and Sims, and the selectors made two rather curious choices. Ames, who had done nothing wrong, was replaced by Duckworth, which considerably weakened the batting, and Maurice Tate came in for Nichols, who

114

had taken 13 wickets in the three Tests. Everybody liked and respected Tate, but he was 40 years old and even if the selectors thought the South Africans had worked Nichols out, it was hardly a constructive piece of team-building. For South Africa, Nourse replaced Siedle.

Smith and Bakewell opened very brightly, but they had a lot of luck. The South Africans had their worst day in the field so far, and dropped each opener twice while they were scoring 71 together. Then Bruce Mitchell did catch Smith off Bell, who had Barber out at once. Hammond came in at 77 for 2, a slightly difficult moment, and began to bat with force and charm. He made 'two of the best strokes we can hope to see', according to *The Times;* these were forcing back-foot strokes off Crisp which fairly whistled to the fence. It seemed that Hammond was himself again, but he tried to force Crisp once more, off a ball of fuller length, and was bowled off the inside edge for 29. Cardus pronounced an elegiac farewell:

'. . . his cricket expressed a tranquil consciousness of effortless superiority. He made hacks of the rest, and after he departed it was only a cricket match'.

Bakewell, 63, and Wyatt soon followed Hammond and at 141 for 5 things looked pretty desperate. Leyland and Robins responded in the style of the Golden Age, setting about all the bowlers and putting on 105 in 75 minutes. Robins played the innings of his life, making ground *across* the wicket to play Langton's off-breaks on the leg-side and driving both Langton and Vincent through the covers. Robins was a forcing batsman who frequently got himself out; he acknowledged no man to be his master, but seldom scored as many as he looked capable of. This was his day of days, and after Leyland got out, Tate had one last fling as a Test batsman, scoring 34. England ended on 357, with Robins on 108. Amazingly, in view of the mid-innings collapse, the runs came in 92 overs in just over 5 hours.

Bad light stopped play for the day at the start of South Africa's innings and on the Monday Hammond and Bowes had a quick wicket apiece. England glimpsed victory, but Viljoen took charge. In no hurry – and there was every reason why he should not be – he batted from first principles, playing very straight and waiting for the loose ones, of which there were enough. He appears to have played Tate particularly well, letting the ball come on to him and taking his runs on the leg-side in a way that had not been found possible by the great players, ten years earlier.

Nourse was just coming into form after a poor start to the tour and managed to keep Viljoen company for a while; then Cameron played in his usual robust, uncomplicated way. He wasn't as aggressive as usual, but he took advantage of some unusually loose bowling from Verity and hit a couple of sixes. When he was out, the score was 223 for 5, with the follow-on saved, an it was apparent that England would have great difficulty in forcing a win. Worse was to come with Dalton settling in to see Viljoen to his 100 and beyond, and do some hitting on his own account. He hoisted one over the top of Bowes at mid-on and gave Cardus the opportunity for one of his most felicitous similes; he wrote, evocatively, that Bowes ran about as if chasing butterflies!

South Africa eventually totalled 318, only 39 behind, and England were 43 for 1 by the close, with plenty to do on the Tuesday. Once again, Hammond had been held back, and this time it was a little difficult to understand. He came in when Bakewell was out at 90 and played a fine forcing innings. Bell was unfit to bowl – he had fluid on the elbow – but South Africa were looking to contain, and Vincent and Langton were the best men for that. Vincent in particular did a good job, bowling all morning and finishing with the excellent figures, against experienced attacking batsmen, of 26-6-78-4.

Hammond played a succession of sparkling off-side strokes and lofted Vincent over long-off but he was never able to run away with the game, and 63 in 90 minutes, good as it was, was not quite enough. Perhaps it didn't matter; Wyatt was always going to declare at lunch and a declaration 20 minutes earlier would only have given him ten extra minutes at the batsmen. England made 188 in the 150 minutes of the morning, Leyland with 37, the other main contributor.

South Africa were set to make 271 at 72 an hour, a pretty unrealistic target for the side that was one up. At tea, they were only 76 for 1 with Rowan the man out and both sides had settled for the draw. Although much of the bowling after tea was done by Leyland and Bakewell, the final score was 169 for 2, and it had been a rather dreary finale to an interesting match. However, South Africa had achieved their objective; the final match would now be played over three days and would take a deal of winning.

★ ★ ★ ★ ★

A week before the final Test at the Oval, the South Africans met Gloucestershire at Cheltenham and suffered their first defeat of the tour. Hammond had a very good match, scoring 38 and 123 and taking four wickets. Reg Sinfield scored 102 on the first day and took eight wickets. The tourists went on to Southend, where they lost again, Stephenson and Nichols taking 16 wickets between them. Bell and Balaskas were injured in these matches and would miss the Test.

116

The England team had already been picked and the selectors had naturally packed the bowling. 'Hopper' Read of Essex, possibly the fastest man in England at that time, had been picked to open with Nichols, and John Clay of Glamorgan, an off-spinner who was having a fine season, had been picked to play his first Test in place of Verity. Robins and Bowes completed the attack. It was a natural corollary of this policy change to recall Ames as keeper and to bat at No 6. Arthur Mitchell was fit again and replaced Smith. South Africa naturally varied their side in the opposite direction and played only three specialist bowlers, though they had little option in the face of their injuries. With Wade coming in at No 7, it was plain that they were looking for a draw, though they would take a chance if it presented itself.

These being the teams, it should have surprised nobody that Wyatt put South Africa in when he won the toss, but he was freely criticised after the event by the less thoughtful. His reasoning was plain enough. If England had batted first, however many they had made, they would have to bowl South Africa out twice on consecutive days, to force a win, for South Africa had already demonstrated that they would not be responsive to a challenging declaration. On the other hand, *if* England could manage to bowl the opponents out for about 300, and *if* they could then make a quick 500, they had the spinners to get them out on a wearing wicket on the last day. It very nearly worked out that way.

South Africa batted none too well at the outset. Mitchell and Siedle began with a stand of 116, but Robins then took two quick wickets and Bowes weighed in with a third at 164. All this time Bruce Mitchell was batting with the utmost soundness. He was naturally taking no risks, but he was confirming, if confirmation were needed, that he was not only the best bat in the side, but now that Woodfull had retired and Sutcliffe was about to, arguably the best crisis batsman in the world. Read got him out after tea and had Cameron caught, but Wyatt may have been at fault in not bowling Robins more; he was more likely than anyone else to bowl the unplayable ball and England needed to make a quick end to the innings. Hammond, too, might have been used more, but Wyatt probably calculated that he would need a fresh Hammond to score quick runs.

South Africa were 297 for 6 at the close, slow going by the standards of the day, but totally understandable. On the Monday, they soon lost Viljoen and Vincent, but Dalton was still there, and he and Langton played the decisive part adding 137 in 70 minutes. Dalton's play was in complete contrast with all that had happened on the first day. Cardus, trying to have it both ways, wrote that he was 'a superb stroke-player even if he flashes riskily at the off-side ball'. Was there ever a superb stroke-player who didn't flash riskily from time to time? Even Bradman did sometimes. South Africa added 179 during the morning and were all out for 476 on the stroke of lunch.

England then had it all to do. To have any chance of winning they had to score 500-odd by lunchtime on the third day and bowl South Africa out very cheaply. They managed the first part of the programme, and it is greatly to their credit that they did, after a poor start. Bakewell and Mitchell went off briskly, but Bakewell was caught behind for 20, and Mitchell and Wyatt both fell at 98.

At this stage, there was a very real possibility of a collapse and a follow-on, but this didn't deter Hammond and Leyland for a moment. Both attacked from the start, though Hammond seems to have been a little streaky. He was a shade lucky when he lofted a ball from Vincent which fell just short of long-on, and he might have been run out, too, but he kept after the bowling and played some characteristic drives.

Together they had added 151 in 100 minutes and effectively insured against any danger of a follow-on before Vincent defeated Hammond for the tenth and last time in a Test. Hammond had been using his feet well against Vincent, but the bowler eventually got him to prop, and he was well stumped by Cameron for 65. Ames came in to attack with enthusiasm, and he and Leyland had taken the score to 313 for 4 by the close. 492 runs had been scored during the day, while eight wickets fell – one of the Test days one would have liked to have seen.

On the last day, Ames and Leyland carried on where they had left off, the wicket-keeper being marginally the more enterprising. Leyland was stumped at last, off Bruce Mitchell, and Nichols and Robins helped Ames to take the score 534 for 6 at lunch, when Wyatt declared. England had added 221 in the morning, Ames scoring 123 before lunch which was, and remains, the Test record though I can find no note of anybody's recognising this at the time. It was a less numerate age!

Read and Bowes made early inroads into the batting and South Africa were 67 for 3, nine runs ahead with two and a half hours to go. An England win was still just possible, albeit highly unlikely. Viljoen and Cameron added 45 quiet runs and the opportunity passed. After tea, the zest went out of the cricket, much as it had at Old Trafford, and the batsmen took some cheap runs off Robins, Wyatt and Leyland. It was pleasing to the tourists' many friends that Wade was on the field at the end, playing his highest innings of the series (40).

England had thus been in a position to declare in four of the five Tests, but had failed to force a win in any of them. They had held the initiative in these four games for much of the time, but that was hardly the point. By mutual agreement, the matches were being played over three days and within those rules South Africa had won worthily, in

118

spite of illnesses and injuries and significantly, England had for the first time been bested at home by a side other than Australia. The England selectors hadn't distinguished themselves but, in truth, the general standard of county cricket was not high in 1935, and any combination might have had difficulty. South Africa suffered a tragic loss when Cameron died of enteric fever only a few weeks later, and their cricket took a long time to recover.

Although Hammond didn't make a century during the series and had now played in 17 Tests without doing so, he still headed the England batting averages and scored more runs than any of his team-mates. He was once more seen as England's leading batsman, but it is interesting to compare his Test and first-class figures for the period 1933 to 1935, including the West Indies tour:

	Innings	N.O.	H.S.	Runs	Average	100
Tests	27	3	87*	800	33.33	None
First-class	164	17	302*	9094	61.86	31

His Test figures were now:

	Innings	N.O.	H.S.	Runs	Average	100	50
1935	8	2	87	389	64.83	–	4
To date	91	11	336*	4531	56.63	13	17

	Balls	Runs	Wickets	Average
1935	421	146	6	24.33
To date	6091	2411	63	38.26

16   Simple and Great

Hammond had batted magnificently in all his games in 1935, except the Tests, though even there he had shown signs that he was returning to form. 1936 was to be a year of mixed fortunes. He had been troubled by septic tonsils for some time and finally took the decision to have them out just before the season started. This kind of operation was not then the routine affair it has now become, and it was some time before he got over the ill-effects. He struggled to find his best form, and was into his sixth match before he made a 50. He bowled only 16 overs in the first five matches, another indication of delicate health.

The England selectors kept faith with Hammond, but he was obliged to declare himself unfit for the first Test against India. This must have been a blow to the selectors, who had decided not to recall Sutcliffe and were left seriously short of experienced batting. They had also gone for GOB Allen as captain in place of Wyatt, and clearly had Allen in view for the 'peacemaking' tour of Australia. Walters was not available and the new batsmen tried in 1935 had really done very little, always excepting Arthur Mitchell who, as we have seen, had been selected by default. In the circumstances, the selectors were very glad that Wyatt readily agreed to play under Allen's leadership, he and Leyland being the only two batsmen in the side who had played in 1934. The brilliant Gimblett came in to open with Mitchell, and the other batsmen were Turnbull and Hardstaff. The bowling was in the hands of Allen, Langridge, Robins and Verity, which meant that Wyatt would be opening with Allen. The side would certainly be batting long with three virtual all-rounders plus Verity, an able batsman at any time.

In the first Test at Lords India were shot out for 147 (Allen, 5 for 35), but England, on a slighty tricky pitch, failed to match even this, being bowled out by Amar Singh for 134. Leyland made 60, and nobody else got as far as 20. Fortunately for the selectors, Allen bowled India out cheaply for the second time, finishing with 10 for 78 in the match, as they were put out for 93. Gimblett and Turnbull made this task look easy enough, and England won by nine wickets, but the England batting had clearly lacked solidity and Hammond's health and form were the subjects of daily bulletins and fervent prayer.

On the third day of the Test the news was that Hammond had made 74 not out against Yorkshire, and the selectors must have begun to hope. He wasn't yet fully recovered; he was still only making 40s and 50s, but he played a brilliant innings of 72 for the Players at Lord's, in the middle of a nasty collapse against the lively JWA Stephenson, on a bowlers' wicket. It was more than enough to win him selection for the Old Trafford Test, and his return was welcomed. *The Times* critic wrote:

'Hammond is back in the side, and he makes all the difference to the balance of any team'.

True and very gratifying, but it added to his burden of responsibility, particularly since the team included two batsmen, Fagg and Fishlock, who were new to Test cricket.

★   ★   ★   ★   ★

Once again India batted first and, once again, they didn't do very well. This time, Verity did the damage, taking four wickets as they were bowled out for 203. Hammond bowled nine overs without a wicket. Gimblett failed and Hammond joined Fagg to play one of his more spectacular Test innings. He hit eight fours in his first 50 runs, and had scored 118 at about a run a minute by the close, when England were 173 for 2. Neville Cardus described his batmanship as being:

'as ripe as the peach mellowing on the sun-stained wall'

and if this sounds a somewhat passive image for a batsman scoring at such a speed, the ripeness of Hammond's technique could certainly not be denied.

The next day was more spectacular still, with more runs being scored than on any other Test match day, before or since. Hammond and Worthington added exactly 100 more runs before Hammond was bowled by CK Nayudu for 167. *The Times* correspondent, probably Major Vincent, summed it up:

'He was simple and great to all the bowling till he played lazily to a ball which may have turned a little but for which, in fact, he was late.'

'Simple and great' is an odd phrase, but it sums up Hammond's batting quite admirably. He *did* make it all look simple when at his best, and it was only when the onlooker saw the difficulties of others that he appreciated the art of Hammond, which concealed art. Cardus, who seems to have been in even more lyrical form than usual this year, wrote of one stroke:

'He flicked a good ball from CK Nayudu round for four with a flexibility astonishing for a man of his powerful frame; it was as though a noble trombone had performed an exquisite little appoggiatura.'

Which was all right if you knew what a appoggiatura was. The rest of the England batsmen hammered away in less musical vein, only Fishlock and Allen failing, and Allen was able to declare at 571 for 8, scored at almost exactly four an over. Merchant and Mushtaq Ali then handled the England attack with equal dexterity, and India were 190 for 0 at the close. A massive 588 runs had come in the day.

On the final day India batted on with every chance of saving the match. Mushtaq Ali, who had outscored his distinguished partner, was soon out, and then Hammond dropped Merchant at slip, one of his rare errors. He soon made amends by having Merchant lbw to a full toss, and over another long day in the field, was the least expensive bowler, with figures of 12-2-19-1. Ramaswami batted soundly for two hours, and Nayudu and Amar Singh took quick runs off Robins and Allen towards the end. The innings defeat had been saved before bad light stopped play. The England attack had done none too well in the second innings and there was some work to be done on the batting, but the general English mood was one of relief that Hammond had returned to his majestic form in good time for the tour of Australia. It was a striking tribute to him.

★　　★　　★　　★　　★

The third Test at the Oval, found Hammond in the form of his life. When it began on 15 August 1936, he had already scored 552 runs in the month, and a century from him was regarded as a foregone conclusion. All too often, such an assumption is followed by total failure – Bradman's duck in his last Test comes to mind – but this time the prophecies were fulfilled.

Hammond came in on the first morning at 19 for 1 and started where he had left off at Old Trafford. To be strictly accurate, he seems to have been just a little uncertain against Amar Singh at the outset, and he gave an extremely difficult chance to short-leg when he had made three, but Amar Singh on the first morning was a good enough bowler to worry anybody. Hammond soon settled and played as well as he had ever done in a home Test, though Cardus made the curious comment that he indulged in:

'variegated play in which the imperfect strokes were as interesting, and as much in character, as the perfect ones.'

This doesn't sound much like the traditional view of Hammond, but reminds one more of Compton – or Botham. Be that as it may, Hammond had scored 160 by tea and the Indian bowlers were looking helpless. He had given another chance, to deep square leg, but the fielder with the sun in his eyes, dropped it. Worthington was well-established by tea and also scoring freely. Fortunately for India, Hammond made a mistake after another hour, flashing at a rising ball from Nissar and deflecting it into his stumps. He had made a magnificent 217. Worthington also played on to Nissar, who took two more wickets before Allen declared, to finish with the evocative figures of 26-2-120-5. He had been hammered by the fourth wicket pair, but had kept his nerve and his length and he was rewarded.

India batted in rather dispirited fashion on the second day. Mushtaq Ali went off like a train, as he often did, and made a quick 52 before being stumped. Merchant and Dilawar Hussain made a dogged stand, but Sims and Verity rattled through the rest and India were following on 249 behind, soon after tea. In the second innings, Hammond made one of his more spectacular catches when Voce deflected the ball and he dived to take the rebound. Nayudu top-scored with 81, but India were all out for 312 and England had all the time in the world to make the 64 they needed.

Fagg was out before the end, and Hammond was at the crease on 5 when the victory was won, the 64 runs coming in just 13 overs. It had been an overwhelming win and England supporters were delighted that Hammond was in such form, though everybody knew that things would be much harder in Australia.

Hammond returned to Gloucestershire, batted consistently in the next three matches, and then signed off his county season with a devastating 317 in 390 minutes against Nottinghamshire in Tom Goddard's benefit match. He had scored 1,281 runs in August, a record which was to stand until Len Hutton beat it in June 1949.

	Innings	N.O.	H.S.	Runs	Average	100	50
1936	3	1	217	389	129.66	2	–
To date	94	12	336*	4920	60.00	15	17

	Balls	Runs	Wickets	Average
1936	216	94	1	94.00
To date	6307	2505	64	39.14

Hammond had now overtaken Herbert Sutcliffe as the second highest scorer in all Test cricket.

17   Australia revisited

It is difficult to realise now that until about 1950 it was really only the Tests against Australia that engaged the attention of the English cricket public. It was true that South Africa had beaten England in 1935, but this was regarded as a bit of a fluke – England had had the better of most of the drawn games and South Africa wouldn't do it again. (This turned out to be perfectly true; South Africa didn't win another Test until 1951, and didn't defeat England in a series until 1965). It was true, too, that the West Indies had beaten England two years earlier, but Englishmen took little account of matches played outside England or Australia, and the losing England side had lacked several of their best players. But the players who set out for Australia in the autumn of 1936 were well aware that theirs was the mission which represented success or failure for English cricket for the next year or two.

This time the tour had a dual purpose. After the turmoil of the Bodyline series, there were still some fences to be mended. The MCC had begun the peacemaking by sending an A team to Australia and New Zealand the winter before, under the leadership of Errol Holmes, and matches against the Australian states had been played in the happiest atmosphere.

The reconciliation was now to be consolidated by GOB Allen, known to his intimates as Obby and to the world as Gubby, the appointed leader of the team. Allen had been born in Australia and was consequently seen as almost one of their own, though they never for a moment questioned England's right to pick him. When he first played for England in 1930, a mischievous journalist tried to stir up trouble on this score, but the matter had died a quiet death. Allen was certainly cut out to be the reconciler.

There was also a little matter of regaining the Ashes; Allen might be a peacemaker, but he was also a good and competitive captain. His team was almost – but not quite – the strongest that could have been picked. Voce, who had in 1933 declared himself unwilling to play for England, had been persuaded back into the fold, and the fast attack looked all the better for him; Allen himself, Farnes and Copson were the other fast bowlers. Verity, Robins and Sims were the spinners.

The batting looked a little short of experience. Hammond, Wyatt, Leyland and Ames had all been to Australia before, and could be relied upon, but there were five who were new to Australia, and also relatively new to Test cricket. These were Barnett, Fagg, Fishlock, Hardstaff and Worthington, who had played 18 Tests between them while making just one century. Sutcliffe had had a poor season, for him, and it was perhaps reasonable to leave him behind, though there were those who would have picked him as long as he could walk to the wicket; there was less excuse for omitting Paynter, who had done well on the previous visit, and had had an excellent season in 1936. People wondered what would happen if one of the experienced men should be injured – most of all of course, if Hammond, the corner-stone, should fall out. In the event, Hammond kept fit, but both Ames and Wyatt suffered serious injuries and Allen had a very anxious time.

The Australians had problems, too, some of their own making. Woodfull, Ponsford, Kippax and Wall had all retired and their tour of South Africa had brought forward only McCormick, a fast bowler with more fire than Wall, but less than his accuracy. That tour had been led by Vic Richardson in the absence of Bradman, but although Richardson had his supporters, it was apparent that Bradman would be the captain now. For reasons that have never been made very clear, Bradman believed that Grimmett's Test days were over, and the attack looked more vulnerable than it had done for some time.

Bradman suffered a terrible personal tragedy early in the season, when his infant son died. It seems insensitive even to mention a game in the context of this awful blow, but Bradman was responsible for Australia's cricket fortunes and he was undoubtedly much affected. It was to be expected that he would come through this, and that Mrs Bradman would be of every possible help to him, but it would take time. It is often alleged that a batsman's form suffers when he becomes the captain, and when Bradman failed as a bat in the first two Tests, the theory was trotted out again. Australia depended on Bradman's batting to a far greater extent than any other country depended on its champion, and this was never more clearly demonstrated than in this series.

Hammond got off to a tremendous start on the tour, scoring four consecutive centuries in the first three games, and following this with 39 and 91 against New South Wales. At this point, he had made 618 runs at an average of 103, but the team had been doing less well, losing to New South Wales and having very much the worst of a draw with an Australian XI which contained several of the likely Test team's batsmen, but none of its bowlers. The Englishman had been cruelly exposed by four slow spinners in as many matches, none of them major

125

weapons in Australia's armoury – so far. Wyatt had broken his wrist and Ames had had back trouble. Only Barnett and Fagg of the new batsmen, had done very much, and Hammond was still England's great batting hope. England looked to him for great things if they were to have any chance at all.

Not for the first time or the last, a struggling touring side came good in the first Test but, oddly enough, Hammond had very little to do with it. England got off to a terrible start at Brisbane. McCormick had Worthington caught, mis-hooking, off the first ball of the match, and very soon afterwards had Fagg caught down the leg-side. Enter Hammond, at 20 for 2, a great weight of responsibility on his shoulders. Exit Hammond, first ball. McCormick bowled him a good-length ball on the leg-stump, which seemed to pop just a little, and Hammond turned it sharply into the hands of short-leg. Short-leg was Ray Robinson – no relation to the accomplished writer of the same name – who was playing in his only Test. He was out for 2 and 3, caught Hammond bowled Voce in each innngs, and this was virtually his only positive contribution for Australia, but it might well have won that match.

Fortunately for England the next batsman was Leyland, never a man to be overawed by a testing situation, and he and Barnett added 99 for the fourth wicket, Leyland digging in while Barnett sensibly played his natural hitting game. Things began to look better and looked better still when McCormick limped from the field, smitten with lumbago after bowling just eight overs. O'Reilly took up his burden again, troubling all the batsmen except Leyland, who always reckoned to have his measure, and now scored 126 in just over four hours. England finished on 358, a very good score after that dreadful start. Whether it would be enough, with Bradman on the other side, was another matter.

Badcock, who seldom did himself justice on the big occasion, played all round a ball from Allen, and Bradman came in rather sooner perhaps, then he would have liked. He crashed Allen for two fours and looked to be on the verge of a big innings, but Verity contained him skilfully. Losing patience, he tried to cut Voce and was caught at slip, a clear case of one bowler getting a wicket for another. McCabe looked safer, and he made 51, but Voce had him, too, as he mis-hooked and was caught at mid-on.

This series was remarkable for the number of wickets which fell as batsmen tried to hook; Maj CHB Pridham wrote a most telling article about the fallacy of the hook-stroke in the *Cricketer,* giving chapter and verse of a great many dismissals, most of them in this series. I think the explanation was that there were several goodish fast bowlers about and that once the bodyline field was banned, batsmen saw the gaps and chanced their arms, but weren't quite good enough to get away with the hook consistently. The next England-Australia series in 1938, was played on some very flat wickets, and hooking became that much easier. Hammond, of course, had eschewed the hook, at least in Test cricket, and he shone the more brightly for the comparison.

Fingleton, never a flamboyant player, had been playing quietly on as the others came and went, and he now lost two more partners before himself falling to Verity for a fighting 100. The tail collapsed and Australia were all out for 234, 124 behind. England's openers were out before the end of the third day, which came with England on 75 for 2, anything but safe with Bradman to bat again.

On the fourth day, the England batsmen again faltered before leg-spin. Bradman opened with Ward – in the continued absence of McCormick, he had little choice – and Fagg was at once deceived and brilliantly stumped. Leyland and Hammond, now together, were England's best hope – if anybody could play leg-spin, they could – but they were very slow and uncertain, and Hammond had made only 25 in 95 minutes when Ward forced him back on his stumps and got him to hit his own wicket as he played an ugly short-arm jab. It didn't augur well either for England's chance of winning the match or for Hammond's prospects in the series.

Ames and Leyland went cheaply, but Allen, with great moral courage, promoted himself and swung the bat freely at both Ward and O'Reilly. It was the innings of his life. He would not be described as a true Test batsman, but this was a triumph of sheer character. He scored 68 and set England on the way to a total of 256. He played O'Reilly particularly well, and English patriots convinced themselves that there were now three men in the party who could cope with the great man – Allen, Leyland and Hammond.

Australia were left to score 381 to win, and had to start their innings in rather poor light on the fourth evening. Fingleton was out first ball and Sievers, a medium-pace bowler playing in his first Test, was sent in, understandably with instructions to appeal against the light and to go on appealing until he got a decision. The players came off at 3 for 1, but heavy rain rendered the wicket practically unplayable, and Allen and Voce skittled the Australians out for 58 the next day. Bradman got a duck, but it would silly to build any theory about his inability on wet wickets on this dismissal; nobody could bat for any length of time on an Australian sticky wicket, though Hammond and Leyland were to have an opportunity, soon enough, to show what could be done. For the moment, the dazed Englishmen were one up, and the Australians had all the problems.

★   ★   ★   ★   ★

The Australian selectors refused to panic, simply recalling the experienced O'Brien for the unlucky Robinson. England boldly brought in a bowler, Sims, for Worthington; they were to be rewarded, though Sims himself did little. Allen won the toss and although Fagg failed, Hammond took advantage of a good wicket and played an innings in the manner of those great constructions of the 1928-29 series. It is amusing to read today the criticisms of his slow scoring; he reached his 100 in 162 minutes, and at the close had made 147 in 266 minutes. We would think it fast enough today, but Cardus saw him as a batsman doing a job of work and perhaps that was how Hammond saw it, too. O'Reilly attacked his leg-stump consistently and this certainly slowed Hammond down. England were 279 for 3 at the end of the first day and in a very strong position.

On the second day, England certainly were slow; they seemed determined to make such a huge score that even Bradman would not be able to top it, but as can happen when a side bats this slowly, they rather passed the initiative to the bowlers. Hammond remained in control, though he batted for some three and a quarter hours for 84, but the other batsman looked very fallible. In those spacious days, the *Sydney Morning Herald* employed no less than four writers to cover the play, and it is interesting to see what some of them thought of Hammond's batting. Jack Hobbs was inclined to give full credit to the Australian bowlers, whose accuracy and skill contained him. Charlie Macartney gave a technical view:

'He played a magnificent innings. . . but his timing was occasionally at fault.'

Dr RH Bettington, the old Oxford Blue, was somewhat harsher:

'He is a batsman with only a limited number of shots, but these are of the highest quality. When he is unable to score from these shots, he seems incapable of adapting himself to make others.'

We would probably say today, with hindsight, that Hammond was not so much incapable of adapting as unwilling to take the risk – he decided to play the percentages. This was rather the view of Neville Cardus, that day in Sydney:

'And all the time, over after over, Hammond went his serene way; I cannot remember batsmanship of surer or more easeful technique than Hammond's this day. There was no strain, even though he was carrying the team; no haste and no lagging; every

128

stroke and every movement of the feet and arms were now the instinctive expressions of a mastery which worked almost like a force in nature needing to labour as little as the sunshine overhead, for the full light it shed on the England innings.'

There were times, such as this, when it seemed that Cardus was made for Hammond and Hammond for Cardus.

Slow as England had been they had arrived at 426 for 6 by the time rain stopped play on this second day, and if the wicket had remained good, Allen would doubtless have batted on, and Hammond might have made a very big score indeed, because the team had virtually no tail; this was one of those England sides of which every member made his first class 100 at some time. However, the wicket was, for the moment, all in favour of the bowlers, and Allen declared at once on the third day. Badcock was ill and unable to bat, and Voce had O'Brien caught off his seventh ball. Bradman came in in his usual place in the order – the sun was shining and there was no point in changing the order and hoping for rain – and he was dismissed just as Hammond had been in the first Test, caught first ball off a leg-stump ball that lifted just a little. For the moment, the batsmen of both sides seemed still to be haunted by the spectre of bodyline.

The collapse continued, Voce and Allen being equally dangerous, and Verity just as effective when he came on. The score had reached 31 for 7 when O'Reilly laid about him and made 37 not out with some free hitting; he had nothing to lose, and took sixes off both Verity and Sims. Australia made 80 in the end leaving Allen with a slightly awkward decision. Most captains would have enforced the follow-on with no hesitation; Australia were down and demoralised and still a man short. But Allen knew that at each rolling the wicket would improve – there was no forecast of more rain – and there was Bradman. What if the great man made 200, and Australia strung together 500, and *then* it rained again? England would struggle to make 100 in the last innings, if it came to that.

Allen took his courage in both hands and put them in again. Fingleton and O'Brien made a sober start against Allen and Voce, then hammered Sims all over the park when Allen put him on to see if he could extract some turn. Allen replaced him with Hammond, who bowled, says Cardus, as well as anybody had done all day. Looking at the scorecard, this is a rare compliment. Hammond had O'Brien caught off a ball which made pace off the pitch, and brought the next one back at Bradman, making him hurry his stroke; but Fingleton and Bradman settled in, and the score was 145 for 1 at the close. It seemed almost as if that nightmare might come true.

Sims did the trick in the morning by bowling Fingleton with the perfect leg-break. He troubled both Bradman and McCabe, and then Bradman aimed a pull at a short one from Verity and was bowled. McCabe played a fine brave innings, as he often did when Australia were in deep trouble, but nobody could stay with him, and Australia, all out for 324, were beaten by an innings. Hammond came back late in the innings to take two more wickets and finish with the best figures of 3 for 29.

This unconsidered England side was now two up and could begin to hope. The more sophisticated observers, Cardus among them, felt that England had had all the luck and that there was in fact very little between the sides. It was noted that Bradman had yet to play a really big innings, but that in the second innings at Sydney, he had shown ominous signs of returning form.

★　　★　　★　　★　　★

There was a curious incident between the second and third Tests when five members of the Australian side were summoned before a committee of the Board of Control and told, in circumlocutory terms, that some people thought them less than whole-hearted in their support of their captain. Their spokesman O'Reilly asked for chapter and verse and the committee couldn't provide them. The players withdrew in some indignation and the Press had a field-day. Before the matter could be taken any further Australia had won a Test and the whole thing died a natural death, but it does indicate the state of Australian morale. Bradman had always denied that he had anything to do with the summons, and it certainly seems that he had his side in hand at all times.

The selectors made wholesale changes, again recalling experienced batsmen in Brown and Rigg. McCormick was unfit, and, instead of calling up another fast bowler, they recalled Sievers, who had previously been omitted.

It was time Australia had some luck and they had it in good measure at Melbourne, in a match which was attended by the biggest crowds ever seen at a cricket match up to that time. Bradman won the toss, but the Australians made nothing of their opportunity. Brown was out at once and Bradman made a cautious start. He was just beginning to look as though he was going to play the big innings that the Australian crowds were waiting and praying for when he edged Verity's arm-ball quietly to Robins at short-leg and was caught for 13.

English spectators could scarcely believe their eyes. Five Bradman innings for a total of 133! As Cardus wrote, England must win the rubber at once, for it couldn't last. The Australian collapse continued, only McCabe passing 50 and when rain brought an early end, the score was 181 for 6. At this moment, England stood on the brink of winning the rubber, two matches up and the third surely half-way to being won. In tennis terms, they were four-one up in the third set on their own service. Could they lose the rubber?

Well, they could, of course. The rain continued to fall all night and the wicket would clearly be difficult next day. Nobody knew just how difficult, but when play began after lunch, it was evident that it was well-nigh unplayable. Bradman continued his innings for a few overs, during which Hammond picked up two wickets and the wicket got worse, if anything. Australia declared at 200 for 9 wickets and waited to see what England could do. The roller did absolutely nothing to improve the wicket and McCabe had Worthington caught without a run on the board. Hammond came in – there was, once again, no point in playing for time – and began to bat with total calm as if the wicket were a perfect one. Barnett, at the other end, laid about him, seeking to get what runs he could before the unplayable ball came along, but Hammond seemed untroubled, although, of course, there were balls which he could do absolutely nothing with, as when O'Reilly bowled one which rose head-high from a good length. Hammond simply moved his head and allowed it to whistle past. Barnett was out, hooking, and Leyland came in to equal Hammond's unruffled play.

Paradoxically, it is possible that their wonderful exhibition did their side no good, for it meant that England batted for most of the day, whereas a few wild hits and a quick end would have got Australia to the crease to face the music. But neither Allen nor Hammond could know the wicket would be any better next day, and the light might not have held up long enough for a full Australian innings on this dreadful pitch. So Hammond and Leyland continued with their slow and masterly exhibition until, one after another, they turned the ball round the corner, failed to keep it down, and fell to agile, skillful catches by Len Darling – another player who never quite fulfilled his promise in Test cricket, but seldom missed a chance in the field. Hammond had scored 32 and Leyland 17. Once again, Allen had to make a fiendishly difficult decision. It was unlikely that the remaining batsmen would make much of batting on this pitch, and if he declared now, at 4.45pm he might pick up some vital wickets. Bradman was certain to change his batting order and send in his tail-enders, but perhaps England could get through them really quickly, and get at the batsmen. On the other hand, the light was worsening, and an appeal in 20 minutes' time might succeed. Allen had been much criticised for his failure to declare, but his critics have the advantage of hindsight, and of having time to think about it. Allen had to decide then; it was a time when even ten minutes could make all the difference. He compromised and sent in Sims, hoping that he and Ames would survive until the light failed, and that Ames and the others would at least make a few runs the next day, if the wicket mended. If it didn't improve, of course, Australia would be in trouble the next day, and who could tell what might happen?

Everything went wrong for poor Allen. His later batsmen got out, without making any runs worth counting, and when he did declare, at 76 for 9, he only got in a couple of overs at those tail-enders before the light completely failed. Next day, the weather continued to favour Australia. England took 5 wickets for only 97 runs, only two them recognised batsmen, but the wicket was improving all the time, and some light showers not only lost Allen time, but gave his bowlers a wet ball to bowl with. Bradman and Fingleton batted out the day; and then, on the fourth day, Bradman, in the very nick of time, recovered all his form and played a most devastating innings. He scored 192 in the day and, just as Hammond on the sticky wicket had played an innings that would have been beyond even Bradman, so Bradman now played an innings beyond Hammond – or anybody else. By the end of this day, Australia were 500 for 6 and the match as good as over. Hammond had bowled 21 eight-ball overs for 82 runs and as he toiled, he must have reflected grimly on the change of fortune.

England went in to score 689 in the fourth innings – a total then thought to be absolutely impossible of achievement – though Hammond's own team were to go close to an even more distant target two years later. They went at their task rather light-heartedly, Barnett playing some very airy strokes. Hammond dug in and seemed ready to play a long innings, without cutting out all his strokes; Cardus described his batting as 'grand and leonine'. But he was defeated by a fine ball from Sievers, which came quickly from the pitch and bowled him for 51. Sievers had taken 5 for 21 on the sticky dog in the first innings, and it is a commentary on that pitch that he was now dropped for good; Hammond's wicket was the last he took in Test cricket, but it was something for him to remember.

Leyland, like Hammond, was giving nothing away, and it was on this afternoon that he made his famous remark to Walter Robins, who had called him for a short run; Leyland called up the wicket 'Wait your hurry, Mr Robins, we can't get them all tonight, you know'. Or words to that effect. England were all out for 323, and had lost their first of three opportunities to make the Ashes their own.

★　　★　　★　　★　　★

England were lucky enough to get one more chance of winning the rubber, but this time they threw it away with no help from Fortune.

Australia, uncharacteristically, had packed their batting, but to begin with, it did them little good. On a hot Adelaide day Bradman won the toss but England's bowlers, with Farnes in the lead, were too much for all the batsmen except McCabe, who scored 88, and by the end of the day Australia were 267 for 7. Bradman was bowled for 26 by Allen as he aimed a vigorous pull – yet again, in this series, a batsman had fallen trying to find a gap on the leg-side. Hammond's contribution was to have Gregory lbw. Ross Gregory, who was not closely related to the other cricketers of that name who played for Australia, was a stylish young batsman who was to play only twice in Tests; he missed the 1938 tour and was killed in the war.

On the second day England quickly disposed of the tail, but then squandered their opportunity. Fagg had had to return home with rheumatic fever and, after Worthington's failures in the first and third Tests, Allen decided to open with Barnett and Verity. Verity was a staunch batsman – he was once memorably described by RC Robertson-Glasgow as batting like 'Sutcliffe gone stale. That is, pretty good' – and he took some shifting in this match, but this did get England off to a slow start. Hammond began slowly and indecisively, by his own high standards. He made only 20 in an hour, his only really characteristic stroke an off-drive from a McCormick no-ball. He was caught round the corner off O'Reilly and once again the technical comments of the ex-players are interesting:

Macartney: 'He lost his wicket playing a round-the-corner stroke not worthy of such a batsman. A full-blooded pull would have been safer and more playable'.

Jack Hobbs: 'On this tour, he has brought into his repertoire a sort of pat stroke with a horizontal bat. The risk is not worth the taking, and this time it got him out.'

Macartney, then, would have liked to see a more dashing Hammond. This would be in keeping with his own very positive approach to the batting art, but it doesn't take enough account of Hammond's responsibility as the head and front of a pretty inexperienced batting side. If Hammond failed, the side was very likely to fail, and it is hard to blame him if this made him rather cautious. Hobbs seems to be describing the stroke we should now call the paddle. Curiously enough, it was often adopted by Colin Cowdrey, a batsman who much resembled Hammond in technique and (in Test matches) in approach. At the close, England were 174 for 2, with Barnett 92 not out. It looked like a good springboard but close observers felt that England should have taken their opportunities and scored faster against tired bowling. They paid the price next day, when O'Reilly and Fleetwood-Smith began to get some turn out of the pitch. Once Barnett was out for an uncharacteristically slow 129, nobody was at all comfortable, and England subsided to 330. A lead of 42 was never going to be enough if Bradman struck form again and with the results of the series depending on him, it was likely that he would strike form. Fingleton got out early, but by the close Bradman had made 26 in an hour. This was slow going for him, but he had been ominously certain.

Bradman settled for around 30 runs an hour on the fourth day, but at this pace he looked totally safe. Allen had strained a leg and could bowl only seven overs, and he elected to save Hammond as much as possible, knowing that if England were to have any chance at all of making a big score in the fourth innings, Hammond would have to lead the way. Verity bowled with admirable steadiness – at the close, he had bowled 32 overs for 54 runs – but if he was turning the ball with his finger-spin, what would O'Reilly and Fleetwood-Smith do in the fourth innings? Bradman was 174 at the close, and Gregory was still there at 341 for 4. A huge Australian score was on the cards, but on the fifth day Allen was driven to use Hammond more and he produced his best bowling in a Test, qualitatively speaking. Just before lunch, he held a thunderous return catch from Bradman (212); it was the third and last time that he dismissed Bradman in a Test, and he must have been glad indeed to see the back of him, even if the match was already lost. Hammond now took three more quick wickets, wrapping up the Australian innings in no time at all – they went from 422 for 5 to 433 all out. Hammond's analysis was 15.2-1-57-5, and on this fifth day he had taken four for 20.

England needed 392 to win and on, a turning pitch, it was very unlikely. Verity again played soundly, and when he got out, Allen sent Hardstaff in, reasoning that Hammond needed rest and protection after his bowling efforts. It didn't profit Hammond much, because Barnett got out immediately, and Hammond had to join Hardstaff at 50 for 2. They at once began to handle the spinners with some ease; there is a suggestion in some accounts that Fleetwood-Smith's accuracy and concentration were affected by Bradman's switching him to the other end but, whatever the cause, Hardstaff was batting better than he had done since he had arrived in Australia and Hammond was calm and masterful. They added 70 with few alarms, and England supporters were beginning to hope when O'Reilly bowled Hardstaff. Leyland looked equally assured, and he and Hammond were still there at the close with the score on 148 and England needing 244. A win was just, only just, possible.

Fleetwood-Smith settled the matter in the first over next day, bowling Hammond with perfectly pitched Chinaman. Neville Cardus quoted an anonymous Yorkshireman as saying 'That's where Wally Hammond isn't Don Bradman. They wouldn't have got Don out third ball if Australia had wanted only 244'. The remark has also been attributed to George Duckworth; I prefer to believe that Cardus made it up himself, but in any case, it's a bit unfair. Bradman did sometimes get out when his side depended on him and it is no great disgrace to be accused of not being Bradman.

Cardus does also say, less arguably, that Hammond was a victim of the 'new' lbw law. Once Fleetwood-Smith had pitched his delivery on the right length, Hammond had to play for both the Chinaman and the arm-ball; he couldn't trust to his pads as he would have done at any time before 1935. Let us leave it that he was out to a beautiful ball when on 39 and take note that once he was gone, nobody else had any chance of saving the game. Leyland and Wyatt fought for a while, but 149 for 3 became 190 for 6 and 243 all out. The score in the rubber was two-all and the odds very firmly on the side coming from behind, unless Allen could win the toss and Hammond could make a big score.

★ ★ ★ ★ ★

Captains in this position never do win the toss. Allen was physically and mentally exhausted and was suggesting to his selection committee before the Melbourne Test, that he should stand down, but they wouldn't hear of it and the only change they made was to replace Robins with Worthington, thus terminating the experiment with Verity as opener. Allen duly lost the toss and Australia made a devastating start. The openers Fingleton and Rigg got out to Farnes, but not before Allen had dropped Fingleton off a relatively easy chance. It was to be the central theme of the day. Soon after McCabe came in, he was dropped, again by Allen; it was a difficult chance, but it would have meant much if Allen could have held it. McCabe was dropped again off Hammond when he had made 63, and yet again off Voce, at 86. The strain of a long tour was beginning to tell on the Englishmen, and they must have realised by tea-time that they had lost the rubber.

Bradman was batting faultlessly all this time and it is perfectly possible that even if McCabe had been caught he would have made the game safe. McCabe was out at last, caught at cover, after they had put on 249. It was rare for McCabe and Bradman to bat for a long time together – McCabe more often shone when he had to play a lone hand, but this must have been a partnership well worth seeing for the uncommitted observer – Bradman the spectacular hitter contrasted with the graceful McCabe.

Badcock came in at the end of the day and he, too, looked in prime form. Badcock made many huge scores in domestic cricket, but this was to be his only substantial Test innings; in fact, it was the only time in his seven Tests, that he got into double figures.

Bradman was out early on the second day, after making 169 in 223 minutes, but Gregory joined Badcock in another big stand, which must have delighted the huge crowd; here were two of their young players – Badcock was 22 and Gregory 21 – following in their captain's wake – it was a good omen for the next series. The Australian crowd were not to know that, come the next series, it would be England's young batsmen who would be the stars. No more catches were dropped on this second day, and the bowlers stuck to their task well, but the damage was done. Badcock made a fine century and Gregory 80, and Australia were all out early on the third day for 604, and the game was won and lost. Farnes in a heroic piece of bowling had taken 6 for 96, and Hammond had bowled 16 overs, a considerable stint for someone who had to carry the main batting burden as well.

Barnett failed to settle at the start of the innings, and Hardstaff was again sent in at No 3. He batted steadily and well, and Worthington was just beginning to show his true form when he swung a ball to the leg boundary and trod on his wicket, a most unlucky dismissal, but one which symptomised the change in England's fortunes since Sydney. Hammond came in at 96 for 2 and concentrated whole-heartedly on defence, which may not have been wise in a timeless Test when the other side had runs in the bank. Finally, on 14, his concentration faltered when he tried to hook O'Reilly. Not many batsmen ever did that successfully, and Hammond found the fieldsman. That was virtually the end of any serious resistance by England. Leyland was out very soon after and Hardstaff and Wyatt batted out time slowly and doggedly, Hardstaff showing true form for the first time in a Test.

Once again the weather was against England. A storm in the night produced a slow turner to begin with, but the pitch got progressively worse as the sun got to it. Hardstaff fell, 17 short of what would have been an excellent 100, Wyatt made 38, but nobody else made very many, and England were all out for 239. Bradman put them in again on a wicket which, nothing like as vicious as those in the first and third Tests, was still one on which they were never going to come within shouting distance of saving the innings defeat.

Worthington and Hardstaff were out almost at once. Barnett played his natural game and made a few before being leg-before to O'Reilly, the ball after he had hit him for a defiant six. Hammond, as he had done in the third Test, played as though the wicket were a good one, and revealed no sort of anxiety; it was a strength of his that he seldom betrayed his feelings about the pitch, an adverse decision or anything else. He made 56 before O'Reilly got one to lift even more than was to

136

be expected on this cranky pitch and Bradman – who else? – took the catch.

That really was the end. England, all out for 165, were beaten by an innings and 200 runs. It had been the oddest of rubbers. An unconsidered England side had had all the best of the luck and had gone two up while Bradman struggled to get his side running smoothly and to regain his own irresistible form. Then the luck changed sides once and for all, and Allen was seldom in the battle with a chance – except for that first innings at Adelaide, when two hours' positive batting might have turned back the tide.

Hammond had had a pretty good series; he was top of the England averages and headed all the Australians except Bradman, but his figures rest very much on that huge innings, whereas Bradman, as he usually did, dominated three Tests with big, fast innings. Hammond also bowled finely and his bowling figures would look even better if he had the opportunity to bowl on the bad wickets.

It has been said by some commentators that England lost this series because Hammond was not in the same class as Bradman. Maybe; nobody was in the same class as Sir Donald, but to be fair to Hammond, we should remember that he did a great deal of bowling in the series. 708 balls at his pace and at the age of 33, was no light task. Furthermore, he fielded at slip throughout, and as I have said, that makes a heavier call on the mental resources than fielding away from the wicket. It demands unremitting attention to every ball, and if Hammond's concentration lapsed in either the fourth or fifth Tests, there was every reason for it. He emerged from the season still a genuine all-rounder and the acknowledged second-best batsman in the world.

	Innings	N.O.	H.S.	Runs	Average	100	50
1936/37	9	1	231*	468	58.50	1	2
To date	103	13	336*	5388	59.86	16	19

	Balls	Runs	Wickets	Average
1936/37	708	301	12	25.08
To date	7015	2806	76	36.92

18 The new generation arrive

Hammond got away to an excellent start in 1937, seeming to be unaffected by his exertions in Australia. He made 121 against Glamorgan, and he graced the 150th anniversary celebrations staged by the MCC with scores of 86, 100 not out, 47 and 45, this against some of the best bowling in England. The two matches were North v South, and the MCC touring team against the Rest, and the Hammond was on the winning side each time. A feature of the festival was the fine batting of two newcomers to the major scene, Hutton and Compton, who would be bidding to fill the vacant spots in the England batting that everybody was identifying following the pretty patchy batting in Australia.

New Zealand were the visitors. This time they had been allocated three Tests, but they made a very shaky start to the season, and came in to the first Test at Lord's having lost five first-class matches and won only one, against Cambridge University. They had some promising-looking batsmen, but their bowling rested far too much on Cowie, a very fine fast-medium bowler who would have to be most carefully nursed by Page, the captain.

Hutton was selected for the first Test and duly opened with Parks, another newcomer. Paynter was recalled, not before time, and Hammond, Hardstaff and Barnett of the tourists, were retained. Allen played very little cricket this year and Walter Robins was appointed to captain England. Robins was by no means an automatic choice as a player and the selection was seen by some as a stopgap one. The other bowlers were Voce, Verity and Gover, who some had though unlucky not to go to Australia. Ames kept wicket.

Robins won the toss and Hutton was out at once, bowled by Cowie without scoring. Hardstaff came in next and batted soundly, though his timing was a little awry. When Parks was out for 22, Hammond was cramped and almost strokeless for a long time. At lunch, the score was only 87 for 2, regarded as abysmally slow by the standards of the day. Cowie twice beat Hammond early on by thumping him on the pads, but it was the slow left-arm Vivian and the medium-paced Roberts who tied the batsmen down. Too much should not be made of the scoring rate, though; Hammond was playing some fine strokes which were brilliantly fielded. Vivian set a very defensive field.

The Cricketer describes the field in detail. There was a mid-off, two extra-covers, a cover and a deep point, plus a deep extra-cover as an 'outpost' – we would probably call him a sweeper today. That is, a ring of six in front of the wicket on the offside. *The Cricketer* doesn't say where the other three were, but there must have been a gap either at third man or on the leg side, and perhaps Cardus's criticism of Hammond's early batting as being 'entirely strokeless and poor of spirit' had some justification.

After lunch the situation changed completely. Hammond had reached 43 before he hit his first four, then he hit one through the covers, followed by three more superb cover drives, a straight drive to the screen and, to quote *The Daily Telegraph:* 'two glorious strokes off his leg-stump'.

In short, he was away, and Hardstaff joined him in savaging the attack; notwithstanding their slow start, they put on 245 in 219 minutes. It was Hardstaff's first Test 100, Hammond's seventeenth. Once they had parted, for 114 and 140 respectively, wickets fell steadily, but Paynter batted freely for 74, and England's 424 was more than enough in a three-day match. Several of the New Zealanders made a good start, but none was able to go on to a big score. *Wisden* was pretty scathing about some negative bowling by England, but New Zealand were all out for 295, and England in a position to force the pace and look for a declaration.

Hammond, alas, was afflicted with water on the knee and it was considered unwise for him to bat. The attack was not a particularly severe one – he was bowling again a fortnight later – but it would have been silly to risk him when England were only going to bat for a couple of hours. The openers failed again, but Barnett, replacing Hammond at No 4, and Hardstaff added 104 in quick time, and Robins was able to leave New Zealand with four hours' batting and no chance of winning. Kerr, the opener, had been injured by a lifting ball from Hammond in the first innings, but he came in fifth wicket down and, with the very youthful Martin Donnelly, saved the game.

One interesting feature of the match was that this was Hammond's first Test 100 at Lord's; prior to this Test, his record there was:
Innings 13, Not Out 0, Highest Score 46, Runs 313, Average 24.07

He had broken the spell now, and was to do greater things in the following year.

★　　★　　★　　★　　★

Although Hutton had made only one run in his two innings at Lord's, it was Jim Parks who was dropped, and dropped for ever. Barnett moved up the order to partner Hutton, and the selectors strengthened the bowling, picking Arthur Wellard, a hard-hitting all-rounder, for his first Test, and recalling Jim Smith, Tom Goddard and Freddie Brown. The last was a slightly odd pick in that he, like Robins, was a leg-spinner and it was difficult to see them both getting much bowling in a three-day match. In the event, the captain didn't bowl at all because he had dislocated a finger in the field.

At Old Trafford, he did, however, win the toss and Hutton and Barnett got England away to a very good start, making exactly 100 at a run a minute before Barnett was out. Hutton went on to his first Test 100 before he and Hardstaff were out within a few minutes of each other. Hammond was slow and out of touch and had only scored 33 before he tried to drive a ball from Gallichan which went with the bowler's arm, and was bowled. England were now 296 for 4, and nobody else made many, Robins declaring overnight at 358 for 9.

On the Monday, New Zealand were soon in trouble, and when Vivian who opened and batted aggressively and well for two hours, was out they were 119 for 5. Walter Hadlee, who had not had a good tour so far, then played a splendid innings for 93, and saw them on to 281. Wellard was the best of the bowlers, maintaining a good length and troubling everybody. England had to go in in poor light, late on the second day, and lost the openers cheaply. Hammond went in at 29 for 2 but fell to Cowie without scoring. He 'quietly pushed Cowie into Moloney's hands at short-leg' to quote *The Daily Telegraph* writer. It was a way in which he did sometimes get out when survival was the only objective, and it was to happen again the following season, with more serious consequences.

This time England retrieved the situation; starting the last day 114 ahead, they lost futher wickets to Cowie, bowling with his tail up, but Ames and Brown pulled the game round with a lively, if lucky, eighth-wicket partnership of 72, Brown being dropped four times. New Zealand were set to make 265 to win, when the target might have been only 170 or so. The wicket was beginning to take spin enabling Goddard to bowl them out for only 134. He took 6 for 29, and only Vivian could resist him, though Donnelly made a brave 37 not out – his class was already clear for all to see, though few would have forecast the brilliancy to come. England were one up.

England took the chance to experiment in the third Test at the Oval by bringing in two young batsmen who were to do great things – Compton

140

and Washbrook – and Austin Matthews, a Glamorgan fast-medium bowler who was never to play in another Test. This time, Page won the toss, but torrential rain on the first day effectively destroyed all hope of a finish. Only half an hour's play was possible on this first day and when play was resumed on the Monday, New Zealand had to contend with a turning wicket – it was bad luck for them, coming at a time when they were beginning to recover from a disastrous start to their season.

New Zealand got into terrible trouble, but the middle-order batsmen, with Donnelly again in the lead, retrieved the position and they made 249, enough it seemed to secure them against defeat, in what was left of the match. Hammond had been placed at No 6 in the order, to give every chance to the young batsmen on trial, and for a time it appeared that he would be needed to shore up a tottering innings. Hutton, Barnett and Washbrook were all out with the score at 36 and New Zealand must have been getting excited, but Compton, at the age of 19, showed the fearless composure that was to be a feature of his batting throughout his career, and he and Hardstaff added 50 more that evening, in appalling light.

Next day, they went on to 161 before Compton was run out. The cynic may think that here, too, Compton was demonstrating a feature of the rest of his career but – at least on this occasion – he was in no way to blame. Hardstaff drove the ball hard back and the bowler deflected it on to the stumps with Denis backing up. It is the unluckiest way of all to get out and when the batsman concerned is on 65 in his first Test, it's enough to break his heart, but Compton was tougher than that, and merely determined to do better next time. As we shall see, he did. Hardstaff did go on to make 100 and Hammond played a little gem of an innings, making a rapid, graceful 31 before skying Cowie to cover as England pressed towards a declaration.

New Zealand did fall into trouble in the afternoon, but their batsmen were learning from their experiences on English wickets, and the ball was doing rather less that on the second day. Hammond put in a fine spell, turning the ball from leg and taking two wickets, but New Zealand were almost safe by tea and saw the day out. The game ended quietly and it can be said that New Zealand had had the worst of the wicket and would have been a trifle unlucky to lose. England had emerged from the series with some promising batsmen, but still looking for a bowler or two. Hammond had had an average series, but he had achieved one most notable landmark. He had overtaken Jack Hobbs as the highest scorer in all Test cricket and, although his own figures have been surpassed by a few players in these days of more Test matches, they are still mightily impressive by any standard.

	Innings	N.O.	H.S.	Runs	Average	100	50
1937	4	–	140	204	51.00	1	–
To date	107	13	336*	5592	59.48	17	19

	Balls	Runs	Wickets	Average
1937	270	101	4	25.25
To date	7285	2907	80	36.33

19   The crown of his career

Hammond had had another great county season in 1937, and his figures for the season 1932 to 1937 were almost Bradmanesque, considering the difference between England and Australian conditions and the sheer physical effort of continuous county cricket. He scored 16,192 runs in those six seasons at an average of 61.10 and he would clearly be England's chief batting hope against Bradman's Australian team in 1938. True he had failed in the Tests of 1934, but surely that wouldn't happen again. The exciting thing for England supporters was that he would now be surrounded by fine young players in Hutton, Compton, Barnett and possibly Hardstaff and Edrich.

There was still a question-mark about the captaincy – Robins had not been very impressive as an all-rounder either in 1936-37 or in 1937, and Allen was getting no younger – but when Hammond was offered a good position with a tyre company which enabled him to turn amateur during the winter, it seemed that the problem was solved, and the selectors didn't hesitate for long before appointing him. They went through the motions of a Test Trial first, but their minds were effectively made up for them when Allen, the appointed captain of The Rest, withdrew from the Trial.

What of the Australians? They appeared to have an immensely strong batting side. Bradman himself was literally worth two men, and most of the younger players distinguished themselves early on. By 24 May they had scored 4,506 runs in the first eight matches, at an average of 80.46, mightily impressive figures.

The Australian bowling was much less of a proposition. Grimmett had been left behind, it being Bradman's view that at 46 he had lost his edge (though Grimmett continued to take a lot of wickets right up to the war). Ward, his direct replacement, did well against the counties but was always regarded as suspect in the Tests, and the attack was going to depend on three men, O'Reilly, whom England knew all about, Fleetwood-Smith, who had had his golden moment at Adelaide on Allen's tour, but who did offer the odd loose ball and was seen as vulnerable, and McCormick, who had also had his moments in 1936-37, but was distinctly injury-prone. At the beginning of the 1938 tour,

143

he developed a new phobia to go with his injury problems – he began to overstep the crease, sometimes two or three times an over, and nothing could cure him. It wasn't a matter of dragging, but he had simply lost his rhythm. He was no-balled 35 times in the opening match at Worcester and it took him weeks to recover any measure of confidence.

England's bowling for the first Test at Nottingham was also on the weak side. Not only Allen, but Bowes and Voce were unfit. Moreover the selectors were very worried about the length of the tail, and spent the first part of the season in a fruitless search for an all-rounder. In this first Test, they picked Reg Sinfield for the part, a worthy county cricketer but one who had never before been seriously considered for England. He was 36 years old and wouldn't do a lot for the fielding of the side. Farnes and Verity were fit and in form, and the Trial had produced a real find in Doug Wright, a leg-spinner with real zip and fire.

However, this left England with a four-man attack and threw an extra bowling burden on Hammond. The wicket was going to be a very easy one – this was a period when 'cow confetti' was Bill O'Reilly scornfully called it, was the most important ingredient in the preparation of English wickets – and both captains would be desperate to win the toss. Hammond was the lucky man and Hutton and Barnett, who had begun their association so profitably the summer before, gave England the most encouraging start.

Barnett was distinctly shaky to begin with – Cardus described his innings as being played 'on the rim of mortality' but he soon decided to trust his eye and the groundsman, and went for everything. He was particularly hard on Fleetwood-Smith, and it was evident that luck was on England's side when Bradman missed a catch – he was normally as infallible as Hammond himself. Barnett was 98 at lunch out of a total of 169, and over-optimistic England supporters probably thought the rubber already won.

The slaughter continued after lunch, Barnett was out at 219 and Edrich failed. Hammond came in now, and, according to Howard Marshall, writing in the *Telegraph* he looked in the mood for a big innings, but after a few beefy straight drives he was drawn forward by O'Reilly and bowled for 26. For a moment, England looked vulnerable at 281 for 4, but Paynter and Compton made the most of this beautiful batting wicket and played out time. The first-day score of 422 for 4 was the kind of figure that was normally only achieved when Bradman had been in all day, but the difference now was that four batsmen had all contributed to the scoring and Hammond, the acknowledged star, had done virtually nothing. England's prospects were bright indeed.

On the second day, Compton went on to his 100 before throwing his wicket away with a careless stroke – it is said that Hammond was far from pleased with him – and then Ames and the bowlers saw Paynter to an excellent 216 made in 320 minutes. This was the highest score yet made against Australia in England. Few dreamed that it would be beaten twice in the next three Tests. Hammond was able to declare at 658 for 8 and send the Australians in to bat for two and a half days to save the game.

The wicket was still excellent, but the batsmen were tired, and Wright and Farnes bowled with spirit and fire. Fingleton got out to one of Wright's bad balls, but the young bowler then tormented Bradman, who looked distinctly out of touch, and almost had him out twice. At last, Bradman succumbed to Sinfield for 51. Brown fell before the close and Australia were in all sorts of trouble – but they had been getting out to bad balls and there was always the possibility that someone would play a match-saving innings.

If anyone had been making a book on the events of this Test – but this was in the long interregnum of purity between Lord Frederick Beauclerk and the Ladbrokes tent – Stan McCabe would have been everybody's choice to provide that match-saving innings. He duly obliged and it was one of the very finest innings ever seen, as Bradman very handsomely acknowledged at the time and on reflection. McCabe scored 232 in just under four hours, under the severest pressure all the time. The score was 263 for 7 when O'Reilly came in, and the last three batsmen scored just 16 runs while McCabe was making 127. He scored all the last 66 runs, in about 25 minutes! I could go on quoting figures, but these will suffice. It was a superhuman piece of batting.

Hammond's captaincy was criticised on two counts. He delayed taking the new ball for a while and it was said that this enabled Ben Barnett to establish himself at the wicket; and he bowled Verity for only 7.3 overs, apparently reserving him for the follow-on. It is very likely that nothing Hammond could do would have subdued McCabe, but other tactics might have got rid of the tail-enders more quickly. The reason he didn't take the new ball was probably that Wright was bowling superbly at the time, having just shot out Hassett and Badcock, and anybody who ever saw Wright bowl will testify that when he was on song he always looked as though he would take a wicket with every ball. Sinfield was used as the stock bowler in the first innings in preference to Verity, and Hammond was of course accustomed to see Sinfield doing the job for Gloucestershire, day in and day out. It was very understandable that he used him now.

Fingleton and Brown batted soundly, if deliberately, in the second innings. They were very freely barracked by a partisan crowd who had not forgotten the treatment of Larwood and Voce, but didn't allow this to disturb their concentration. When Fingleton was out for 40, most brilliantly caught by Hammond off Edrich, Bradman came in and played a most uncharacteristic innings, batting for 365 minutes for 144. Verity bowled 62 overs in this innings, and perhaps his workload was oddly distributed, but the wicket, although it began to crumble, remained slow, and England never looked like forcing a win. At the close, Australia were 427 for 6, 180 ahead, and it was evident that if the wickets were to be like this, neither side was very likely to win in four days.

★　★　★　★　★

England made only one change for the Lord's Test, Wellard, a fast-medium bowler, replacing Sinfield, an off-spinner. This may have been an acknowledgement that Hammond was getting a little too old to open the bowling in a Test, for he had not looked at all the part in the first match. He won the toss again and McCormick had one of those fiery spells which he produced all too seldom. He fired one in at Hutton, who was caught at short-leg, and then Edrich hit all across a good-length ball.

Hammond came to the wicket to face a real crisis at 20 for 2, saw Barnett fall to McCormick at 31, and then played the innings of his life. By common consent it surpassed even his two great double-centuries in 1928-29, though like those innings it was achieved by his concentrating on the strokes which were totally safe – basically, crashing hits through the covers and through the V between mid-off and mid-on. He was stoutly supported by Paynter, who made 99, and although Compton failed, Ames joined him in a stand of 186, which was then the record for the sixth wicket for England against Australia. It has been recorded in some accounts that Hammond scored 70 before lunch, 70 after lunch and before tea, and 70 after tea, but he was in fact 139 at tea and made 71 afterwards. It is worth quoting one or two contemporaries on this innings, the crown of Hammond's Test career. Sir Pelham Warner wrote:

'Hammond was at his best, cool and unruffled and masterly both in defence and stroke-play.'

Howard Marshall, in *The Daily Telegraph:*

'His innings must rank with McCabe's as one of the greatest ever played in Test matches. . . we have always thought of him as the potential answer to Bradman and to see him. . . forging inevitably on to his 200 was heartening indeed'

146

It is interesting that Marshall was seeing Hammond as the *answer* to Bradman, some indication of the understandable awe in which English followers of the game held the little man.

Hammond pulled a muscle in his leg towards the end of this first day and was very lame the next morning. He wasted little more time at the wicket, but rattled up another 30 runs in as many minutes before being bowled by McCormick for 240. Cardus thought him even more brilliant on this day than on the Friday and, in an eloquent passage too long to quote here, brought out all his musical metaphors in one last elegiac tribute – it was almost as if Cardus had the gift of prophecy and knew that Hammond was never to make another 100 against Australia. The innings rather subsided after he was out, and England, after being 457 for 5, were all out for 494. It hardly looked to be enough.

Fingleton and Brown started a little shakily, but settled after lunch and made 69 at a run a minute. Farnes looked mediocre, certainly lacking McCormick's zest and fire, but Wright troubled all the batsmen. He beat Bradman once or twice and it was a surprise when Hammond replaced him with Verity; but before the critics could sharpen their pencils, Verity bowled the Don as he tried to cut, and once again the rather under-rated England attack seemed to have found the answer to the Bradman problem. This was to be disproved in due course, but for the moment Australia had all the problems.

Brown was looking very safe, and McCabe began as though he was going to repeat his Nottingham masterpiece. He played all the bowlers with consummate ease, till he fell to a catch by Verity in the gully which evoked the memory of Chapman's great catch to dismiss Bradman in 1930. Hassett and Brown were rather more pedestrian, but they added 124, and Australia began to feel more comfortable. There followed a nasty little collapse, Badcock failing for the third time in the series, and it needed an inspired burst of hitting from O'Reilly who, with his immensely long reach and his daring spirit, could be a very awkward customer in a crisis, to avert the follow-on. Brown carried his bat for a cultured and chanceless 206, and Australia were only 72 behind.

A sharp shower late in the Australian innings freshened the wicket, and McCormick and O'Reilly took the wickets of the two openers in the last half-hour. Suddenly, it was England who faced a crisis, especially as Hammond would be very much hampered by his leg-strain.

And, indeed, England did get into real difficulties on the last day. Verity had come in overnight, and Hammond sent Paynter in at No 5, but he himself had to bat at 64 for 4, when Edrich and Verity were out, and he failed, playing an awkward-looking one-handed sweep (he had been hit on the elbow in the first innings as well as pulling a muscle, and was clearly batting under great difficulties). He was out for 2 and

147

England were 76 for 5. But Compton now showed his greatness in a Test for the first time, batting resolutely and assertively for 76, and he was still undefeated when Hammond was able to declare and set Australia to bat out time – it was clearly impossible for them to make 315 to win in under 3 hours, but Hammond was unlikely to make a more challenging declaration with Bradman on the other side. Australia did manage to get into some temporary difficulties but Bradman was equal to the challenge, and he made 102 in two and a half hours, for the first time looking reasonably secure against Wright. Hassett made 42, but the other batsmen failed and Australia, 204 for 6 at the end, were perhaps a little lucky to escape. Cardus, pessimistic as ever, pointed out that England had now had the enemy on the ropes twice and hadn't managed to finish him off. 'Frankly' he wrote 'I think we have lost our chance in the rubber.'

★   ★   ★   ★   ★

The third Test due to be played at Old Trafford, was completely washed out, and the captains didn't even exchange teams. This was hard on Frank Smailes of Yorkshire who had been picked, at least for the squad of 13 by selectors who were still looking for the missing all-rounder. He wasn't picked for the fourth Test at Leeds, and had to wait eight years for his first and only cap.

Ames had had a finger broken in the course of the Lord's Test and the selectors had to look for another wicket-keeper who could bat well, if they were not to have too long a tail. Paul Gibb, the Cambridge wicket-keeper, had been playing for Yorkshire in place of Wood, who was reckoned to be just a little out of form, and he was picked for the game at Manchester. He would doubtless have played at Leeds too, but in a fateful game at Lord's on a very lively pitch, he, Hutton, and Leyland were all injured. Hutton was by now a fixture in the England team and Leyland, who had started the seaon with shoulder trouble, was now fit and in form. He would almost certainly have been picked on his own ground, for it was acknowledged that he played O'Reilly better than anybody else – and O'Reilly was the threat.

The selectors had now to regroup, without these three players and in the knowledge that Hammond would not be fit to bowl. They picked Edrich and Barnett to open, and brought in Hardstaff. Bowes was now fit and they went for an attack of four specialist bowlers, plus Edrich. Price of Middlesex was the wicket-keeper – he had opened for the county some seasons earlier, but his batting had largely left him, and he was nobody's idea of a Test No 7. The tail would be long, but it is difficult to see what else the selectors could do. They could of course

148

have packed the batting and hoped for a draw. The Oval Test was now to be played to a finish, since the result of the series would be undecided when it began and most people expected the toss to decide the match, on the sort of wicket that could be expected. The Leeds wicket would not favour the batsmen and the selectors possibly reckoned that there would be a finish in any event, and they had better go for broke.

Hammond won the toss for the third time, but things went badly for England from the start. The pitch was a slow turner, but it was Waite, a worthy but uninspired medium-pacer, who troubled the batsmen to begin with. Two chances went down off him in the first half-hour and the batsmen may have thought that fortune was on their side – but Bradman brought O'Reilly on early and he bowled Edrich with a googly, with the score at 29. Hardstaff was at once run out after getting into a dreadful muddle with Barnett, and once again Hammond was coming in to right the ship. It was a slow business, but he made his mark.

The score was only 62 for 2 at lunch, abysmally slow by the standards of the day, and not long afterward Barnett was caught at the wicket. Paynter, expressionless and sound as ever, joined Hammond in a stand of 54 which was decorated with two consecutive and splendid off-drives for four by Hammond, and some audacious cuts by Paynter. O'Reilly seemed to be the only bowler to trouble Hammond, and at last he drew him forward and bowled him with a well-flighted googly.

Hammond had made 76 out of 108 scored while he was in, and there was little more resistance by the batsmen. Verity and Wright hit out bravely at the spinners and added 41 for the eighth wicket, but nobody else did much, and 223 was an inadequate score on this wicket. Brown tried to pull Wright and was bowled before the close, and Bradman made his own comment on the wicket by sending in a night-watchman. Surely, he seemed to be saying, the wicket would improve on the morrow.

Barnett, the night-watchman, batted finely in the morning and scored 57. The light got steadily worse after lunch, but Bradman refused to appeal. The wicket would get worse if it rained and after all he was seeing the ball perfectly; it was for his other batsmen to look after themselves, and if they didn't come off, England would do no better either in the dark or on a rain-affected wicket. That, roughly speaking, was his philosophy, and it won him the match. He made a wonderful 103 in just under three hours and his side got a lead of just 19, Badcock failing yet again – he was having an inexplicably bad series – and nobody else, after Barnett, making 20.

Edrich and Barnett batted serenely in the evening light, which was considerably brighter than it had been for most of the day, but they were separated early on the second day. Hardstaff was bowled by O'Reilly when he had made 11 and, yet again, Hammond was coming in to try to save the innings. This time he didn't manage it. O'Reilly bowled him a googly with his first ball, which may well have popped a bit – Hammond played a tentative stroke and was well caught by Brown at short-leg for a duck. The fat was in the fire and England's young batsmen could do nothing about it. Paynter put up a fight, but that long tail wasn't equal to the task of supporting him. England were all out for 123, Paynter 21 not out, leaving Australia needing only 105 to win.

The path of a Test captain is never smooth, and this time Hammond was criticised for not bringing Wright on soon enough, and for not keeping him on when he had taken two wickets – but Wright was a bowler who generally sent down one bad-length ball in every over, and Hammond had no runs to play with. He was inclined to trust to Farnes and Bowes and hope that the wicket would do the job for them, and he only put Wright on when it was evident that the wicket wasn't as bad as all that – or as bad as O'Reilly and the England batsmen had made it look.

Wright did dismiss both Bradman and McCabe, and Australia were faltering at 61 for 4, but Hassett played a brave and skilful innings, to borrow a phrase from Cardus, and effectively saw them home to a win by 5 wickets. England could tell themselves that they had had the better of two Tests out of three, but nevertheless Australia had kept the Ashes. They had probably managed their slender resources rather better than had England, and Bradman's superbly consistent batting – when it mattered – had been the decisive factor, as it had been in 1930, 1934 and 1936-37.

$$\star \quad \star \quad \star \quad \star \quad \star$$

Perhaps because English supporters felt their side had been a little unlucky, there was still immense interest in the last Test at the Oval, and a very extraordinary game it was. Since it was to be played to a finish, it seems all the more remarkable that both sides packed their batting, England going into the match with only three specialist bowlers and Australia with only two! McCormick was said to be ill, but he had not looked in good shape since that opening burst at Lord's and Hammond's great riposte, and of course the Australians had brought no spare fast bowler. Their opening attack would be Waite and McCabe, possibly as undemanding a pair as they had ever fielded.

All England's invalids were fit again, though the unfortunate Gibb was not selected. Arthur Wood was now thought by Yorkshire to be keeping better than Gibb, and he now got his first England cap at the age of 39. England dropped Barnett, possibly thinking his glad methods unsuitable to a timeless Test, but also needing Edrich's bowling in support of Farnes, Bowes and Verity. Leyland – the natural counter to O'Reilly – came in at last and Hardstaff was retained.

The wicket was going to be the truest ever seen in England, the pundits said, and nothing was more certain than that the side which batted first would make a great many runs. Hammond had won three tosses in a row, and must have feared the worst, but the law of averages doesn't always work in the shorter term, and he won again. The story of this Test is well-known – Edrich got out early, but Hutton and Leyland batted for the rest of the first day with only one mistake, a stumping chance offered by Hutton and muffed by Barnett. At the close, they were 347 for 1 and the Australian attack, such as it was, in tatters. It was true that the wicket was, as predicted, almost sinfully easy, but Australia had only themselves to blame, having gone into the match with so weak an attack.

Leyland was run out on the second day for 187 with the score at 411, and Hammond had the rare luxury of coming in with his side in an invulnerable position. (This was his twenty-ninth test against Australia, and this was only the third time he had come in with as many as 150 on the board.) He began forcefully, almost frivolously, scoring 20 in his first 15 minutes – but after lunch, he bethought him that this *was* a timeless match and Bradman *was* playing on the other side, and he quietened down, coming almost to a halt in fact. It took him two hours to reach his 50, in spite of that tearaway start, and when he was out to Fleetwood-Smith for 59, Hutton had actually outscored him in a partnership of 135. Hutton went on to 300 exactly by the close. Paynter and Compton had failed, but Hardstaff had settled in and was looking like playing another big innings. England couldn't lose now, but it wound be intriguing to see what the quality of Australia's reply would be.

It all ended in anti-climax of course. After Hutton had broken the records of Bradman and Hammond and then got out from sheer weariness at 364, Bradman broke his ankle, and Hammond declared at tea on the third day. It is alleged that he asked for a sight of a medical certificate on the state of the ankle before he did so, but I am sure this is apocryphal. It is amusing, nevertheless, to speculate on the course of the match if Bradman and Fingleton, who had strained a muscle, had not been injured. To begin with, Hammond wouldn't have declared. Hardstaff was still very much in and he and Verity would have been good for a few more runs against Hassett and Barnes. England would have made a thousand and we can be pretty sure that Bradman would have led a vigorous reply. My view is that Australia would have made

500 or 600 and that England would have batted again, and made 400 – the mind boggles!

In the match itself, Australia virtually surrendered, only Brown and Barnes playing in their accustomed style in the first innings. Barnes, who had been waiting a long time for his chance, played soundly again in the second innings, and Barnett made the top score of 46, but the rest of the team recognised and accepted inevitable defeat. It was a pretty un-Australian performance and the margin of defeat – an innings and 579 runs – the greatest ever in a Test. It remains the record margin and one hopes that it will remain so for ever. Farnes and Bowes, with 11 wickets between them, were the most successful bowlers.

Hammond's first season of captaincy had been a mixed one. England's new batsmen had done wonders and in three matches there had been little that even O'Reilly could do against them. But Australia had got away with it once again, by virtue of that snatched win in the match at Leeds, which had been by a long way the best match of the series. Hammond's tactics had been generally approved. His handling of Wright had sometimes been a little uncertain, but Wright's bowling method was such that it was never easy to make the best use of him. Hammond had generally batted well, apart from that crucial dismissal in the second innings at Leeds. He was clearly set for a long spell at the head of affairs – if Herr Hitler allowed it.

	Innings	N.O.	H.S.	Runs	Average	100	50
1938	6	0	240	403	67.16	1	2
To date	113	13	336*	5995	59.95	18	21

	Balls	Runs	Wickets	Average
1938	198	67	0	–
To date	7483	2974	80	37.17

20   Ten days of tedium

For his first tour abroad as England's captain, Hammond was given a strong side, very nearly the strongest that could have been picked. Compton was playing football for the Arsenal but otherwise, of the side that had been playing against the Australians, only Leyland, Hardstaff and Bowes were left at home. The selectors, very reasonably, wanted to look at some younger batsmen, and selected Bartlett, Valentine, Yardley and Gibb, who was also the reserve wicket-keeper. Perks of Worcestershire came in as an opening bowler, and the side had four spinners, Verity, Wright, Goddard and Wilkinson, a most promising leg-spinner from Lancashire who was destined to have a short and not very successful career.

South Africa were trying to rebuild their attack, Bell, Crisp and Vincent having played their last Tests. They had lost poor Cameron and Herby Wade and Siedle had retired. England would be well advised to look for an early lead in the series before the new men could establish themselves. The tourists began very strongly, either winning their games or having the best of draws, but faltered in the last match before the first Test against a strong Transvaal team, every member of which played for South Africa at one time or another. The MCC were 160 behind on the first innings, but there was a good deal of rain during the match, and there was never any prospect of a finish. More seriously, Hutton was hit on the head and had to miss the first Test at Johannesburg.

Hammond had been batting quietly in the preliminary matches, leaving it to his young men and to Eddie Paynter, to pile up some massive totals – but he had made a splendid 122 against Natal and was expected to be on form in the Tests. He was; it was his best series against 1929. He was also in form as a spinner of the coin, continuing his run of success begun against Australia.

In Hutton's absence, Edrich and Gibb opened for England, and Edrich was out at once. Paynter batted third, as he was to do throughout the series, and he and Gibb made a huge stand, Paynter scoring 117 out of 184. This really set the tone for the series. Paynter was in the form of his life and seldom failed when it mattered, and Gibb, a slow and

153

not very attractive player, proved very difficult to shift. His nuisance value, to use a phrase not then in vogue, was considerable. The South Africans regarded him as a lucky player and he certainly seemed to profit from more than his share of dropped catches, but he had the priceless virtue of putting a mistake firmly out of his mind and addressing himself to the next ball. As WG said, the bowler can only bowl one ball at a time.

In this match, Hammond didn't stay long. He looked good while he was in, but Gordon, a fast-medium bowler making his first appearance, had him lbw for 24. Ames batted freely, and when Gibb was out at last for a stubborn 93, the total was 278 for 4. A pity, said the critics, that Gibb should miss getting a 100 in his first Test by so little, but he was to miss a greater prize than that. Yardley, also playing in his first Test, failed, but Valentine made a vigorous 97, and England totalled 422.

The South African debutants were less successful than Gibb had been, van der Bijl, another obdurate bat, being out for 4, and Melville, captaining South Africa on his first appearance, failing to score. Mitchell had been batting freely at the other end while van der Bijl struggled, and he and Nourse pulled the game round with 73 apiece, but there was a sensational collapse at the end of the second day. Goddard caught and bowled Nourse at 160. Gordon was sent in as night-watchmen, and was stumped off the first ball (which rather makes one wonder if he was the right choice for the part), and Billy Wade, the new wicket-keeper, was bowled, also first ball. Goddard, not everybody's choice for the touring team, had his hat-trick.

Next day, Viljoen and Dalton led another recovery and Langton knocked the tired bowlers about at the end of the innings, scoring 64 in 95 minutes. South Africa finished only 32 behind, and a draw was the only possible result. Gibb made sure of his 100 this time, batting with much more assurance, and Paynter made a second 100, a very rare feat by an England batsman. Hammond came in to force the pace before making a token declaration, and scored 58, batting, according to the critics, in a delightfully aggressive way and going yards down the pitch to the slow men. It was all to no avail. He was never going to set South Africa an attainable target – captains just don't do that in the first match of a Test series – and the game petered out in a draw.

★   ★   ★   ★   ★

Hutton was fit for the second Test at Cape Town and replaced the unlucky Yardley. Wright came in for Wilkinson, who had had an unhappy time in the first Test. Hammond won the toss again and opened with Hutton and Gibb. Hutton fell to Gordon, who was

154

beginning to look quite a prospect, and Paynter failed for almost the only time in the series. Hammond went in at 30 for 2 and made a shaky start. Gordon shaved his stumps and he responded by cracking the next ball through the covers for four. He settled down and was soon taking runs freely, while Gibb played his usual patient game.

When Gibb was out at 139, Ames came in and batted in his very best form, actually outscoring Hammond in a scintillating partnership. They put on 197 in 145 minutes, of which Ames made 115. Each was missed once, Hammond offering a screaming slip catch off Davies to which the fielder couldn't get a hand. Edrich failed again, but Valentine was in fine form too, and made 112 in quick time. Hammond was out for 181, scored in five and a half hours with 16 fours, mostly crashed through the covers off the back foot. It was an awesome display, and he was able to declare at 559 for 9, after batting for just one over on the third day to get the advantage of putting the heavy roller on the pitch.

Mitchell and van der Bijl made a solid start, but the pitch was beginning to offer the spinners just a little help, and the weary South Africans struggled. Melville had been injured in the field and couldn't bat until the fourth day but Nourse saved his side with a fine fighting 120. They were all out for 286 and followed on before lunch on the last day, but Rowan and van der Bijl saved the game very easily as the pitch slowed. South Africa were 201 for 2 at the end and it was beginning to look as though neither side could win in four days. The last match was to be played without a time-limit if the result of the rubber depended on it, and it seemed that the rubber would be decided at Durban.

★   ★   ★   ★   ★

It was indeed decided at Durban, but in the third Test, not the fifth. England still depending on spin, brought Wilkinson back for Goddard, which seems a little hard on the Gloucestershire man, and retained the same batsmen. Yardley may have felt a little hard done by – here were England playing both their keepers, quite rightly on their batting form, but also persevering with Edrich who had now failed in his first six Tests. Yardley had made an excellent 126 against Border – but he was destined to wait for seven years before playing for England again. Melville was fit to play for South Africa, but only just it would seem – he batted at No 8.

Yet again Hammond won the toss, and again things went well for them. Hutton was out to Gordon for 31, scored out of 38, but Gibb and Paynter wore the bowling down. The newspapers were critical of the slow going before lunch, when the score was 101 for 1, but they must have been looking at Gibb and not at Paynter, who was 'on song' from the start. Gibb made only 38 in two and a half hours, but he had done his job in his usual unobtrusive way, for the score was 153 for 2 when Hammond came in. He got a no-ball from Davies and drove it for four, and he was away. By tea-time, the score was 225 for 2 after that South Africa were never in the match. 17 minutes were lost to the rain after tea, but Paynter and Hammond scored 148 in the shortened session and had mastered all the bowlers well before the close. Paynter was 197 overnight, Hammond 99.

One wonders if either of them lost any sleep over this – they had both been there before – and they came up for the second day looking fresher than the bowlers. Hammond touched an outswinger to slip when he had made 120 in under three hours, again with 16 fours, but Paynter careered on to 243 before being caught. It was the highest innings ever made in England-South Africa Tests, and it remains so to this day. Hammond declared at 469 for 4, a bold declaration by today's standards, for the wicket was still playing well, as far as could be seen.

Mitchell and van der Bijl batted serenely enough, but when they were parted Farnes ripped the heart out of the middle batting and South Africa were all out for 103. It was the first collapse of the series and it was decisive. They batted much better in the second innings, Mitchell, Rowan and Viljoen all making runs, but somehow it always seemed that England would have time to bowl them out. Only bad light seemed likely to frustrate England, but the South Africans declined to appeal – which may seem Quixotic to the modern reader, but was by no means unusual then. Two catches by Hammond are singled out by *Wisden* as being brilliant and decisive, and his captaincy was highly praised by the South African critics who noted that in this second innings he was always switching his bowlers and giving the batsmen no time to settle. We shall return to the question of his tactical ability, but *at the time* he was regarded as being as good as anybody.

★　★　★　★　★

England, then, went to Johannesburg for the fourth Test one up, and it was generally thought that they could escape with at worst a draw, and that they could therefore do no worse than halve the rubber. It very nearly went wrong, South Africa having distinctly the better of a drawn match much interrupted by rain. Edrich had saved his place with a sparkling century in Rhodesia, and England continued to shuffle their spin bowlers, bringing Goddard back for Wright. South Africa introduced a new wicket-keeper, Grieveson, who was to have a distinguished two matches, the whole of his Test career.

Hammond won his eighth Test toss in a row – surely his luck must run out some time? – but his batsmen failed to take advantage of it. Gibb failed for once, Hutton and Paynter added 78, and then a short shower freshened the pitch and two crucial wickets fell. Paynter was caught off Langton for 40, and Hammond got a brute of a ball from Gordon, which moved in to him and popped. He played a correct enough defensive stroke, but got it too high on the bat and was brilliantly caught, one-handed, by Newson at short-leg for 1. It was the third time Gordon had dismissed him and the new man was earning his keep – to this point, he had taken 15 of the 30 England wickets to fall. Hutton played his best innings of the series, scoring 92, but England were all out for 215 and in real trouble.

On the second day rain delayed the start. The wicket was difficult to begin with, but Melville and van der Bijl, opening together for the first time survived their early difficulties and made 108 together, by which time the pitch was playing more easily. Rowan, Mitchell and Nourse all played well and South Africa were ahead by the end of the day with seven wickets in hand. But the rain returned and washed out the third day altogether, and South Africa had a great deal to do if they were to force a win. They really didn't make much of a fist of it, losing five wickets while they added 100 at a run a minute and leaving themselves less than four hours to get England out and knock off the runs.

It was never on – Paynter failed for once, but the openers made runs and Hammond played beautifully, making a calm 61 in not much more than an hour and a half. England were 203 for 4 at the close and had escaped without alarm. If the third day had not been lost, they might have been in trouble – it is unlikely that they would have made more than say, 350, and South Africa might have had time to win, but it would have been a close-run thing.

So the series came down to a timeless Test after all. South Africa could only share the rubber, but they were naturally very keen to do so. For Durban they retained the side that had done so well at Johannesburg, while England for the first time, picked a balanced attack of two pacemen – Farnes, and Perks, making his Test debut – and two spinners, Verity and Wright, with support from Hammond and Edrich. The Middlesex batsman had saved his bacon again with a fine 150 against Natal, but he had now scored only 87 runs in his first ten innings and was reckoned to be lucky, or perhaps unlucky, to be there. The pressure on him must have been immense.

Now, at last, Hammond lost the toss. It was a beautiful wicket and he must have felt that his luck had run out at just the wrong time. South Africa began very slowly, making only 49 before lunch, but speeded up afterwards and had made 229 for 2 by the end of the day. Van der Bijl had batted all day for 105, often very slowly, but astonishing everybody by scoring 22 off one over from Wright – he was that kind of batsman and, one must say, Wright was that kind of bowler.

On the second day, things slowed up again, only 17 runs coming in the first hour for the loss of Mitchell's wicket. Van der Bijl was out for 125 made in 438 minutes, which seems slow by today's standards, and was then regarded as downright funereal. Bob Crisp, writing in *The Cape Times* wrote on this day, a Saturday, that the match might well last till Wednesday – but which Wednesday? and he was the first to suggest that the boat might have to be delayed to enable the Englishmen to finish the game. Many a true word is spoken in jest. By the end of the day, South Africa were 423 for 6, Wright and Perks having shared the wickets, while Verity bowled accurately and tirelessly, keeping the runs down – he conceded less than two runs an over throughout the match – and these were eight-ball overs!

Grieveson distinguished himself on the Monday, making 75 in his first Test innings – he had not batted in the fourth Test, though he had taken five catches. South Africa were all out for 530, Verity taking two wickets at the end to give him figures of 2 for 97 in 55.6 overs. It was one of the more remarkable statistics of this remarkable match that each of the specialist bowlers took at least one wicket and no bowler took 'none for a hundred' in an innings. England cannot have been looking forward to batting after two and a half days in the field, were relieved when heavy rain stopped play soon after tea with the score at 35 for 1, Gibb being the man out.

On the fourth day England struggled against tight bowling, and by the end South Africa seemed to have the match won. Hutton and Paynter went easily along to 64 before Hutton was run out, he and Paynter getting into a muddle over what should have been an easy run. Hammond started a little shakily against Gordon, but seemed to have got over his difficulties when he went down the pitch to drive Dalton, missed and was stumped, floundering outside his crease in a highly uncharacteristic way, for 24. The score was now 125 for 3 and things looked bad.

Ames began well, but Paynter was completely tied down. He was out at last for 62, made in 260 minutes, which gives some idea of the tempo of the innings, for Paynter was usually the most enterprising of batsmen. Edrich failed – the crowd and the critics had come to expect this by now – but Ames and Valentine put up a fight and when Valentine and Verity

158

were out, Wright hung on with Ames till the close came at 268 for 7. England were going to be a long way behind, but it was very unlikely that Melville would enforce the follow-on, with all eternity before him – and it was beginning to look as though all eternity would be needed.

England were quickly out next day for 316, and South Africa went in again to drive home their advantage. This time, Mitchell opened with van der Bijl, and they made 191 for the first wicket. The match now seemed to be right out of Hammond's reach but there came a turning-point when Verity got Mitchell to hit his wicket, and immediately had Rowan splendidly caught by Edrich, whose fielding, at least, was impeccable throughout the tour. South Africa hardly needed to use a night-watchman, and Nourse came next – but he saw van der Bijl caught at short-leg in the last over of the day, for 97. Even then, another wicket might have fallen, but Hammond of all people, failed to hang on to a hard drive from Nourse. It may be said in extenuation that Hammond was not accustomed to field at mid-off, and it had been a long day.

Viljoen batted well next day, strongly supported by Nourse and Melville, and when he was out, the score stood at 346 for 5. Surely the match was won and lost – South Africa were 560 ahead already, with some good all-rounders to bat in support of Melville, who was still there, lame, but seeing and timing the ball well. The England bowlers had by no means lost heart though, and Farnes came back for one last fling, dismissing Melville, Grieveson and Langton. Hammond made a fine slip catch to get rid of Langton, and he deserves credit for husbanding Farnes' strength for this final effort; Farnes bowled 'only' 22.1 overs in a long innings. South Africa were 481 all out, and England needed 696 to win. It was an astronomical total – more than ever had been made in the fourth innings of a first-class match – but it might have been bigger still if the bowlers, well handled, had not stuck to the task so doggedly. Hutton and Gibb had faced only one ball when bad light stopped play at the end of the sixth day.

It may well be asked how this consistently high scoring was possible, and whether the pitch was not beginning to wear. At least part of the answer lies in the unusual weather during the match. The pitch had been a very good one to start with and after each burst of heavy rain on the third and fifth evenings, it had rolled out virtually plumb. More rain was to come to help England in their struggle, but for the moment, matters were in the good hands of Hutton and Gibb. Apparently unruffled by the huge task, they batted serenely, Hutton taking runs freely, Gibb his usual obdurate self.

Hutton played on when he had made 55 out of 78, and now Hammond produced a daring stroke of captaincy. Edrich, after failing as an opener in the first Test, had been dropped to No 6 and sometimes

No 7 in the order, and had looked increasingly tormented by self-doubt. Now Hammond restored him to No 3, his normal position for Middlesex, a gesture which said more convincingly than many words that his captain still believed in him. Edrich responded magnificently. He hit his first ball, from Bruce Mitchell, to the fence and went for all the bowlers in the style he had been showing in the non-Test fixtures throughout the tour. Gibb at the other end, was perfectly happy to give Edrich his head and by the end of the day, they had taken the score to 253, Gibb 78 and Edrich 107. Edrich had been given a wonderful ovation by the crowd when he reached his 100 – they knew a fighter when they saw one. They were the first Test crowd to see Edrich in fighting mood, but he was to have a long and distinguished Test career.

It rained heavily on the Saturday morning, but the pitch rolled out well, and the game was set to begin when the rains returned and the eighth day of the match was lost altogether. This worked to England's advantage, because the pitch could be rolled again on Monday morning, and with so much rain and two rollings with no wear and tear in between, it emerged as good as ever. On the other hand, it was now distinctly possible that England would run out of time – the team had to leave for their boat on Tuesday night – but it was much too soon to start taking risks. 443 runs were still needed and nobody really believed they could be got.

Edrich and Gibb went steadily on on Monday morning, Edrich continuing to hammer all the bowlers, and Gibb nudging and defecting, but always looking for the short single. He was out at last, soon after lunch, after batting nine hours for 120. Gibb, on this tour, probably made more of his talents than any England player for years past, much as Trevor Bailey was to do in the 1950s. The score was now 358 – England were more than half-way there! Hammond was in and would at least be able to assess the situation at first hand. As in one or two of the Tests on this tour, he began shakily – he was having a hard tour and he was no longer young – but nothing actually went to hand. At the other end, Edrich was now playing the spinners with some ease, going yards down the wicket to both Mitchell and Dalton. At tea, the score was 422 for 2, and Hammond was into his stride, but the weary Edrich was out very soon afterwards for 219, a classic of perseverance and courage. Paynter was next and still in the splendid form he had shown throughout the tour. Hammond was 58 not out at the close and England needed exactly 200 to win. For the first time in the match, the two sides could be said to be on level terms, but the weather forecast was far from good.

So the match went into its tenth and last day, the only Test in history to last so long. Play began under threatening skies and a full day's play was unlikely, but Hammond and Paynter dared not launch an all-out

160

attack in poor light. They added 39 in the first hour, 82 before lunch, but with only 118 now wanted and the skies darkening they went for everything after lunch. Hammond's hundred came up. Paynter was well caught low down by Grieveson, and at last Hammond fell when was on 140, dashing down the pitch to Dalton and being stumped as he swung at the ball, a stroke he would not have played if urgent runs had not been the only priority. Valentine hurried to the wicket to join Ames but he had hardly taken strike before the clouds opened and the match which was to be played out to settle the series ended in an honourable draw. England would almost certainly have won if the rains had not come – they needed only 42 more – but as I have tried to show, the earlier rain had helped them by, in effect, re-making the pitch.

Hammond had had a most distinguished series – his best since 1928-29. He had made three fine 100s and topped the Test averages, though Paynter actually scored more runs. He was universally praised for his clever and inspirational captaincy and particularly for the way he handled a rather unbalanced attack. England looked to have a solid, well-founded side which would be a match for any country for years to come – but of course it was not to be.

	Innings	N.O.	H.S.	Runs	Average	100	50
1938/39	8	1	181	609	87.00	3	2
To date	121	14	336*	6604	61.71	21	23

	Balls	Runs	Wickets	Average
1938/39	480	161	3	53.66
To date	7963	3135	83	37.77

21   The lights go out

1939 was a strange season. Nobody could be sure that the Tests would take place – it was obvious that war was imminent and the only question was whether Hitler would wait to get the harvest in first. He did, and the season was almost completed. The West Indian tourists had to cancel their final few matches and catch the last available boat, but they got home safely. In the circumstances, the cricket received little attention, but the players had no choice but to go on doing their job, and the matches were not without interest.

The West Indians were a reasonably strong team. Headley was at his best, and there were several good young batsmen in support. Constantine was available for the whole tour and he had now adapted his bowling style, producing every kind of variation short of bowling left-handed, and still able to slip in a fast ball which was as fast as anybody else in England that summer could produce. Martindale and Hylton were in the team, but both proved to have gone back a little since 1935. CB 'Bertie' Clarke, a leg-spinner, did a great job as stock bowler. He stayed in England to pursue his medical studies, was a popular member of the British Empire XI and other war-time years and later played with distinction in county cricket. Cameron, Tyrrell Johnson and Rolph Grant the captain, also had their bowling successes.

The tourists made a moderate start to the season, but ran into form when the warmer weather arrived in June, and had beaten three counties before the first Test at Lord's. Hammond, tired after the South African tour, started slowly too, but he was soon into his stride and played two huge innings before the Test, 192 not out against Warwickshire, and 302 against Glamorgan, the second time he had made this precise score against the Welsh county. He was naturally re-appointed as captain of England – more surprisingly, six players who had not toured South Africa were picked. These were Gimblett, Compton, Hardstaff, Copson, Bowes and Wood, who kept wicket because Ames was unable to keep throughout the season – his back was troubling him again and he could bat, but not keep – and Gibb didn't play first class cricket at all in 1939. Edrich was more than a little unlucky to be dropped after that splendid 219, but he was no longer opening for Middlesex, and a place had to be found for Compton.

Grant won the toss and went in first himself with Jeff Stollmeyer, making his Test debut. It was a bitterly cold day and the pitch had little life, but Bowes and Copson attacked with spirit. Grant made a quick 22 and got out to Copson, who must have been relishing getting on the field for England at last after being considered more than once, and touring Australia in 1936/37 without playing in a Test. Headley came in and played elegantly but without risk; he and Stollmeyer added 118 before the opener was out, and it looked as if the West Indies were in for a big score. However, Sealy failed and then Copson, who had been carefully nursed by Hammond, ripped out the heart of the batting with the second new ball. Headley made a good 100 in 250 minutes, but he too fell to Copson and the innings closed at 277.

Hutton and Gimblett batted quietly until the close, and although Gimblett, Paynter and Hammond were all out pretty cheaply on the Monday, Hammond brilliantly caught by Grant at mid-off for 14, Hutton and Compton came together in an exciting and heart-warming stand of 248, made in only 140 minutes. The outstanding English batsmen of their generation, these two didn't often have a big partnership, but this one was worth travelling miles to see. Between them, they gave three chances very early on, but all were terribly difficult and all went down. After that, all the bowling came alike to them. Compton made 120, with 16 fours, and Hutton 196 with a five and 21 fours.

Hammond was able to declare at the overnight score of 404 for 5, and give himself the whole of the last day to get the West Indies out, and make whatever runs were needed. He was well served by his bowlers. Headley made another fine century – the second time he had made two 100s in a match – but nobody else scored 30 and the side were all out for 225, Copson again the main destroyer. He took 9 for 152 in the match, but it was Wright who got rid of Headley, and his burst of three wickets in two overs was the knock-out punch. Again, Hammond was praised for his skilful management of the bowling and the field. Note this – for with hindsight, many people came forward to say that Hammond had never been much of a captain.

England had to make 99 in 110 minutes to win, and the openers batted light-heartedly. Both were out before the runs were made, and Gimblett might not have been so light-hearted if he had known that in only his fifth first-class season, he was playing his last Test match. Paynter and Hammond finished it off, Hammond, who made 30, making the winning hit, a glorious off-drive.

Fagg, who was having a good season, came in for Gimblett at Old Trafford, and, as I have said, Gimblett never played for England again, although he was selected in 1950 but he had to withdraw with, of all things, a carbuncle on his neck. He really ought to have gone to Australia in 1946 and again in 1950, and it was perhaps a matter of selectors distrusting a player of genius, and preferring the steadier batsmen. Goddard replaced Verity at Old Trafford, and this seems, at a distance, to have been a slightly odd choice. Verity never let England down and it wasn't a question of trying out a youngster. Goddard was 38. The West Indies introduced Gomez and Foffie Williams for the first time.

The match was effectively ruined as a contest by heavy rain which permitted only 35 minutes' play on the first day. Grant put England in, and Hutton and Fagg survived those 35 minutes. Wickets fell rapidly in poor light on the second day and, although Hammond went for quick runs off Clarke trying to hit his way out of trouble, he was stumped off a beautiful ball from the leg-spinner, who beat him in the flight. England were 62 for 5 when he was out, but Hardstaff and Wood added 88 in a fine fighting stand, which could hardly have been more sharply contrasted with their partnership of 106 on the feather-bed at the Oval the year before – a most striking example of the variety which is the charm of cricket.

Hammond declared when Hardstaff was out at 164 for 7, and Grant then launched a courageous attack on the bowlers. Hammond brought Goddard on early and although he got Stollmeyer and Grant out, he took some heavy punishment in the context of a low-scoring match, coming out with the bizarre analysis of 4-0-43-2. Headley and Sealy were together at the close, when the score was 85 for 3. It seemed impossible that there could be a finish, but there might be some excitement nevertheless.

Bowes and Copson were soon among the wickets on the third day, only Headley playing them with any confidence. Hammond was criticised for not bowling Goddard, but it is difficult to see why. Bowes and Copson were getting the wickets and getting them inexpensively, the West Indies lost 7 wickets for 48 during the morning. Hammond needed a big a lead as he could get, to give him some room for manoeuvre, and a few minutes of Constantine against Goddard's bowling could have upset all his calculations. As it turned out, Bowes bowled Constantine for a duck and Headley was last out for 51. England led by 31 runs.

Now England did lose their way a little. Hutton and Fagg were quite unable to get on top of the bowling and Paynter was out for nought. England made only 32 for 2 in their first hour, and there was even a possibility of a West Indian win. Hammond had to dig in for a while and was barracked for almost the only time in a Test in England. The pitch was far from easy and the bowlers' tails were up, but Hammond and Compton gradually got on top, and when Hammond was out for 32 at 89 for 4, bowled by an off-break from Constantine at which he played no stroke, the danger of defeat was past, although too much time had been lost by now for him to have the remotest chance of forcing a win.

His declaration left the West Indies to make 160 in 70 minutes in poor light, and they scored 43 for 4. Hammond took his hundredth Test catch with a slip-catch, which came to him by way of Wood's gloves, to get Headley out. He was the first fielder to reach this total and the list is still a short one. England had had the better of an interesting draw.

★　　★　　★　　★　　★

England made some odd changes for the final Test played at the Oval as the clouds of war were gathering over Europe. (The pact between Russia and Germany, which was the final blow to any hope of stopping Hitler peaceably, was signed the day after the match finished.) Paynter was left out in favour of Oldfield, a younger Lancashire player who might well have had a good run in the England team, but for the war, and Keeton replaced Fagg as Hutton's partner, a change more difficult to understand, since Keeton was ten years older than Fagg. Bowes was unfit, and he and Copson were replaced by Nichols and Perks. The West Indies brought in Victor Stollmeyer, elder brother of Jeffrey, and Tyrrell Johnson, a fast left-arm bowler who showed real promise, but had not been as successful so far, as his talent suggested.

Hammond's luck with the toss returned and England batted first on a very good wicket. At once, there was a sensation, Johnson taking Keeton's wicket with his very first ball in Test cricket. Oldfield batted with Paynter's own aplomb, and he and Hutton put on 131 for the second wicket. Hutton was hardly recognisable as the earnest professor who had batted for 13 hours the year before; he cut and drove with vigour and elegance – but this was a three-day match and the runs had to be made reasonably quickly. Timeless Tests were a thing of the past. When Hammond came in, at 133 for 2, he looked comparatively careworn. DR Jardine commented 'Hammond, though not in difficulties, never found runs easy to get. He played as one a trifle stale, or as one a little out of love with Test matches'.

Well, everybody would be out of touch, if not out of love, with Tests soon enough, and no doubt Hammond's thoughts were elsewhere, but he was to have one last fling before the match was over. He scored 43

165

in 105 minutes before being smartly taken at short-leg by Grant off the bowling of – who else? – Constantine. It was the last time they faced each other in Test cricket, and on the whole Constantine had had slightly the better of it. He dismissed Hammond eight times in ten matches, not a bad record. After their earlier differences, they came to respect each other thoroughly, and it was fitting that they were the opposing captains in Constantine's very last first-class match, in 1945. Compton was also rather out of sorts and fell for 21, but Hardstaff scored a fine 94, and was only out when he had to have a fling with the last man in. England scored 352, and the West Indies were 27 for 1 at the end of a lively day.

The second day produced riveting cricket, played in great heat. Jeffrey Stollmeyer and Headley began slowly by their standards, against good bowling from England's new opening attack and from the spinners, and it was Hutton, coming on as third change, who had Stollmeyer caught with his score at 128. Victor Stollmeyer came in and committed the crime that all West Indian batsmen must have dreaded in the thirties.– he ran George Headley out. He played the ball to square-leg and, apparently failing to see Hardstaff lurking near the umpire, he called Headley for a run. Headley hesitated then went, and was well short of the crease. He had made 65 very good runs, but when Gomez failed, they were 164 for 4, and not well placed.

Stollmeyer put the misfortune behind him and was batting well when KH Weekes came in to play the innings of his life. Weekes, a sturdy left-hander and a cousin of Everton Weekes, had a very short first-class career – he played in only 30 matches, and had made his way into the touring team with two aggressive innings in the 1938-39 inter-colonial matches, his first two first-class appearances. He now lived up to his nickname, 'Bam Bam', racing to his 100 in 110 minutes. The England bowling fell apart under the bombardment and Nichols and Perks went for 43 in four overs when the second new ball was taken. England were relieved when rain stopped play for an hour after tea, but 368 runs were scored in the day and there was more to come.

Constantine had come in just before the close and in the morning he set about Nichols and Perks in his own characteristic way, playing all the strokes in the book, and a good many that were in no book that was ever written. The statistics of this last day tell the story – 92 balls were bowled, and the last four wickets fell for 103, of which Constantine scored 78, with 11 fours and a six, a drive to the distant Vauxhall end off the back foot.

Hammond was criticised for his management of affairs, but he was helpless. Runs were coming swiftly off the fast men, but he had every reason to suppose that the slow bowlers would have been maltreated even more savagely – and he had scattered his field in every possibly defensive deployment. It was simply a matter of genius taking over from normal players, and Constantine's end typified the whole spectacular performance, when he hooked at Perks, top-edged, and was caught by Wood, the wicket-keeper, haring back towards the pavilion and catching the ballooner as it fell over his shoulder. As the capricious Wood announced, it was lucky that he was standing back.

England had to go in again 146 behind with nothing to play for but a draw, plus a certain moral obligation to play attractively – it would probably be the last Test match that many of the crowd would ever see. Keeton and Oldfield were soon out, but Hutton who was batting faultlessly, was joined by Hammond, and they treated those present to a sample of classical batmanship which could hardly have been bettered. They added a huge 264 in three hours, though some of Neville Cardus's remarks read oddly:

'Hammond made many excellent strokes without satisfying us that he was feeling consistently at his happiest'.

Was anybody feeling consistently at his happiest in August 1939? Cardus also referred to the 264 being added at 'a respectable rate'. 88 an hour would seem something better than respectable, now or at any time in cricket' history, but perhaps Cardus had been dazzled by Constantine's brilliance. At all events, Hammond was bowled by Bertie Clarke, and thus brought down the curtain on his pre-war career with a thoroughly commendable 138. Hutton was undefeated to the end, finishing on 165. It would have been appropriate if Hammond, the premier England batsman in the thirties, had been on the field at the end of the match, but if this was not to be, it was fitting that Hutton and Compton, who were to carry on the great batting tradition into the 1950s, were together. England made a token declaration at 366 for 3, and perhaps the groundsman had had the last word, 1,216 runs being scored in the three days of the match.

Hammond had gone out on a high note and was still acknowledged as the finest batsman in England, Nobody could say whether he would ever play Test cricket again, and this match does of course mark the end of an era – 14 of the participants were playing in their last Test. Happily, Hammond did return, together with five of his side. This is not the point in the book at which to sum up his career, but it may be stressed that at *this* moment, nobody doubted his capacity as a leader, and he had only lost one Test out of the 12 in which he had led England. The perfect wickets of the day had frustrated his efforts to win more

167

than three matches, but England had generally been on top. He was undoubtedly one of the game's major figures.

	Innings	N.O.	H.S.	Runs	Average	100	50
1939	6	1	138	279	55.80	1	–
To date	127	15	336*	6883	61.45	22	22

Hammond did not bowl in the 1939 Tests.

22   Joyous Cricket

During the First World War, very little cricket had been played in public in England – that is to say, few matches had been arranged by way of public entertainment. At the outset, there was a feeling that any able-bodied man should be rushing to the Colours, and later on, all the able-bodied were in France or other overseas theatres of war, and not available to play. In the last two years of the war, this changed just a little, and one or two charity matches were played at Lord's, CG Macartney appearing, to the general delight, but by and large, cricket was in abeyance.

It was otherwise in the 1939-45 War. Conscription was in force from the outset and recruitment went ahead in a more orderly fashion, with rather less moral pressure on young men to join up at the earliest possible moment. Then, during much of the war, a large proportion of our army was training in Britain and available to play or to watch, as the case might be, while the RAF or much of it, was operating from Britain, and players such as WJ Edrich were flying on operations one day and available to play at Lord's the next! It was seen that organised sport could be a morale-builder and, as far as possible, it was encouraged. The cricket matches were all friendlies of course, except for League cricket in the North and Midlands, and teams were apt to be changed at the last moment because a player was on duty, but all the matches were played in the happiest spirit, the more so because, for players and spectators alike, they were a happy relief from the horrors and tedium outside the grounds.

Hammond took little part in the first four years of wartime cricket though he played a few games in 1940. He had joined the RAF at the outbreak of war, and was initially stationed in Sussex, where he played a little, and then in Devon, where he both organised and played. At the end of 1940, he was posted to the Middle East and he played there, in Central Africa and in South Africa, actually playing in a first-class match at Johannesburg in December 1942, scoring 60, on Boxing Day, and 18. He was lbw to Gordon, whom he had last encountered in the Timeless Test, and he made a catch off the bowling of Eric Sturgess, who was to play Davis Cup tennis for South Africa after the war.

Hammond returned to England in time for the 1944 season. Most of the big matches that year were between Service teams, and a new element had been introduced in 1943, in the shape of a distinctly strong Royal Australian Air Force team. This included several State players, notably Keith Carmody the captain, Sismey, the wicket-keeper, and the enormously promising Keith Miller. Hammond encountered them very early in the season when he captained a side billed as 'The Rest (of the World)' against 'Australia' on Whit-Sunday, and played for 'England' against the same opposition, but under the captaincy of GO Allen, on the Monday. The Rest lost an exciting match, England won their match, and Hammond scored 46 and 1. The Australians had put up a remarkable performance considering their relative lack of experience, and it was already being freely said that, like the AIF team of 1919, they would form the nucleus of Australia's post-war Test team. It didn't work out like that – there were some even better cricketers in the Far East – but these Australians were to give England a great fight in 1945.

Hammond continued to delight the cricketing public, scoring a carefree 100 against a West Indies XI a few days later, and another hundred for 'England' against 'Australia' in August, but he missed some games when suffering an attack of fibrositis, and this was not a good omen for his future in cricket. He was in fact invalided out of the RAF in December, and went back to his pre-war employer, Marsham Tyres. It seemed that his playing days were nearly over, but he was to have two more fine seasons.

When the war in Europe ended in May 1945, a programme which had already been arranged centring round the Australian team, was rapidly expanded into a series of five three-day 'Victory Tests' which were accorded first-class status. The Australian airmen were joined now by an AIF (Australian Imperial Forces) team, based at Eastbourne. The Eastbourne unit's primary task was the rehabilitation of Australian prisoners of war as they were released from German camps, and cricket was to play an important part in that rehabilitation. The AIF team, led by Lindsay Hassett, played matches separately from the RAAF side, whose captain Carmody, had himself been taken prisoner in 1944, but resumed the leadership when he was released.

The two parties came together to make up the Australian side for the Victory Tests and Hassett, who was of course the senior in cricket terms, led the side. The AIF also had its State players, including Whitington and Williams, who had played for South Australia for some years, and Cecil Pepper, a formidable all-rounder who probably would have played in Test cricket if he had not made a habit of falling out with Authority. Nevertheless, it was hardly to be expected that this Australian side would meet virtually the full strength of England on

170

equal terms, unless there were some really outstanding new players in the party, or the England selectors made the mistake of underrating them.

The matches turned out to be fascinatingly even contests. Several of the England players were past their best, though Hammond who was the unanimous choice as captain, was not one of them. The selectors did make the odd mistake, but the main reason for Australia's success in holding England to a 2-2 draw was that the Australians played above their form and, in particular, fielded superbly. It was a triumph for youth. Although the matches were not official Tests, they were so interesting that they deserve a brief description.

For the first match, the England selectors picked an unbalanced attack and paid the penalty. The opening bowlers. Gover and Stephenson, were both 37 and, for the first three-day match for six years, this was a little too old. The other bowlers were Edrich, not yet the formidable slinger he was to become, and Wright and Robins, two attacking leg-spinners. In other words, there was nobody who could contain the batsmen. Hammond was unfit to bowl thoughout the summer. Nevertheless, the batting looked strong, with Hutton, Washbrook, Robertson, Hammond, Ames and Edrich, and a draw was on the cards.

Hutton was out for 1, but the other England players batted brightly, the difficulty being that none of them settled down to make a big score – but the match began only 11 days after VE-day, and no doubt they were all pretty light-hearted. Hammond made a rapid 29 and was bowled by Graham Williams, another returned prisoner. England were 267 all out, and Australia 82 for 2 by the close, with Hassett and Sismey together. On the second day, Hassett made a solid 77, and Miller fulfilled the promise he had shown in the previous two seasons with an elegant 105. Most of the later batsmen made runs, Williams continuing to celebrate his liberation with a hard-hit 53. He was having a match to remember. Australia were all out just before the close for 455, and England were in unexpected trouble.

On the final day, Hutton and Washbrook began well enough, but Pepper dismissed them both, and Ellis, a slow left-arm bowler who had had Hammond three times in 1944, had him lbw again. Robertson and Edrich fought hard, but the tail collapsed and Australia were set to make 107 in 70 minutes. Hammond really had no alternative but to use Gover and Stephenson with defensive fields – the runs would have come too freely from the leg-spinners – and Pepper saw Australia to a win in the last over. England had perhaps paid the price for taking their inexperienced opponents too lightly and would certainly have to field a different kind of attack.

The second match was to be played at Bramall Lane, still bearing the marks of heavy bombing. It was a less glamorous venue than Lord's, but the Yorkshire public turned out in their thousands for what was to be one of the best games of the season. England picked a new opening pair in Pope and Pollard, experienced seam bowlers who had been playing in League cricket and were match-fit. WB Roberts, a left-arm bowler who was to do well for Lancashire after the war, but to die tragically early, and Wright completed the attack, and Errol Holmes replaced Ames as a batsman. SC Griffith kept wicket for England throughout the series.

Hassett won the toss and put England in on a drying pitch and, as *Wisden* put it 'events moved quickly'. Wickets fell, and Sismey was laid out by a rising ball from Cheetham, evidence of a mischievous pitch. Hammond batted calmly and resourcefully, giving the young Australians a lesson in playing the turning, swerving ball off the back foot. Five wickets fell for 141 before George Pope joined him in the stand that was to win the match. They saw off the pace bowlers and took quick runs when the slow men tossed the ball up, and they put on 107, Hammond making the lion's share. He was out for exactly 100, one of his finest innings in adversity.

England made 286, an excellent score on such a wicket, and Australia could only score 147 in reply, Pope taking 5 for 58. Hammond made two slip catches look easy, and Miller, Australia's best hope of a score, was run out by Robertson trying for an impossible single. Hutton and Washbrook made 56 for the first wicket, though not without some alarms against fiery bowling from Miller, who hit both of them. Hammond batted calmly again for 38, in the midst of a collapse, which was halted by a vigorous little stand of 55 for the eighth wicket by Griffith and Pollard. England made 190 and Australia were set the daunting target of 330.

A formidable task indeed, but the wicket was now as good as it had been at any time and the Australians, if they got a good start, had every incentive to give it a go. Two up and three to play, in an English summer, would be a wonderful position. They did get a good start, Whitington and Workman making 108 for the first wicket. There were a few streaky ones, and Hammond actually dropped Whitington when he had made 7 – it was a very cold morning and slip-fielding wasn't easy. Jim Workman had never played in first-class cricket before this year, and this was only his third first-class innings, but he played like a veteran. Whitington outscored him, but he, Miller and Hassett were all out with the score at 171, and Workman was still there. Carmody hesitated when Workman called him for a sharp single to Hutton and was run out, and at last Workman edged Pollard to Hammond, and

Hammond wasn't in the habit of dropping two catches in one day. It was 221 for 5 and Australia still had a glimmer of hope, but none of the later batsmen were able to settle to the sort of solid innings that was needed, and Australia were all out for 288, Pollard 5 for 76. It had been a magnificent effort, but England were on terms, thanks largely to that fine century by Hammond on a vile wicket.

★   ★   ★   ★   ★

One thing about this Test series was normal. The selectors didn't please all the people all the time. They had been freely criticised for picking the veterans Gover, Stephenson and Holmes in the earlier games, and they now went right to the other extreme and picked three 18-year-olds for the third Test at Lord's. This seemed at the time and does still seem, to be an error. One youngster, yes. Two, perhaps, but not three.

The three new boys were Donald Carr, who was to have a distinguished career as a player and administrator, John Dewes, who didn't in the event fulfil all his promise and retired early, and the Honourable Luke White, an Etonian who never played regularly in county cricket. All had done well for their schools in the preceding season, but to bring them in at the expense of Robertson, Holmes and Pope did seem to be over-doing the search for talent. Pope was mysteriously unavailable in any case – he was said to have a prior engagement for his League club, but there were stories of a brush with authority. In his absence, the selectors might have done better to pick another tried professional, but it wasn't the bowling that let 'England' down.

England batted first, and didn't make much of it. Hutton played beautifully, but everybody else struggled. Dewes made 27 but never looked comfortable, and Hammond was stumped for 13 off a lovely ball from Pepper which drew him forward and left him. Hammond had looked stiff and uncomfortable while batting and it was no great surprise when he reported sick with lumbago on the second morning and took no further part in the match. Griffith took over the captaincy. In spite of Hutton's skilful 104, England had made only 254, but Australia did worse. Hassett made 68, but Pollard troubled most of the others and Australia finished 60 behind, Pollard taking 6 for 75. Carr bowled very little; with Roberts, another slow left-armer, in the side, that was to be expected, but one wonders what Carr had been picked for.

The England second innnings was a triumph for Bob Cristofani, a leg-spinner who had had only one previous first-class match. His figures of 5 for 49 were the best he was ever to achieve. Hutton made 69, Edrich 58, but the side were all out for 164. Hammond couldn't bat and the three youngsters made only five runs between them. Washbrook batted under severe handicap, with a badly bruised thumb, and the debacle was all very predictable.

Australia had still to make 224, and when Pollard had Whitington caught for a duck, their chances looked slender, but Workman and Sismey made a solid 82 together, and then Miller again showed his class, scoring 71 not out, in spite of a strained back muscle which was to affect his bowling for the rest of his long career. Interestingly, *Wisden* says that he took few risks, but he scored his runs in just under two hours, some measure of his outstanding quality. Australia won by four wickets. England had been unlucky with injuries, but had contributed to their own defeat by an inept piece of selection.

★　　★　　★　　★　　★

England had learnt their lesson and went firmly for experience in the fourth Test at Lord's. Pope had settled whatever differences he had had with the selectors and he came back for Carr. Robertson, who should never have been dropped, returned and Fishlock came in for the first time. In spite of Miller's injury, the Australians asked him to open the bowling, and so were able to strengthen their batting line-up by playing Pettiford, who was to do well for Kent in later years. They batted first and were extremely solid. Some English journalists, taking the England setbacks a little hard, suggested that Australia played for a draw from the outset and were pretty dull into the bargain, but this was less than fair. Certainly, they made a solid start. Sismey, batting at No 3, scored a slow 59, but this was simply to prepare for the hitters. Miller scored 118 in 200 minutes, and Pepper a rapid 57. Overall, Australia scored at three an over, and there was nothing wrong with that. They just made a lot of runs.

England had to look for a big lead in quick time and they certainly went for it. They had one thing in their favour. Sismey had bruised a thumb during his long innings and couldn't take the field, and Workman who replaced him, was not much at home behind the stumps. Miller was bowling short, with a lot of life, and a few balls went over Workman's head. Eventually, Hammond suggested to Hassett that Carmody, the twelfth man, who had some experience as a keeper, should take over, with England's ready consent, and this reduced the flow of extras and prevented the match degenerating into farce. Hammond's courteous offer was very much in the spirit of the series and was not forgotten by Australians.

Fishlock led the England assault, strongly supported by Hutton and Robertson, and when he was out for 69, the score was 173 for 3. On the third day, Hammond brought out all the well-remembered off-side strokes in a magnificent 83, and after he was out, Washbrook and Edrich saw England to a lead of 80. The critics' derogatory remarks about the Australian scoring rate read even more oddly in conjunction with *Wisden's* description of Washbrook's innings as 'brilliant'. He scored 112 in four hours. England's scoring rate was little better than Australia's and the game petered out into a draw. I was there and can remember being slightly relieved, in a sense, that Australia batted circumspectly enough to make sure they didn't lose. There would have been something false and unnatural about a 'Test' series in which a side which was 2-1 up *didn't* sit on its lead – up to a point.

★　★　★　★　★

The cricketing caravan now moved on to Old Trafford, where England played a very modern attack of three seamers, plus Wright and Edrich, introducing Eddie Phillipson of Lancashire, a good all-rounder who lost some of his best years to the war and may perhaps have been unlucky never to play in an official Test. Australia played four spinners, including Pettiford.

The wicket was always helping the bowlers, particularly on the first day, when the three seamers had Australia out for 173. Only Miller could handle them. He scored 77 not out, and perhaps he should have batted higher up the order than No 6. Hutton was solidity itself, but he lost Fishlock and Robertson quickly before Hammond, in the words of *Wisden*, put the England batting on a different plane. Hammond scored 57 in 70 minutes, driving the fast-medium Williams for three straight fours.

It rained on the second day, and when play began Cristofani and Pepper were a difficult proposition, but Washbrook, always a good wet-weather batsman, held the innings together with a 38 which was worth more. England led by 70 and when the seam bowlers took six wickets before Australia drew level, it looked as though the series would end in an anti-climax. But Cristofani, the inexperienced leg-spinner, now played one of the great last-ditch innings of cricket history, scoring 110 in 143 minutes, and adding 95 with Williams for the ninth wicket at a run a minute. England still needed only 141 to win, and got them for four wickets (Hammond scoring 16) but the match belonged to Cristofani. It had been a very remarkable series. Australian self-confidence and panache enabling them to share the honours with a far more experienced side.

★　★　★　★　★

I cannot leave 1945 without describing one more match. The game between England and the Dominions which brought down the curtain on a most intriguing season at Lord's, was one of the finest games ever played there, and Hammond decorated it with one of his finest performances. The Dominions side was basically the Australian side which had halved the series, reinforced by DR Fell, a talented South African; Martin Donnelly, the New Zealand batsman who had toured England as a youngster in 1937; and Learie Constantine, encountering Hammond for the last time – and playing, in fact, in his very last first-class match. Hassett was ill and unable to play and Constantine was elected by the players to lead them, quite a significant gesture at a time when the West Indies side had never been captained by a black man.

England were just a little weaker than in the Victory Tests, Hutton, Washbrook, Pollard and Pope all being unavoidably absent, but the reinforcements were all good players, although the attack was to be exposed as a little unbalanced. The Dominions batted first and got into trouble, Miller failing for once, but Donnelly played superbly for 133. He was one of the best players ever produced by New Zealand and it was a pity that the claims of business brought his playing career to an early end – but he will not be forgotten by those who saw him at his best. Pepper scored 51, and the final score was 307, a good one on a pitch that was always rewarding the good bowler. The pitch, in fact, was the key to this match; fast but true, such as is always referred to as a good cricket wicket. We all know what we mean by the term and it is a pity that we don't see such pitches more often.

Gimblett was suffering from cramp and couldn't open, and when Fishlock and Robertson were out cheaply, Hammond changed his order perhaps a little too radically, batting Langridge, Phillipson and Griffith at three, four and five. Wickets fell early on the second day and the score was 96 for 6 when Edrich joined Hammond. The captain was in superb form, however, and he scored 121 in 160 minutes without a mistake. He drove Cristofani into the pavilion three times and, to the general delight, was right back to his form of 1939. To the onlookers, it must have seemed that he was immortal; nobody could have guessed that his career had less than two years to run. He and Edrich added 177 and England finished only 20 behind. It was still only teatime on the second day, and the Dominions had time to score 145 for 3 by the close. Miller had made 61 in 75 minutes and the third day promised to be a good one.

Nobody could have foreseen how good it would be. Miller and Donnelly began brightly and when the New Zealander got out and Constantine came in, Miller threw caution to the winds and set about the slow bowlers. The crowd were in ecstasy. Constantine pulled two sixes into the Grand Stand, but Miller outshone him, driving six sixes in the course of the morning, one of them to the very roof of the broadcasting box on the top deck of the pavilion. With hindsight, one can understand how it all happened. Phillipson was injured and Hammond had no choice but to keep the slow men on. Slow bowlers take a little longer to get 'match-tight' than the faster men, and there is very little margin of error when a hitter is in such resplendent form.

Miller and Constantine added 117 in 45 minutes, of which Constantine made only 40, and when Miller was out on the stroke of one o'clock, he had made 124 in 90 minutes on the day, 185 in all. Fortunately for the spectators, the tail got out quickly, and England were left to score 357 in 270 minutes – the perfect equation in a match of this kind, where both sides were out for a win and had no thought of a draw.

Once again the openers failed, but once again Hammond was in his very best form. He was missed twice in the deep, but that was scarcely to be wondered at when he was chasing everything. He scored 102 in two hours, and it was in this innings that he struck a famous blow, which pitched on the pavilion steps, careered through the open door into the Long Room and hit a showcase without breaking the glass. (I should explain for the benefit of younger readers that there was then no sightscreen at the Pavilion end.) He got out at last, through sheer exhaustion, but the match was still not over.

Colonels Davies and Griffith added 83 in 58 minutes in the best amateur style. Then Constantine brought down the curtain on his sensational first-class career by throwing the wicket down from cover to run Phillipson out. Now it *was* all over; Wright and Hollies weren't quite up to batting out the last quarter of an hour and nobody who was there really wanted them to.

The Dominions had deserved their win, but the match had really been a showpiece of everything that was best in cricket – four magnificent centuries, good batting in support, ten wickets in 60 overs from Doug Wright, and some marvellous fielding. All seemed set fair for the resumption of regular cricket, and Englishmen could winter comfortably knowing that they had at least a fine batting side, led by Hammond whose form was as good as it had ever been, but whose fitness was more doubtful.

23 Back to normal – rain stopped play

After the exciting Victory Tests and other charming moments of the 1945 season, English cricket followers were hardly able to wait for the full resumption in 1946. The Indians were to be the first tourists, and they brought a few old favourites and some players, like Modi and Mankad, whose fame had gone before them, Modi in particular having done great things in domestic cricket. More than this, England were to tour Australia in 1946-47, and there was an urgency about the building of a team. Would there be new stars – in particular, new bowlers – to blend with the young men who had come to the fore in 1937-39? It could be assumed that most of the pre-war players of a slightly earlier vintage, such as Paynter and Leyland, wouldn't be around, but everyone was hoping that Hammond would be available and at his best.

It was very unfortunate that 1946 turned out to be one of the wettest in living memory. This was particularly hard on the Indians, playing in totally unfamiliar conditions, but it was no help to the England selectors, trying to assess old and new players in the space of three three-day Tests. Several of the established batsmen started in their very best form, but none did better than Hammond.

He had wound up the 1945 season with those two centuries against the Dominions, and he now began the 1946 season with a thumping 100 against a rather indifferent Oxford University attack, in which Martin Donnelly was actually the most successful bowler, and 134 against the much more formidable Lancashire side. Ominously, he missed the second innings of the Lancashire match with a strained back and missed the next two county games, but he was back against Warwickshire and was 59 not out when rain washed out the third day. This is noteworthy because he then scored 100s against Yorkshire and Somerset, batting only once in each match, so that if he had gone on to his 100 against Warwickshire (which must have been on the cards – they had a weak attack) he would have made seven successive centuries, a world record. We must note that he didn't make these runs by careful acquisition; only against Yorkshire is he recorded as having been 'steady' and even then he scored at 30 an hour against some excellent bowling. In short, he was at the top of his form and the only doubt was about that back.

The Indians had struggled rather on the wet wickets, but had produced one extraordinary performance when their last two batsmen, Sarwate and Banerjee, made 249 for the tenth wicket against Surrey, the highest ever partnership by Nos 10 and 11. They had also beaten a weakish MCC team by an innings, and most of their specialist batsmen had played a big innings or two before the Lord's Test. Vijay Merchant, in particular, was in most majestic form, and he was to average 74 on the whole tour, second only to Hammond in this bowlers' season.

The captain, the Nawab of Pataudi, whom we last sighted playing for Jardine's team and refusing duty in the leg-trap, had had a series of niggling muscle ailments and was barely fit for the Test, and the attack looked unbalanced, with two of the all-rounders, Amarnath and Hazare opening the bowling. Much would depend on Mankad, the excellent slow left-arm bowler but, for the first Test at least, he was also to open the batting since Mushtaq Ali was hopelessly out of touch. It was a lot to ask of him.

Hammond was the obvious choice for the captaincy and it is worth making the point that nobody seriously considered anybody else. When things went wrong in Australia, there were plenty of people to say that somebody else should have been given the job, but if he hadn't been appointed, there would have been a howl of protest that would have made some recent captaincy controversies look like a choir practice. He was by far the most experienced Test player in the offing, he was in prime batting form, and he had at this time, a good record as a captain.

He was joined by Hutton, Washbrook, Compton, Hardstaff and Gibb, who had all proved themselves before the war, and by Ikin, a batsman who bowled a little, rather than an all-rounder, who had already shown himself in a few games for Lancashire to be a most brilliant fielder close to the wicket. Only one new bowler had come to the fore, but he was potentially great. Alec Bedser had had a couple of games for Surrey in 1939, and had come to the fore in wartime matches. He had been abroad in 1945 and had missed all the Victory Tests, but he was on everybody's list as a potential England opening bowler. Wright was another obvious choice, but no other new bowlers had come to the fore, and the selectors picked Bill Bowes, who had spent much of the war as a prisoner, but seemed to be recovering his form, if not his full fitness, and Smailes of Yorkshire, who had been picked for that washed-out Test in 1938, but had never actually played for England. Bowes and Smailes were 37 and 36, respectively and had the unenviable look of stopgap selections.

Pataudi won the toss and, on a wicket that was always giving the bowlers a little encouragement, his batsmen struggled. Merchant was lured into an edged stroke at an outswinger from Bedser and was caught behind, and Amarnath was lbw to Bedser at once. Thereafter, nothing went right until Modi and Abdul Hafeez came together at 87 for 6. They fought hard and bravely and took the score to 144, and then the tail helped Modi to an innings of exactly 200, Modi 57 not out. Bedser had done nearly all the damage, taking 7 for 49 in a most impressive first appearance, but neither Bowes nor Smailes had made any impression, and it was clear that the selectors would be looking elsewhere for bowlers to play in the next Test, and indeed in Australia.

Amarnath, a phenomenally accurate medium-pace bowler with a curious action which made it appear that he bowled off the wrong foot, was soon troubling the England batsmen. He had Hutton caught for 7, and Compton came in in a tense silence. Poor Compton was in the middle of the worst spell of form of his whole career. It happens to every batsman – except Bradman – but this was a particularly spectacular 'trot', Compton having made nine runs in total in his last five innings. In the circumstances, it was a little odd that he batted first wicket down, but the only other regular No 3 in the side was Jack Ikin, and he was playing in his first Test and perhaps stood in even more need of protection. Amarnath was hardly the bowler an out-of-form batsman would have chosen to face – no chance of a loose one from him – and, sure enough, he sent down a good length inswinger which bowled Compton first ball. (It is pleasing to record that he scored a very good 100 in the next county match.)

Hammond came in on a hat-trick and played his first ball quietly back to the bowler. In the same over, he drove Amarnath almost to the boundary. Washbrook almost lapped Hammond as they ran, and Hammond was all but run out by a fine throw from Gul Mahomed. It was time to settle down and they batted quietly for a while, though always troubled by Amarnath's nagging length. He struck again at 61, having Washbrook caught at short-leg, and then at 70, came what seemed the terminal disaster, as Hammond shaped to push an inswinger to the leg-side, but was bowled as it moved back off the seam – a fine piece of thoughtful bowling.

England were 70 for 4 of which Hammond had scored 33, and in serious trouble. Hardstaff played handsomely and correctly, but the crowd died a thousand deaths as Gibb scraped forward at Amarnath and Mankad, playing and missing over and over again. It seemed that he must get an edge at any time, but he survived till the close, when the score was 135. Hardstaff looked the complete master on the Monday, driving and hooking in his finest form. Possibly the wicket was a little easier, but it was still an impressive display and seemed to have established Hardstaff in the England side for some years – once again it wasn't a good omen for the future, for he was approaching 35. Gibb made 60, Smailes and Bedser made healthy, if lucky, contributions, and England totalled 428, Hardstaff undefeated with 205. It was likely to be more than enough.

Bedser again bowled well in the second innings and took four more wickets. This time, Smailes took wickets too, but he was perhas a little lucky when Amarnath played all round a half-volley and was bowled. He had made a hard-hit 50 and had been one of the few Indian successes, with 5 wickets in 57 overs. Mankad, who had been steadiness itself with the ball, also passed the 50, and it was evident that the Indian side had potential; but in this match, they were clearly not going to make enough runs once Merchant and Modi were out, and they were all out for 275. England had only to make 48, and Hutton and Washbrook took a little quiet practice. The match was won, but some problems remained.

★   ★   ★   ★   ★

The selectors retained the same batsmen, most of whom picked themselves. Ikin hadn't done much, but he was clearly worth persevering with, and Compton had emerged from his bad spell. Bedser and Wright played again, but Bowes and Smailes had to go. Their replacements were Voce and Pollard, neither of them a man for the future – Voce had first played for England in 1930 – but the fact was that there were no new fast bowlers coming forward, and there wouldn't be for some years. India brought back Mushtaq Ali and introduced Sohoni and Sarwate. Their results between the Tests had been mixed, but Merchant and Hazare had played big innings, and if the wicket was a good one, there might be plenty of runs.

It was hardly to be expected in a wet summer that Manchester would be blessed with good weather, and it wasn't. There was a lot of overnight rain, and there was a further problem in that Manchester's heavy roller had been requisitioned by the Army (Heaven knows what for) and no replacement was yet available. The groundsman would have to do his best with the lighter model.

Pataudi won the toss and put England in, probably more afraid of what Bedser and Pollard might do, than confident about his own bowlers' powers. In the event, Amarnath and Mankad did all the work, taking all the 15 England wickets which fell. Hutton, variously described by those present as getting over a chill and troubled with his back, was slow at the outset, but Washbrook played more freely and had made 52 out of 81 when Hindlekar caught him after some nerve-racking juggling. Compton was a changed man from the zombie of Lord's, and scored 51 out of 75 for the second wicket before Amarnath got him again. Hutton was still grafting along, but when he and Hardstaff were out, it was time to rebuild. Hammond and Gibb were there at the close, England 236 for 4, no bad score in the conditions. England were, at any rate, unlikely to lose.

Towards the end of the first day, Hammond had been rounding into his best form – he had hoisted Amarnath over the square-leg fence, and driven him to long-off – but there was more rain over the week-end and on Monday the wicket was described as black and dead. Maybe a heavier roller would have squeezed more moisture out of it, but as it was, there was nothing for the stroke-player. Amarnath and Mankad had showed at Lord's that they were adept on such a pitch and were soon winkling their way through the order. *The Times* critic said that even Hammond had to pay them some respect, but, he added:

'There is no bowler living, however, who can utterly subdue Hammond.'

The remark reads oddly now when we know how Hammond was to struggle against the Australian spinners just a few months later. He fell at last to Amarnath for 69, and England were all out for 294 – happy no doubt to be bowling on this treacherous pitch.

To begin with, the England bowlers made little impression, as Merchant and Mushtaq turned back the clock and made over 100 for the first wicket as they had done at Old Trafford ten years earlier, almost to the day. Doubtless they were aided to begin with, by the effect of the roller, such as it was, but they mastered all the bowlers by thorough, correct cricket. The worth of their effort was manifest when Pollard at last bowled Mushtaq, and the rest of the side collapsed like a pack of cards, only Pataudi with 11, getting into double figures. Pollard, playing in his first Test at the age of 34, had the remarkable figures of 27-16-24-5, and Bedser took 4 for 41. Hammond bowled 1 over for three runs – the very last over he was to bowl in Test cricket.

India were soon out for 170, 124 behind, and England needed quick runs; the Indian innings had ended early on the third day and Hammond wanted to declare as soon after lunch as he could safely manage. Scoring quickly was not going to be easy against three bowlers as accurate as Amarnath, Hazare and Mankad, and Pataudi wisely didn't risk his less experienced men. Amarnath had strained a knee, and was in great pain, but he bowled unchanged for 30 overs, a brave and remarkable effort. Hammond came in at 48 for 2 and was out almost at once for 8, caught in the deep as he tried to force Mankad away. When Hardstaff and Gibb followed him and England were 84 for 5, it looked almost as if they might have overdone the adventure, but Compton was there,

182

showing his rare skill in defence as well as improvising some typically daring strokes. Ikin helped him in an invaluable little stand and Hammond was able to declare, leaving India to make 278, or to survive for three hours.

Pollard struck the all-important blow at once, having Merchant caught without scoring and then he bowled Mushtaq almost immediately. Bedser bowled Pataudi and India were 5 for 3. It looked as though they were going to collapse ignominiously and that the match would end in total anti-climax, but Hazare and Modi retrieved the situation magnificently. There was now certainly nothing left for the Indians to play for but a draw, but they wisely took what runs were offered by Hammond's attacking fields, and added 74 at a run a minute. England still needed seven wickets at tea, but Bedser put in a fine spell, dismissing four specialist batsmen in six overs.

Hammond was handling the game with great skill – he rested Bedser briefly, then brought him back to dismiss both Mankad and Hafeez, who had looked like saving the game, and then Sarwate was caught by Gibb. There were 15 minutes to go and India's last pair were together. It looked as though Hammond – and Bedser – had brought it off, but Hindlekar, the last man in, was equal to the occasion, and he and Sohoni played out time. India had done well to save the game, for they had had the worst of the conditions, but Bedser had again taken 11 wickets, and England had clearly found a great bowler.

★   ★   ★   ★   ★

England made wholesale changes for the Oval Test, some of them enforced ones. The England touring team had been announced by now – the side had to sail to Australia rather earlier than usual, taking advantage of whatever boat was available – and the selectors were anxious to give all the tourists a game. Fishlock, Edrich, James Langridge and Evans came in, and when Wright and Voce were injured, Peter Smith and Pollard were selected. Pollard in turn reported sick, and Gover, who was not in the touring team, replaced him – it was an appropriate gesture to a faithful servant of Surrey cricket. All this meant that Edrich, now playing in his first Test since he had scored that 219 at Durban, would be operating as the third seamer and that the spin-bowling would be in the hands of Smith and Langridge, steady rather than penetrative.

Once again the game was ruined by the weather. Play could not start until five o'clock on the first day and would probably not have started then if the match had been against Australia – but the umpires were anxious to give the large crowd some reward for their patience. The

183

wicket was totally dead, though Gover, bowling his heart out as he always did, got enough life out of it to have both Merchant and Mushtaq dropped. They survived the day and made a good start on the Monday, until Fishlock ran Mushtaq out with a sharp throw, hitting the single stump he had to aim at.

Edrich now showed his value as a bowler for the first time in a Test, beating Pataudi and Amarnath for pace, and Compton caught Hazare off Gover. Suddenly India were 162 for 4, but Merchant was as safe as the Bank, and he and Modi added 63. Mankad also batted soundly, and Merchant was well past his century when he was freakishly run out. He was backing up well, as Mankad drove past the bowler – but Compton reached out a foot at short mid-on and deflected the ball on to the stumps. It was reported as a brilliant application of Compton's footballing skills, but it was more probably a bit of a fluke. Mankad and Sohoni hit about them a little and India totalled 331, their best batting effort of the series.

Amarnath again troubled Hutton and Washbrook, but it was Mankad who dismissed them both cheaply. Fishlock was splendidly caught by Merchant off Nayudu, and Hammond who had dropped himself to No 5, came in and batted quietly to the close, when he had scored 9, and England were 95 for 3. The rain had the last word, washing out the Tuesday altogether. Nobody could know it at the time, but Hammond had played his last Test innings in England.

	Innings	N.O.	H.S.	Runs	Average	100	50
1946	4	1	69	119	39.66	–	1
To date	131	16	336*	7002	60.88	22	23

	Balls	Runs	Wickets	Average
1946	6	3	0	–
To date	7969	3138	83	37.80

Hammond was, of course, the first man to score 7,000 runs in Tests.

24   One tour too many?

Everybody agreed that the MCC party which toured Australia in 1946/
47 had its weaknesses. Very few young players had emerged during the
1946 season and the side was therefore made up of pre-war heroes,
some of whom were a little past their best. This is not to say that
Hammond, the oldest member, should not have gone. He was in
splendid form throughout 1946 and the only doubt was whether his back
would stand up to the strain of a hard series. In the event, it didn't
quite, but he also had other troubles which were not foreseen when the
team was picked.

The batting looked strong. Hutton, Washbrook, Edrich, Compton
and Hardstaff picked themselves, Ikin was a young player of great
promise, and it was clearly necessary to pick a vice-captain who would
be ready to succeed Hammond in due course. Norman Yardley was the
obvious choice and he did well in Australia, the success of his
innocuous-looking bowling an unexpected bonus. In retrospect it is a
little surprising that the selectors were not content with eight batsmen,
particularly as they picked Gibb, a wicket-keeper who had shown in
South Africa what a good batsman he could be in Test cricket.
However, they picked Laurie Fishlock, who had had an excellent
season, and this did leave them a bowler short. The team was to regret
this.

The opening attack looked vulnerable, but it isn't easy to see what
the selectors could have done about it – no new fast bowlers had come
forward and Bedser, the real discovery of 1946, had to be supported by
Voce and Pollard, the one distinctly over the hill, the other perhaps
rather too much like Bedser in style. Perhaps it would have been
sensible to have picked a stock bowler such as Gladwin or Ray Smith
who would have borne a big share of the burden in the State matches
and might possibly have forced his way into the Test team. As things
turned out, Yardley sustained this role and Edrich did better as a bowler
than anybody expected, but it was asking a lot of them.

The spin bowlers were Wright, an obvious choice, Peter Smith of
Essex and James Langridge. Here again, one feels that Langridge's best
days were behind him and that a younger man might have been a better

bet, but spin bowlers do take a while to mature, and Jack Young, himself 34, was perhaps the only man who could reasonably have replaced Langridge. The second wicket-keeper, Godfrey Evans, was the other newcomer to first-class cricket who had made the team. He was very soon established as the first-choice keeper, and remained the England first choice for the next 12 years.

The tour began well enough both for the team and for Hammond. After a couple of minor matches, MCC had the better of a high-scoring draw against Western Australia, not then a major power in Australian cricket, and the captain played a majestic innings of 208. He stood down from the next match, the usual fixture against a combined XI, and this time MCC had the worst of the draw, batting with ominous shakiness against Dooland and Ian Johnson. This weakness against a well-flighted spin was to be a feature of the team's batting throughout, and Hammond has been much criticised for instructing his batsmen to play it from the crease and not to go down the wicket. It is said that Compton found this particularly unsettling, and certainly most batsmen are better advised to play their instinctive natural game whenever they can – but Hammond himself had always been successful against the spinners in Australia, by staying on the back foot, and he must have thought that others should do the same.

MCC next encountered South Australia – and for the first time, Bradman. Don's fitness was very much in question at this time and it was severely tested when he had to field for two days before getting his chance to bat. Hutton and Washbrook had a long, slow stand, and Compton, Edrich, Yardley and Ikin all made runs. Hammond missed out; this time he did go down the wicket to Dooland, missed, and was stumped, which may have confirmed him in his opinion that this wasn't the way to do it. Bradman batted competently and at least as briskly as any of the Englishmen, and it looked increasingly likely that he *would* play in the Tests. South Australia saved the match with some difficulty, and it was noted that when Bedser and Wright were not playing, there was little penetration in the English attack.

Bedser and Wright were back for the match against Victoria and they contributed to a good win over a strong State side, Wright taking ten wickets. Both Hutton and Compton made centuries, and Yardley was also in good form. The next match, against 'An Australian XI', was less encouraging. McCool, another flighty leg-spinner, took 7 for 106, including all the leading batsmen, and MCC were out for 314. Hammond played McCool with great care, but eventually had a crack at him and was caught for 51. In the scratch team's reply, Bradman scored 106, hardly in his pre-war form but soundly enough – he would be on parade at Brisbane, there was no doubt.

The game against New South Wales was virtually washed out, and only the Queensland game remained before the Test. Queensland had distinctly the better of it, scoring 400 in the first innings against what was virtually the Test attack, and putting the tourists out for 310. Once again, McCool was the trouble, taking 6 for 105, and at this moment, most commentators supposed that here was another Grimmett, come to trouble England for ten years (McCool was already 31.) It was not to be, but there were other hazards ahead. Hammond was out for 8, and there were beginning to be a few doubts about his form. Queensland were never able to set a realistic target, but MCC with Hutton absent nursing a cold, got into a little trouble after Washbrook and Edrich had made a good stand. Hammond failed again and nobody could be very happy about English prospects for the Test.

Bradman led an almost entirely new side for the first Test, at Brisbane, only Barnes and Hassett having played before the war. Six of the others had made their Test debut in a single match against New Zealand a year earlier, but it was a formidable-looking side. The bowling would be opened by Miller, whom the Englishmen knew something about, and Lindwall, a fast bowler with a glorious action reminiscent of Larwood. Toshack, medium left-arm, and Ian Johnson, off-spin, would be the stock bowlers, and there were two back-of-the-hand men in McCool and Tribe, right and left hand respectively. It was a splendidly varied attack, and nine of the side could bat to Test standard. Six of them were to make 100s in this very series, and a seventh, Don Tallon, the wicket-keeper, to score 92. It was in fact one of the very strongest sides ever to play for Australia and, with the aid of a little bit of luck, was about to give England a terrible thrashing. England played seven batsmen, omitting Fishlock and Hardstaff, and relied on Voce, Bedser, Wright and the occasional bowlers to get Australia out.

Australia had their first piece of luck when Bradman won the toss. Bedser got Morris out at once, caught by Hammond, and then he caught Barnes off Wright. England had taken 2 wickets for 46, and were doing better than they had expected. Then came Australia's second piece of luck – or was it? Bradman had started cautiously and not altogether certainly, and when he had scored 28, he chopped at a ball from Voce which was caught by Ikin at second slip. Bradman seemed unmoved and the Englishmen, who assumed that the ball had been fairly caught, appealed. Bradman was given not out, and it is fair to say that the majority of those on the ground disagreed with the decision. However, nobody's opinion mattered but the umpire's and Bradman batted on to score 187 without another chance. Hassett scored 128, and he and Bradman added 276 at a run a minute. The rest of the batsmen cashed in on this great start and Australia totalled 645, early on the third day (the Tests in this series were played over six five-hour days).

The 'Bradman incident' had several consequences. It virtually ensured Australia's win in this Test, since rain fell and ruined the wicket for England. It meant that Bradman made a big score, which helped him to decide to stay in Test cricket; it is at least possible that; if he had failed twice in this first Test, he would have retired there and then. But sadly, it soured relations between the two captains, if not between the teams, for Hammond was firmly of the opinion that Bradman was caught, that he knew he had been caught, and that he should have walked. There are, and always have been, two opinions about the ethics of walking, and Bradman was perfectly entitled to let the umpire decide, but it is a fact that Hammond was extremely unhappy about the whole incident.

The rain had fallen on the second evening when Australia were 595 for 5, and the wicket was playing tricks from the start of the third day. The roller damped it down for a while, but Hutton was out before the rain returned and England were 21 for 1. A great deal more rain fell in the night and on the fourth day the wicket was a beast. Edrich was hit four times in one over from Miller, who was in no sense aiming at the batsman, but simply had no control over the high bounce. Washbrook and Compton were both out to Miller, and Hammond joined Edrich at 49 for 3. He began to play one of the finest bad-wicket innings ever seen, own brother to his remarkable 32 at Melbourne ten years earlier, and those two fine innings at Bridgetown in the 'declarations match' in 1934-35. It was noticed that whereas Edrich had taken a knock for every run he made, Hammond was hardly struck at all; nor did he ever poke the ball up near the close fielders. Bill O'Reilly described his technique very eloquently:

'He played the dead bat so well that one might have been excused for thinking that his right arm was either broken or made of jelly, so little pressure did it have upon his bat.'

It is always said that the way to play on a sticky wicket is to withhold all strength from the bottom hand thus to keep the ball down, but it is very much easier said than done. Hammond lost Edrich and Ikin before the close, but Yardley kept him gallant company until the players were driven off by bad light at 116 for 5. Miller had taken all five wickets.

If ever a batsmen deserved some good fortune, it was Hammond on 4 December 1946. If there was any justice at all in cricket, the pitch would have rolled out into a smooth lawn and enabled him to turn his hard-won 30 into a typical Hammond 100. But when the luck changes

188

sides at cricket, it generally does so thoroughly, and so it was this time. Another night of rain produced a wicket that was, if anything, even worse than the day before's. Hammond was out at once, for 32, lbw to Toshack's faster ball. Yardley was caught three minutes later and that was that. England were all out for 141 and followed on half an hour before lunch – the timing was important, for the roller had to go on before the wicket had had a real chance to dry. Hutton and Edrich were out before lunch and Washbrook soon after.

The position was hopeless and Hammond decided to have a hit at everything. He hit Toshack for two sixes and a four in one over, but it couldn't last, and he was bowled for 23 by a ball which came back on him, against the normal direction of Toshack's movement off the seam. The later batsmen made a few, as the wicket eased just a trifle, but England all out for 172, were beaten by an innings and 332 runs, the record innings margin for Australia against England. Australia had had all the luck, but it must be said that they did score 645 and might well have won even if it hadn't rained.

★   ★   ★   ★   ★

Lindwall had been off the field in the England second innings and it turned out that he had chicken-pox. He was replaced for the match at Sydney by Fred Freer, playing in his only Test. Voce had made little impact at Brisbane and he was replaced by Peter Smith. Hammond won the toss this time, but England's batsmen, Hammond included, made very little of their opportunity on a wicket which seemed good enough, though some observers claimed after the event that they had detected spots. Freer bowled Washbrook at once, but Hutton and Edrich took the score to 88 before Ian Johnson, bowling for the first time in a Test although it was his third appearance, had Hutton caught off the ball that floated away, which Johnson knew so well how to disguise.

Compton came in and now McCool, who was still the bowler most feared by the Englishmen, struck two decisive blows, having both Compton and Hammond caught at the wicket. Hammond scored only one run – he played back to a leg-break and the general view was that he should have been down the wicket to it, but he had already made up his mind to play the spinners from the crease. Edrich and Ikin went grimly about the business of hauling the innings back from 99 for 4, and they were very slow about it – Johnson bowled 11 overs for 3 runs at one time. Their effort was in vain, Edrich falling at last to McCool for 71. Johnson took all the last five wickets, and England were all out early on the second day for 255. Johnson, with 6 for 42, had the figures, but McCool had made the vital break.

There was a lot of rain about on this second day and Barnes appealed against the light as soon as he got to the wicket. The umpires allowed his second appeal and heavy rain fell soon afterwards. As often happens in Australia, the wicket dried quickly, and some more play was possible at four o'clock. Morris was out to Edrich and Barnes embarked on a series of appeals. There was then no restriction on the number of times a batsman could appeal – the law was later changed, partly because of Barnes' behaviour in this match. The situation was becoming a trifle farcical, with endless conferences between the umpires, when they yielded at last to Barnes' fifth appeal in this period of play. It is fair to say that the light *was* bad, and an earlier abandonment could have been defended, but a less thick-skinned man than Barnes might not have persevered.

The next day was a Sunday, and the England party had the frustration of looking at an obviously difficult wicket and not being able to bowl on it. By Monday the wicket was as good as ever, but Edrich soon got rid of Johnson, the night-watchman. Bradman had injured his leg in the field and held himself back in the order, and Hassett now joined Barnes, who was batting very slowly. Edrich, who was something of a find as a bowler on this tour, had Hassett caught at 96, one run behind the position England had reached at the fall of the third wicket – but Bradman was still to come. He didn't bat, even now, but he did come in when Miller was out, at 159. At this stage, Barnes had scored 71 in just over four hours – very slow going, but he had been much interrupted and England's cheap dismissal had given Australia plenty of time to play with. Hammond's chief preoccupation was the nursing of Wright who, as he often did, was bowling very well but with no luck at all. He was the likeliest man both to dismiss Bradman before he got going, and to go through the tail. Hammond was therefore making free use of Edrich and Smith, but Edrich, in particular, was likely to fade in the course of a long innings.

Bradman started very slowly, by his own standards, scoring only 14 in his first hour, but then he opened out, and had reached his 60 before the close, when the score was 252 for 4. Barnes had made 109 in six hours. England needed quick wickets on the fourth day, but they didn't get them. Bradman looked very uncomfortable against Wright early on, but nothing went to hand, and no other bowler troubled him. By the afternoon he was playing all the bowling much as he pleased and Barnes, too, was accelerating. After tea, their tempo fairly ran away with them, 130 runs coming in the last 90 minutes of the partnership before Bradman swished at Yardley, the seventh bowler tried, and was lbw for 234. He had just overtaken Barnes and the two had added 405, a record for any wicket in a Test in Australia. Barnes was out a few

190

minutes later, also for 234 – there were some who saw this as a generous gesture by one who didn't want to be seen to outdo his captain, but I think that this is unlikely. Australia were 571 for 6 at the close.

Australia batted on on the fifth morning, giving Freer his only chance of a Test innings, which he took with alacrity, scoring a rapid 28. Bradman declared at 659 for 8, leaving England with an awful lot to do. Hutton now played a brilliant cameo of an innings, scoring 37 in 24 minutes, with six fours, before being out very unluckily when his batting glove slipped off causing him to hit his wicket. It is intriguing, if unprofitable, to speculate on what might have happened if he had batted on. A two-hour 100? It might have saved the match for England, and rehabilitated the whole side, but it wasn't to be.

Washbrook batted on in more solid style, but he was out at 118. Edrich was in excellent form – at this point in the tour he was batting better than any of the team – and he and Compton batted almost to the end of the day. If they had lasted it out and got a start in the morning, England might have saved the match, but Compton edged an outswinger from Freer when he had made 54, and was caught by Bradman fielding, unusually for him, at second slip. Hammond scorned to hide behind a night-watchman, came in himself and hit a no-ball from Johnson for a towering six. It was almost his last characteristic gesture of the series.

Next morning Hammond started confidently and England supporters allowed themselves to hope that this was to be the day when his fortunes revived. However when he had made 33 he seemed to decide that McCool, who had troubled him more than had anybody else, must be mastered; he crashed him straight for four, McCool very wisely taking his hand away from the ball, and then tried to loft him for another four, miscued and was caught at mid-on. This 37 was his highest innings of the series, but his dismissal was the beginning of the end.

Edrich went to an excellent 100 – his first against Australia – but he lost Ikin and was finally bowled by McCool for 119. McCool's day had come. He had taken 0 for 85 up to the moment when he had Hammond caught, but he now finished off the innings in quick time ending up with 5 for 109, as England lost by an innings, once again. England could not blame bad luck this time, except in the matter of Hutton's glove – they had been fairly and squarely beaten by a better team.

★　★　★　★　★

I have taken the narrative thus far without referring to Hammond's troubles off the field, but they must be discussed because they had a profound influence on the course of the rubber as well as on

191

Hammond's own future. His marriage was breaking up and he knew that while he was in Australia his wife would be petitioning for a divorce, which he would not contest. She would be citing a Miss Ness Harvey, a lady whom Hammond had first met in South Africa, eight years before. They had fallen in love, and one can only guess at the tensions and troubles of the war years. Now it had all come to a head and Miss Ness Harvey had come to England to stay with Hammond's mother while he was away. She telephoned him in Perth to say that this arrangement was not working out, and this understandably knocked the stuffing out of him. He was much criticised during the tour for his aloofness, his failure to guide young players, his failure to knuckle down to his batting, but we who know more of the underlying reasons will understand and sympathise. It is important to appreciate this personal tragedy, because Hammond is seen by history as an unsympathetic and unsuccessful captain – but nobody saw him in this light when he was happy and untroubled.

Smith had been rather hammered at Sydney and England brought Voce back for the Melbourne Test; this was to turn out unhappily, but it was a soundly-based decision. Lindwall was fit again for Australia and Dooland replaced Tribe, to give Australia an attack of two leg-spinners. Englishmen remembered Grimmett and O'Reilly and shuddered.

Bradman won the toss, but Australia didn't prosper as they had done in the first Test. England, in fact, put up their best performance of the tour on this first day. They suffered two literally crippling blows, but surmounted them for the time being. Barnes hooked a ball at Edrich fielding at short-leg and brought him crashing down with a very badly bruised leg – this before he had bowled. Edrich was off for the day and then after lunch Voce strained a muscle and he too left the field. This was a risk that England had always had to face – Voce was now 37 and liable to strains, especially when he tried to bounce the odd delivery in his old style. England were left with only Bedser, Wright and Yardley. Morris was out before Voce's departure, but Barnes and Bradman were still together and it seemed that Australia must make a huge score. However, Barnes and Hassett were got out and the score was still only 143 for 3. There was hope yet.

Yardley put in a long economical spell before tea and then he turned the course of the day when he bowled Bradman with a ball that kept a little low, and had Johnson lbw first ball. At the other end, Miller tried to cut Wright and snicked the ball to Evans, and suddenly Australia were 192 for 6. It looked like the Sydney Test in reverse only with Australia at the losing end, but Australia batted very long indeed in this series and McCool and Tallon calmly set to work to rebuild the innings. Yardley, who had already had a long spell, had to share the new ball with Bedser – something he wouldn't have pictured in his wildest dreams aboard the *Stirling Castle* – and he made no further impression on the Queensland pair. At the close, Australia were 255 for 6. Bedser had bowled 22 eight-ball overs in the day. He had sent down 87 overs in the first two Tests and was finding out what Anglo-Australian cricket was all about when the selectors left you a bowler short and the luck wasn't on your side.

After a hard night's treatment Edrich came up as good as new in the morning and he had Tallon caught by Evans off his first ball. Here was a fighter indeed. Lindwall didn't stay long, but Dooland, a remarkably good batsman to encounter at No 10 – he averaged 24 in first-class cricket and twice did the double when he played for Nottinghamshire – stayed and stayed while McCool played a fluent innings. He took two hours to score 50, but rattled up his second 50 in just 51 minutes. Not for the first or last time, an Australian late-order batsman had succeeded when runs were most needed, but it would be quite unfair to blame Hammond's tactics for the reversal. Voce was still absent on this second day and Bedser was looking very weary. It was the indomitable Edrich who took the last two wickets, leaving McCool on 104 not out. Australia had made 365.

Lindwall had Hutton caught almost at once – by McCool – and England's leading batsman had made only 85 in five innings, two of them on the gluepot at Brisbane. Washbrook and Edrich came together in a really fine partnership, Edrich in particular handling all the bowlers with the utmost confidence and being especially hard on Toshack, although he did offer an extremely sharp chance to short-leg off him. At the close England were 147 for 1 and beginning to entertain hopes.

Alas for those hopes! Edrich was out lbw to Lindwall, very early on the third morning. The decision was bitterly criticised by English journalists, one of whom made rather an ass of himself, alleging that Edrich had played the ball on to his pad, and claiming to have verified this by inspecting the mark on Edrich's bat. It took English cricket-writers a long while to live this one down.

Wickets tumbled after this, Compton was also out lbw and also to a much-disputed decision, and then Hammond, after opening with two firm hits, failed to get to the pitch of a flighted ball from Dooland and was caught and bowled for 9. This was a particularly interesting dismissal, for Hammond had been preaching to his young men the virtues of playing the spinners from the crease, yet here he was going down the wicket and not getting there. Norman Preston wrote that: 'he failed to get that vital last margin of distance when jumping out to drive.' Jumping out? My own feeling is that he was trying to get down the wicket to the spinners, but that his speed of foot was no longer there. At all events, he was out, and when Washbrook followed him for a hard-won 62, England were 179 for 5.

Yardley and Ikin were perhaps the least-considered of England's batsmen before the tour, but they seldom failed to give of their best, and this was their best joint performance. Sometimes in difficulties against the spinners, but generally playing the fast men confidently, they batted almost till tea-time before Yardley became too ambitious against McCool and was bowled. He had scored 61 and they had added 113. Ikin was out soon afterwards. Voce was hardly fit to bat and unsurprisingly made a duck, but Bedser swung the bat vigorously and the total reached 351, more than had seemed likely when all the top men were out for 179. Australia came in and made 33 without loss before the close of play.

Voce was still off the field on the fourth day and it seemed that England's only chance of restricting Australia for a second time was to take quick wickets for the attenuated attack would surely be worn down by this very long Australia line-up. The wickets didn't come at first, and Australia got to 68 before the incredible Yardley struck again, having Barnes caught behind. If the word incredible sounds a little overstated, it is worth noting that Yardley had bowled only 31 overs for Yorkshire in the previous Championship season and hadn't taken a single wicket. Now he had dismissed Bradman twice and Barnes once, and was by a long way the least expensive of England's bowlers.

The virtues of line and length, as the sage Trueman was to point out many years later. Bradman again looked uncertain against him now though nothing went to hand, but there were a couple of encouraging edges. Morris looked much sounder, and after three failures he was beginning to play to his reputation.

An hour before lunch, it happened again. Bradman played forward at Yardley and gave him an easy return catch. Nobody could explain it, but when, four years later, Freddie Brown caught and bowled Miller twice in the same Test, when bowling in his medium-paced style, Jack Fingleton pointed out that there was a slight fall at one end at Melbourne, and that many a medium-pacer had induced the lifted stroke as batsmen pushed out. It is possible that this is what happened to Bradman.

Morris was in complete command by now, although he was batting slowly. Wickets fell steadily at the other end and when Morris was out after half an hour of the fifth day, Australia were 333 for 5. England still had just a chance and when the score was 341 for 7, that chance looked better, for the wicket was still playing perfectly. But the English bowlers were really running out of steam now. Voce had gallantly taken

194

the field on this fifth morning, but his fire was absent, and Bedser and Wright were visibly wilting.

Tallon and Lindwall now turned the screw with a most brilliant piece of batting, adding 154 in 88 minutes. There was very little that Hammond could do about it except to spread his field and put on whichever bowler looked freshest and most willing, Looking at the score today, one may wonder why he didn't bowl Compton at any time, but Hammond was desperately trying to contain the batsmen by now and this definitely wouldn't have been the moment for Compton's allsorts. Tallon got out for 92 – which remained his highest score in Tests to the end of his 21-match career – and Lindwall may have had a nasty moment when Dooland failed and Toshack, the one undisputed tail-ender, came in. Lindwall still needed 19 for his 100 but Toshack stayed, and Lindwall wasted no time, rattling up the last 19 in 14 minutes. Australia were all out for 536, and England with no chance to win, now had to bat for seven hours just to save the game.

Washbrook and Hutton made an excellent start on the fifth evening. I put Washbrook's name first, contrary to the usual order of naming these two, because on this occasion he took the lead in decisive fashion, hooking Toshack repeatedly and eluding a carefully-set leg trap. Washbrook had made 60 out of 91 for 0 by the close and continued to outscore Hutton next morning. Bradman had tried all his bowlers and was beginning to look desperate when Hutton holed out off Toshack. He had scored 40; it was his best score of the series so far, and he was overdue for a big score. Washbrook had already scored 90, and he arrived at his 100 after batting for 193 minutes, an excellent rate of scoring in the circumstances. A horrid little collapse followed: Edrich was lbw to McCool and then Compton was run out.

Compton had the reputation of being a terrible runner between the wickets, but on this occasion Washbrook refused to run on Compton's call, and most observers thought the blame at least evenly divided. It could of course be argued that runs no longer mattered and that the batsmen should not have been taking the slightest risk. Hammond came in at a very awkward time – 186 for 3 with more than 3 hours to go. He started confidently, sweeping McCool for four, but then the weary Washbrook was out for 112, and England were back in crisis. McCool and Dooland were now bowling in tandem – the light was poor and Bradman was too shrewd to use his fast bowlers – and they were getting some turn at last. Ikin looked unhappy and when after a brief stoppage for rain, the light improved and Bradman took the new ball, he cocked one up off Miller and was caught. 221 for 5. Hammond was, by common consent, batting as well as at any time during the series, and although Yardley was more chancey, it began to look as though the captain and vice-captain would save the game with ease and dignity. It was not to be – Hammond, after batting quite serenely for 77 minutes for 26, was beaten for pace by Lindwall and bowled. England supporters were exasperated and frustrated by way in which, innings after innings, he appeared to be thoroughly set and then fell. He himself must have been much more frustrated and disappointed.

England had to survive for 90 minutes and with Voce only able to bat under difficulties, they seemed to be in great peril, but there came a brief shower which meant that not only did the Australian bowlers lose a quarter of an hour, but they had to bowl with a wet ball when they returned. It was enough. Bedser made a staunch 25 and then Yardley and Evans batted out time. Evans was not yet the batsman he was soon to become, but he could defend with the best, as he was to demonstrate at Adelaide. Yardley was unbeaten to the end, with 53 runs against his name. He had had a really excellent match, scoring 114 for once out, and taking five wickets, including Bradman twice, Barnes and Miller. The Ashes were lost, but there might still be some honour to be won in the series. England had done well to restrict Australia's batting with their depleted attack and this had owed a good deal to Hammond's skilful management.

★   ★   ★   ★   ★

The tourists now travelled to Tasmania, but Hammond did not lead the party there, staying on the mainland for a rest and, no doubt, some treatment for the fibrositis which was troubling him again. He was criticised for this decision by some of the tabloid papers – one can only assume that their reporters had no conception of the strain placed on a touring captain, especially one in failing health. Hammond had stood down from only one first-class match since the team had left Perth.

Compton returned to his finest form in Tasmania, scoring two centuries, and Hardstaff also made a big 100. The side now met South Australia for the second time and Hammond demonstrated that the rest had done him good, scoring a majestic 188. In the course of the innings, he completed his 50,000 runs in first-class cricket, a total reached by only six players before him and none since. Sadly, it was his last first-class 100, but it was a fine one. James Langridge also made a 100 and enjoyed a big stand with Hammond. He might well have been picked for the Adelaide Test on the strength of it, but he aggravated a groin strain while batting and played in no more matches on the tour.

The tour selectors took the odd decision to play Hardstaff in the Test, but at the expense of Voce, so that the attack was reduced to Bedser, Wright and the all-rounders. This was surely taking too big a risk.

196

Edrich and Yardley had bowled better than anyone had a right to expect, but surely they couldn't keep it up? Barnes was unfit, and Australia brought in Mervyn Harvey, elder brother of Neil, who was only just beginning to make his mark.

Hammond won the toss and batted. For the first time Hutton and Washbrook struck their best form in the same innings. Bill Bowes has told how he motivated Hutton by telling him that the Australians had concluded that he was 'afeard of them' and he now played finely. They started slowly, as was only prudent in a six-day Test, but were into their stride by lunchtime. Hutton scored 50 in two hours and the 100 partnership came up in 133 minutes without a chance, though there had been some risky running. Washbrook accelerated now and overtook Hutton at one moment, but he was caught at the wicket off Dooland when he had made 65 out of 137. Edrich started brightly, but Dooland got him too, and Hammond entered at 173 for 2, to an emperor's reception.

He was off the mark right away, with a three to the third-man boundary, but Bradman immediately brought on McCool, who had had him out four times on the tour and was thought to be his bogeyman. McCool got what we must describe as the greater prize when he had Hutton lbw for 94. Hammond now hooked McCool in the air, but too quickly for the fielder to sight it, and was then beaten and bowled for 18 by Toshack with a fine, thoughtful piece of bowling. Toshack tied him down with a leg-stump attack which it seemed that Hammond could play all day provided that he took no risks, and then he produced an off-cutter outside the off-stump which totally deceived Hammond. England were 202 for 4, a disappointing score after their good start. Compton had not been himself in the Tests so far, and a big innings from him was very much needed.

This time Compton didn't disappoint his admirers. He began cautiously, scoring only 15 in an hour before the close, but he looked safe enough – meanwhile Hardstaff, at the other end, played and missed once or twice, but was still there at the close. Bradman took the new ball early on the second day and both men looked much happier. Compton was still slow and was now being outscored by Hardstaff, but both men had reached their 50s before Hardstaff was out. 320 for 5 was a much more promising score and Compton now began to open out. He and Ikin added 61 in 45 minutes, and Compton reached a chanceless 100 in 232 minutes, on the slow side by his standards, but fast enough to satisfy most people. Whether or not he had his captain's permission, he now began to go down the wicket to the slow bowlers, and it paid off, for he added another 47 at a run a minute before being caught and bowled by Ray Lindwall, who then finished off the innings by taking three wickets in four balls. England were all out for 460 – a good score, but not perhaps enough on a perfect pitch – but the excitement wasn't over for the day. Bedser bowled Harvey with the score at 18, and then bowled Bradman for a duck. Bradman said it was the best ball he had ever received and, making due allowance for his disappointment, it does seem to have been a good one, swinging in late and cutting away off the seam.

Morris and Hassett repaired the damage next day. Morris was still in the same prime form he had demonstrated at Melbourne, and Hassett in his usual dogged Test match mode – he could be a very hard man to dismiss, infinitely patient and with a sound idea of the whereabouts of his off-stump. It was gone 4.30pm before he fell, caught by Hammond off Wright, the last catch Hammond was to take in an Ashes Test. Morris soon followed his partner, for a splendid chanceless 155, and England were back in the game at 222 for 4. Miller and Johnson stayed until the close, when the score was 293.

Miller began the next day dramatically. Wright bowled a no-ball with his first delivery and Miller, hearing the call early, hit it over square-leg for six. This got him away to a good start and when Johnson was out for 60, Miller had made 57 in just under the first hour of the day. Yardley applied the brake after lunch, and Miller's batting was more erratic – he offered three chances after reaching his 100 and was outscored by Lindwall during a bright little eighth-wicket stand. But Miller was undefeated when the innings ended on 487; it had followed much the same erratic course as England's, the later batsmen bringing it from mediocrity to a respectable, but not a match-winning score. It looked very like a draw.

Hutton and Washbrook again started well. Hutton scored 20 runs before his partner received his second ball, and retained that lead to the end of the fourth day, when they had made 96 in 82 minutes. England were perhaps ahead on points at that moment, but early on the next day Washbrook was out, just after they had completed their third successive century partnership, equalling a Hobbs-Sutcliffe record. England then fell into trouble, Hutton getting out for 76 and Edrich for 46. England were 178 for 3. Hammond had come in when Hutton was bowled and had batted as well as at any time in the series but just as in the second innings at Sydney, he seemed to become over-confident, swatted at Toshack and was caught at mid-wicket for 22. Tom Goodman wrote that it was almost as if he overlooked Lindwall altogether, for he hit the ball straight at him. Hammond walked slowly back to the pavilion, out for the last time in Australia, though he was, perhaps fortunately, unaware of this. The last innings is a poignant moment for

198

any cricketer and the batsman who plays his last without knowing it is the lucky one.

Hardstaff failed and so did Ikin, and England were facing defeat at 215 for 6. Compton was again in good form, but he lost Yardley at 250 and Bedser at 255. Evans walked in to face the sternest of tests and played finely, if uncharacteristically. Usually the most adventurous of batsmen, he set himself to stay, and do no more than that. Compton farmed the bowling with the greatest skill – he *could* run well between the wickets, when he was concentrating – and when six o'clock came they had added 19 runs in 45 minutes. Significantly, Compton had faced 60 balls, and Evans only 20, from which he had not scored.

On the final day Compton and Evans stayed together all morning. The latter didn't get off the mark until he had batted for 95 minutes, but he was playing a great innings for his side. He was also playing well technically; one has to play very straight not to get a run or two off the edge in 95 minutes. Compton reached his second 100 of the match just before lunch, and Hammond after batting on for just one ball after lunch, to deprive Australia of 12 minutes' or so batting, declared.

The target was 314 in 195 minutes, a difficult but not impossible one. Australia were in no danger of defeat – they had plenty of batsmen to close the game down if they got into trouble – but Bradman was content with the draw. This time, Harvey made 31, while Morris batted very fluently at the other end – he was on 84 when Harvey got out. He reached his 100 in only 124 minutes, and he and Bradman quietly played out time when Bradman could have picked up some cheap runs and did not. He could so easily have made the four runs he was to need at the end of his career, to give him an average of 100 in Tests. Equally, of course, he might have got out!

Bradman was much criticised for not sending Miller in first to try to get on top of the bowling, reserving Harvey and Hassett to secure the draw if need be, but Test cricket simply isn't played like that. It was an oddity that nobody had scored two 100s in an Ashes Test since Hammond did it in 1928-29, and now two players did it in the same match. Nobody has done it since, which says something about the pressures.

Hammond played in the next match at Ballarat, but retired from the field stricken with fibrositis, and didn't play again until the team reached New Zealand. Yardley took over the captaincy and the team did decidedly well in the fifth Test at Sydney, which rather encouraged those critics of Hammond's captaincy who laid all the blame for the defeat at his door. It wasn't quite as simple as that. England had a better-balanced side for the last Test, bringing back Smith for Hardstaff (Fishlock replaced Hammond) and the match was played on a more 'English' pitch than the first four Tests. Hutton made his long-awaited 100, but had to retire from the match with tonsillitis when he had made 122. England only scored 280 in their first innings, but Australia failed to match this. Wright produced this best bowling of the tour, taking 7 for 105, and Australia were all out for 253, Barnes making the top score of 71.

With Hutton absent, Fishlock had to open with Washbrook, and he fell lbw to Lindwall, for 0. England never got over this, only Compton (76) getting past 30 and McCool finished the series with another fine piece of bowling, taking 5 for 44. More irony – he was never to play against England again. Australia only needed 214, but they made dreadfully heavy weather of it. Bedser and Wright gathered themselves for one last effort; Morris was run out at 45, and when he had made 2, Bradman was dropped at slip off Wright. It wasn't the easiest of chances, but it was one which the unlucky Edrich would normally have caught, and of course everybody said that Hammond would certainly have held it had he been there. Bradman went on to score 63 before Bedser had him caught and Australia won by 5 wickets.

Nothing had gone right for England in the series, but they were more than a little unlucky to lose so heavily. Looking back at the side, it looks very powerful in batting, and indeed it made some sizeable scores – but for the most part, too few batsmen were 'firing' simultaneously. The real deficiency was in the bowling, and I have already suggested that more could have been done to help Bedser and Wright by resting them in the lesser matches. Hammond was much criticised for his pedestrian leadership, but England were to do no better in 1948 against the same strong Australian team, reinforced by Harvey and Bill Johnston.

Hammond had a disastrous series with the bat; there were medical, technical and psychological reasons for this, and his failure should not obscure his wonderful record over the years.

★　★　★　★　★

Hammond made a good recovery from the attack of fibrositis and played in both the matches in New Zealand which preceded the sole Test, at Christchurch. For the first time on the tour England played four specialist bowlers, Pollard joining the three who had played at Sydney. Hutton had gone home following his illness, leaving Yardley to open the batting with Washbrook. The Test was scheduled to be played over three days, but when the third day was washed out, an extra day was added. In vain – the rain prevented any play on that day also, so the match was inconclusive; Hadlee and Bert Sutcliffe, New Zealand's new star, made 133 for the first wicket, but then Bedser and Pollard took a grip on the game, and it needed a breezy 45 from Cowie to see New Zealand to the comparatively healthy score of 345 for 9. Hadlee declared when he himself had scored 116, his only Test 100. He was a fine batsman and a fine Test captain, undaunted by a long sequence without a win – it was fitting that he should have one day of glory.

When England batted Jack Cowie showed all the accuracy and fire which had inspired the Editor of *Wisden* to write in 1937 that, 'had he been an Australian, he might have been termed the wonder of the age.' He got Washbrook and Yardley out cheaply and when Edrich fell to Scott, England were 79 for 3. Hammond came in to a tremendous reception from the crowd of 20,000 who knew that this would his last Test appearance in New Zealand, and sensed that it could be the last Test of his career. Hadlee called for three cheers from his players, as Yardley was to do at the Oval 17 months later, when Bradman batted for the last time in a Test.

Hammond's last innings was more noteworthy than Bradman's, or at least it lasted rather longer. He was at home with the bowling from the start and showed that he had recovered his fitness as he stole cheeky singles. Compton was out soon after he came in, but Jack Ikin stayed while 97 were added. Hammond hit ten fours in his 79. Fittingly, he fell to Cowie, and left the field for the last time in a Test, to another rousing ovation. England were still 80 behind at the close, and although Hammond announced that he proposed to declare overnight, to make a game of it, nothing more could be done when the rain came down.

Hammond missed the last match of the tour against Auckland, in which Compton scored 97 not out and took 11 wickets, and he must have been pleased, at any rate, that the New Zealand visit had gone well. He returned at the head of a team which, though well beaten, had not been disgraced. He announced his retirement from first-class cricket, married quietly as soon as he returned to England and started life over again.

	Innings	N.O.	H.S.	Runs	Average	100	50
1946/47 (A)	8	–	37	168	21.00	–	–
1946/47 (N.Z.)	1	–	79	79	79.00	–	1
Record	140	16	336*	7249	58.45	22	24

	Balls	Runs	Wickets	Average
Record	7969	3138	83	37.80

Hammond held 110 catches in Test cricket, an average of 1.29 per match.

25   In the final analysis

I said in the opening chapter that Hammond combined grace and majesty in a way that no other batsman has quite managed – perhaps, on reflection, Viv Richards has come very close to him. How did that style reveal itself in performance? He was clearly and unarguably the greatest batting force ever revealed in county cricket – he was the leading English batsman in eight consecutive seasons, averaging 65.42 over the seasons from 1933 to 1946. Considering the varied conditions to be encountered in an English season, and the constant pressure of time in three-day matches, the figures are worthy of Bradman himself.

But did he reproduce this form in Test matches, winning matches by his own achievement? On the whole, he did. It was his misfortune that he started sensationally against Australia in 1928-29, and that the unthinking counted him as a failure when he didn't always measure up to this standard. One would say that no-one *could* measure up to such a standard, were it not for the undoubted fact that somebody did. It was Hammond's second misfortune that his career coincided almost exactly with Bradman's and that Bradman's performances were so incredibly consistent that he easily outshone every other batsman in history. The relative performance of the two men generally dictated the course of Anglo-Australian cricket in their time. Consider the rubbers, one by one.

In 1928-29 Bradman was slower to get going than Hammond and England won easily against a side which improved as the matches went on.

In 1930 Bradman was at his absolute peak. Hammond had a moderate series with one century and Australia won comfortably.

In 1932-33 Hammond had a good series. Bradman, in theory, did better than Hammond, but in fact he was demoralised by the bodyline attack, as were the other Australians, and England won 4 games to 1.

In 1934 Bradman started moderately enough, but came good when it mattered. Hammond had a dreadful time and Australia won.

In 1936-37, Hammond began well by playing a great innings at Sydney, but fell away, as Bradman came through with the big scores to win the series for Australia.

In 1938 both men did well. Hammond played the innings of his life at Lord's, and also made two 50s. Bradman scored three 100s, all when they were most needed. Both men were strongly supported by younger batsmen and the series was drawn 1-1.

In 1946-47, Bradman was almost as good as ever, but Hammond fell away sadly and Australia won easily.

Of the two, Bradman had the greater influence on his side's fortunes – Australia won 17 matches against England in which he played, and he scored centuries in 13 of them. Hammond was on the winning side 13 times and scored centuries in six of those matches.

Hammond, then, was outshone by Bradman, but by nobody else – it can be said that if Bradman had never existed, or had decided to play for Australia at lawn tennis and not at cricket (this is not a fanciful thought, as he was a very fine tennis player) Hammond would be seen as the finest batsman of his day, and certainly as the best between the eras of Hobbs and of Sobers. His performances against the other countries were often overwhelming – his two great innings against New Zealand in 1932-33, two big 100s against the Indians in 1936, and his consistency in the rubber of 1938-39, will never be forgotten by those who were lucky enough to be there.

He is universally acknowledged to have been the most handsome batsman of his age – unfortunately, there are no prizes for this – and he was also the finest player of his time on a turning wicket. He may well have been the best of all time on a real gluepot. He gave three impeccable displays on wickets which defeated nearly everybody else. They hardly show up in the scorecards – 43 and 29 not out at Bridgetown in 1934-35, 32 at Melbourne in 1936-37, 32 and 23 at Brisbane in 1946-47 – and two of the three matches were lost, but his stoicism and his skilful technique have been recognised down the years. In many ways, it is a great pity that we never have the chance today to see a great Test batsman at bay when the pitch is the bowler's friend. It may not have always been fair, but it was great to watch.

Hammond was for many years acknowledged to be the finest slip-fielder ever seen in Test cricket. He held 110 catches in 85 matches, a high average. Fielding at slip, with the need to concentrate on every ball, must at times have affected his batting. For example, only five of his 22 Test centuries were made in the second innings. His bowling too, while being a great asset to his side, was an additional tax on his magnificent physique; ten times, he bowled more than 150 balls, at a good fast-medium pace, in a Test innings, and, significantly, he never made a century in the same match. He wasn't *quite* a genuine Test all-rounder, but that was because his captains had more sense, generally, than to push him to the limits of his bowling endurance.

What, now, of his captaincy? His last tour to Australia in 1946-47, was a disaster, largely for the several reasons which I set out in the chapter dealing with that tour. The venture came one year too early for English cricket, in that new players had not had time to establish themselves; the team as picked lacked balance; Hammond himself was suffering from ill-health, and his private life was in turmoil. Critics have tended to project backward from this tour, and to argue that Hammond was never a good captain, but was this really the case?

If we look at what experienced observers were saying, *before* the 1946-47 debacle, we encounter a different range of opinions. Louis Duffus of South Africa described his leadership in 1938-39 as 'exemplary'. RC Robertson-Glasgow, writing in the 1942 *Wisden* at a time when it seemed possible that Hammond wouldn't play again, deliverd a balanced judgement:

> 'As a strategist he would not rank among our great leaders; but he was safe, observant and experienced. His colossal achievements commanded the respect as his social nature invited the confidence of every sort of cricketer'.

'Crusoe', then, saw him as a safe strategist *and* a leader of men – not the judgment of others. It may seem that the comment on his acumen smacks of damning with faint praise; but another very experienced judge, Ray Robinson of Australia, writing a chapter on Anglo-Australian captains between the wars, actually placed Hammond first among Englishmen. Ahead of Chapman, ahead of Wyatt, ahead even of Jardine. Robinson wrote, in 1946:

> 'Hammond carried his poise into his captaincy. There has been nothing fidgety or ostentatious to irk his players. He gives them credit for knowing the game, does not regiment them with detailed orders, and gets the response such understanding leadership deserves.'

Well of course it was said in 1946/47 that he *did* regiment his players and particularly Compton, with detailed orders about staying in the crease against the slow bowlers, but we are for the moment considering his pre-war performance. He was appointed to captain England as soon as he turned amateur in 1938. He had very little experience of captaincy and wasn't even at that time, captain of his county. Gloucestershire had used him as vice-captain a few years earlier in the closing period of Beverley Lyon's reign, but it is an altogether different business to lead on a match-by-match basis, and it hadn't worked out.

How did Hammond perform as captain in 1938? In the first Test, he was criticised for under-bowling Verity in the first innings while McCabe was cutting loose, but Hammond could argue that the wicket was absolutely perfect, that he had to bowl Australia out twice to win, and that Verity was the most likely man to winkle them out on the last day. It didn't come off, but it might have done.

Curiously, after Hammond had been accused of over-bowling Wright in this first Test, he was told he should have used him sooner in the fourth, when Australia needed only 105 to win. The fact is that, as Warner points out in his account of this great match in *Cricket Between Two Wars,* Wright was a very difficult bowler for a captain to handle. Not because he was temperamental – he was never that – but because he could and did bowl the unplayable ball and the rankest of long-hops in the same over. With so few runs to play with, Hammond had to use him with discretion. Again, in 1939, it was said that Hammond should have made more use of Tom Goddard when the West Indies had to be bowled out quickly, but the facts are on Hammond's side here, as I have discussed in Chapter 21.

As against his tactical errors, if errors they were, we may look at and admire Hammond's strategic handling of his attack on the 1938-39 tour. He was given a rather unbalanced set of bowlers, including four spinners and only two fast bowlers, and his own inability to bowl very much set him some pretty problems. He juggled his bowlers with some skill and came out ahead on points. Admittedly, South Africa made a great many runs in the final Test, but they never seized the initiative and I have already commented on the way Hammond nursed Farnes, and produced him, *relatively* fresh, at the very last moment. Overall, the very worse that can be said of Hammond is that he was just occasionally uncertain in handling his spinners – but this is a failing of many England captains. At the pinch, most of them have preferred to use their faster men. Think of Hutton, of Dexter, of May, of Brearley, above all of Jardine. If it was a fault of Hammond's, he was one among many.

Still considering the pre-war Hammond, what about his handling of his men? What sort of psychologist was he? There is some evidence. In the first Test of 1938, he is supposed to have taken Compton to task for getting himself out when he had made a 100, instead of taking guard again and settling down to make 200, but it is difficult to take this too seriously. It is far more likely that Hammond smiled and said something like 'what did you think you were doing – wasting an opportunity like that?' In any event, Compton was, and is, an ebullient character who would have been on a high after making a 100 in a Test, and very unlikely to be thrown into despair by a chance remark. Putting it another way – what better time to point out that an opportunity had been lost than when it would do no harm to the man's morale?

Let us now consider Edrich, and Hammond's effect on him. It was at Hammond's pleading that the selectors persevered with Edrich during the summer of 1938 when he couldn't make a run in the Tests. Hammond said he was 'good at the bits and pieces' – another way of saying that he was a thorough cricketer, always likely to make his impact in one way or another – like Hammond himself, who was persevered with in 1934 and 1935, for much the same reasons. Then in South Africa, Edrich's run of failure continued, but Hammond retained his confidence in him, and in the last innings of all restored him to the No 3 position and told him he was capable of great things. The rest is history.

My case rests: in my view Hammond was a thoughtful and wise captain, possibly lacking the outstanding flair for the job of a Brearley or a Benaud. After the war, it all changed. He was sound enough in 1946, but on that ill-fated tour of Australia it all went wrong. He was in failing health, his private life was in disarray and he was facing a team of the highest quality, shrewdly led by the greatest cricketer of all time. To compound the problem he tended to shy away from close contact with his team by doing much of his travelling by car and his tactical advice to his men was not always sound; the main misunderstanding seems to have between him and Compton, two very different personalities. Amidst all this though, he played two of his very finest bad-wicket innings, and it was especially pleasing that this last Test appearance of all, against New Zealand, was a successful one.

It is impossible to say how Hammond might have performed as player and captain on that last tour if fortune had favoured him – but we can look at his whole career and recognise a complete all-round cricketer and a shrewd leader – the greatest personality in English cricket in his time. It would be idle to try to place him within any kind of all-time order of merit. Let us leave him with one last tribute, from Sir Pelham Warner, who had had the advantage of seeing all Hammond's contemporaries and most of his Test predecessors:

'I admired his cricket beyond measure. Everything he did was graceful with a tremendous sense of power. There was majesty about his batting, he made the most difficult catches look supremely easy and his bowling action was perfect in rhythm, swing and delivery. A Very GREAT CRICKETER, one of the Immortals.'

'Here was a Caesar! When comes such another?'

(Julius Caesar III ii)

Walter Hammond – Statistics

Batting

Test figures against each country

Opponents	Matches	Innings	N.O.	H.S.	Runs	Average	100	50	0
Australia	33	58	3	251	2852	51.85	9	7	2
South Africa	24	42	7	181	2188	62.51	6	14	1
West Indies	13	20	2	138	639	35.50	1	1	–
New Zealand	9	11	2	336*	1015	112.77	4	1	1
India	6	9	2	217	555	79.28	2	1	–
Total	85	140	16	336*	7249	58.45	22	24	4

Test figures on each ground, and in each country

Trent Bridge	4	6	–	25	107	17.83	–	–	–
Lord's	12	19	1	240	772	40.63	2	–	–
Old Trafford	10	14	1	167	543	41.76	1	3	1
Headingley	5	10	1	113	496	55.11	1	4	2
Oval	12	17	4	217	930	71.53	4	3	–
Edgbaston	1	2	1	138*	156	156.00	1	–	–
In England	44	68	8	240	3004	50.06	9	10	3
Sydney	5	7	2	251	808	161.60	4	1	–
Melbourne	6	12	–	200	505	42.08	1	2	–
Adelaide	4	8	1	177	482	68.85	2	1	–
Brisbane (Ex)	1	2	–	44	72	36.00	–	–	–
Brisbane (W)	3	6	–	32	114	19.00	–	–	1
In Australia	19	35	3	251	1981	61.90	7	4	1
Johannesburg	6	11	1	75	450	45.00	–	5	–
Durban	6	10	2	140	637	79.62	3	2	–
Capetown	3	5	–	181	360	72.00	1	2	–
In South Africa	15	26	3	181	1447	62.91	4	9	–
Christchurch	2	2	–	227	306	153.00	1	1	–
Auckland	1	1	1	336*	336	–	1	1	–
In New Zealand	3	3	1	336*	642	321.00	2	1	–
Bridgetown	1	2	1	43	72	36.00	–	–	–
Port of Spain	1	2	–	9	10	5.00	–	–	–
Georgetown	1	2	–	47	48	24.00	–	–	–
Kingston	1	2	–	34	45	22.50	–	–	–
In West Indies	4	8	1	47	175	25.00	–	–	–

Hammond was out thus:

Bowled	38	(30.6% of all dismissals)
LBW	12	(9.6%)
Caught	62	(50%)
Stumped	7	(5.6%)
Run Out	4	(3.2%)
Hit wicket	1	(0.8%)

As compared with the generality of batsmen of his period, he was stumped just a little too often, but the other figures are about the norm. But the total of dismissals in one man's *Test* career is too small for valid comparison to be made. It *is* significant that he was stumped in 7 per cent of his first-class dismissals.

The bowlers who dismissed him most often in Tests were:

CL Vincent	10 (in 17 Tests)
WJ O'Reilly	10 (in 19 Tests)
LN Constantine	8 (in 10 Tests)
CV Grimmett	6
TW Wall	5
DPB Morkel	4
EL Dalton	4
SJ McCabe	4
ERH Toshack	4

Hammond scored 22 Test centuries; at the time of his retirement, he was second only to Bradman, then on 23. His 7,249 runs, and 46 innings over 50, both constituted records at the time of his retirement.

Bowling and fielding

Opponents	Balls	Runs	Wickets	Average	Runs/100 balls	Best bowling
Australia	3958	1612	36	44.77	40.72	5/57
South Africa	2811	1041	34	30.61	37.03	5/36
West Indies	414	178	3	59.33	42.99	1/20
New Zealand	507	188	6	31.33	37.08	2/19
India	279	121	4	30.25	43.46	3/9
Total	7969	3140	83	37.83	39.40	5/36

Hammond's figures may not look impressive, but he was largely used as a defensive bowler, and did well in the role; for example, in the five Anglo-Australian series between 1928-29 and 1936-37, runs were conceded by the England bowlers at the rate of 42.54 per 100 balls, Hammond being less expensive than that, at 41.09. Moreover, he was often bowling at times when the other bowlers were exhausted and the batsmen on top. He got most of the leading batsmen of his time out, some of them more than once. His most frequent 'victims' were:

B Mitchell	6
RH Catterall	4
SJ McCabe	4
VY Richardson	4
DG Bradman	3
WH Ponsford	3
TW Wall	3

WJ O'Reilly	3
EL McCormick	3
HW Taylor	3

and he also dismissed Woodfull, Fingleton, Cameron, Viljoen, Rowan Dempster, Merchant, Challenor, Donnelly and Constantine.

His pattern of dismissals was an unusual one, and emphasises that he bowled very much at the wicket:

Bowled	35 (42.1% of all dismissals)
LBW	11 (13.2%)
Caught at the wicket	14 (16.8%)
Caught elsewhere	19 (22.8%)
Stumped	4 (4.8%)

Walter Hammond made 110 catches in Tests, which remained the record for many years, and is still high on the list. He took catches off 38 different bowlers, including himself (he was, naturally enough, a very fine fielder to his own bowling) and his leading collaborators were

H Verity	13
W Voce	12
K Farnes	10
AP Freeman	10
WE Bowes	6
DVP Wright	6

He thus took more than half his catches off these six very considerable bowlers. He and Freeman only played together in nine Tests, and their joint achievement is quite remarkable.

Bibliography

I have listed only those books consulted in the course of writing the book; this is not intended to be a comprehensive bibliography covering the period, even if it looks like one.

THE PLAYERS
WR Hammond
Cricket My Destiny   WR Hammond
WR Hammond, Cricketer   David Moore A statistical survey
Walter Hammond   Ronald Mason
Walter Hammond   Gerald Howat

FE Woolley
Woolley – the Pride of Kent   Ian Peebles
The King of Games   Frank Woolley

Sir Jack Hobbs
The Test Match Career of Sir Jack Hobbs   Clive W Porter
Jack Hobbs   Ronald Mason

E Hendren
Patsy Hendren   Ian Peebles

Sir Donald Bradman
Sir Donald Bradman   Irving Rosenwater
Bradman the Great   BJ Wakley
Farewell to Cricket   Sir Donald Bradman

WJ Edrich
The Cricketing Family Edrich   Ralph Barker

DCS Compton
Denis Compton   Peter West

Sir Leonard Hutton
Hutton and Washbrook   AA Thomson
Len Hutton   Gerald Howat

AD Nourse
Cricket in the Blood   Dudley Nourse

WJ O'Reilly
Time of the Tiger   RS Whitington

Lord Harris
Lord Harris   JD Coldham

Lord Constantine
Learie Constantine   Gerald Howat

Sir Pelham Warner
Plum Warner   Gerald Howat

Sir George Allen
Gubby Allen-Man of Cricket   EW Swanton

AL Hassett
The Quiet Australian   RS Whitington

210

KR Miller
Keith Miller   Mihir Bose
Keith Miller – the Golden Nugget   RS Whitington

THE MATCHES

1928-29
The Fight for the Ashes, 1928-29   MA Noble
The Turn of the Wheel   PGH Fender

1930
The Tests of 1930   PGH Fender
Bradman's First Tour   Rigby Publishers
Don Bradman's Book   DG Bradman
Close of Play   Neville Cardus

1932-35
The Fight for the Ashes, 1932-33   Jack Hobbs
In Quest of the Ashes   DR Jardine
And then came Larwood   Arthur Mailey
Body-Line?   Harold Larwood
Express Deliveries   Bill Bowes
Defending the Ashes   RWE Wilmot
Bradman and the Bodyline Series   EW Docker
Cricket Crisis   JH Fingleton
The Bodyline Controversy   Laurence Le Quesne
Ashes in the Mouth   Ronald Mason

1934
The Fight for the Ashes, 1934   Jack Hobbs
Good Days   Neville Cardus
Ashes – and Dust   DR Jardine
Kissing the Rod   PGH Fender

1934-35
Game of a Lifetime   Denzil Batchelor

1935
In Search of Cricket   JM Kilburn

1936-37
Australian Summer   Neville Cardus
From a Window at Lord's   EHD Sewell
1937 Australian Test Tour   Bruce Harris

1938
The Essential Neville Cardus   Neville Cardus

1938-39
Talking about Cricket   William Pollock
Ten Great Innings   Ralph Barker

1945
The Match I Remember   Denzil Batchelor

1946
Indian Summer   John Arlott

1946-47
With England in Australia   Bruce Harris
Cricket Controversy   Clif Cary

GENERAL CRICKET HISTORY
A History of Cricket   HS Altham and EW Swanton
Cricket Between Two Wars   Sir Pelham Warner
The Cricket Captains of England   Alan Gibson
Between Wickets   Ray Robinson
England v Australia   David Frith
The Fast Men   David Frith
The Slow Men   David Frith
West Indian Cricket   Christopher Nicole
The West Indies: 50 Years of Test Cricket   Tony Cozier
Classic Centuries   BJ Wakley
Cricket Tours   Peter Wynne-Thomas
Who's Who of Test Cricketers   Christopher Martin-Jenkins
The Wisden Book of Test Cricket   Bill Frindall
The Wisden Book of Cricket Records   Bill Frindall
Australian Cricket – the Game and the Players   Jack Pollard
Cricketers of the Veld Louis Duffus
To the Wicket   Dudley Carew
Batsman's Paradise   Ronald Mason
Mainly Middlesex   Terence Prittie
The Charm of Cricket Past and Present   CHB Pridham
Gloucestershire Road   Grahame Parker
Wisden Cricketers' Almanack   1922-1940, 1942, 1945-1948
The Cricketer   various years
Various newspapers, but chiefly *The Daily Telegraph, Manchester Guardian* and
   Sydney Morning Herald.

INDEX

Only cricketers and administrators are included in the index, together with historical figures, and members of the Hammond family are excluded. Entries on the statistical pages are also excluded.

214

215

Scott, R. H. *201.*
Sealy, J. E. D. *163, 164.*
Sellers, A. B. *112.*
Shepherd, T. F. *12.*
Sibbles, F. M. *10.*
Siedle, I. J. *54, 56, 58, 106, 109-111, 114, 115, 117, 153.*
Sievers, M. W. *127, 130, 132.*
Sims, J. M. *112-114, 123, 124, 128, 129, 132.*
Sinfield, R. A. *12, 36, 52, 116, 144-146.*
Sismey, S. G. *171, 172, 174.*
Skelding, A. *13.*
Smailes, T. F. *148, 179-181.*
Small, J. *22.*
Smith, C. I. J. *100-103, 140.*
Smith, D. *112-115, 117.*
Smith, H. *12.*
Smith, H. D. *78, 79.*
Smith, R. *185.*
Smith, T. P. B. *183, 185, 189, 190, 192, 200.*
Sobers, G. St. A. *203.*
Sohoni, S. W. *181, 183, 184.*
Spooner, R. H. *1.*
Stanyforth, R. T. *15, 17, 18.*
Staples, S. J. *17, 18, 24.*
Stephenson, J. W. A. *116, 121, 171, 173.*
Stevens, G. T. S. *18.*
Stollmeyer, J. B. *163-166.*
Stollmeyer, V. H. *165, 166.*
Sturgess, E. W. *169.*
Sutcliffe, B. *201.*
Sutcliffe, H. *4, 12, 15, 16-21, 24, 25, 27, 30-34, 38-40, 42-44, 46, 48-50, 53, 59, 61, 62, 64-68, 70, 73-75, 77-84, 87-89, 92-94, 96, 97, 107, 108, 110-113, 117, 120, 123, 125, 133, 198.*

Tallon, D. *187, 192, 193, 195.*
Tate, M. W. *21, 22, 24-26, 30-32, 34, 37-39, 42, 44-47, 51, 53, 54, 56, 57, 64, 78, 114, 115.*
Taylor, H. W. *18, 40, 54, 56.*
Tennyson, L. H. (Lord Tennyson). *8.*
Thompson, F. C. *26.*
Thomson, J. R. *1.*
Toshack, E. R. H. *187, 189, 193, 197, 198.*
Townsend, D. C. H. *100, 101, 105.*
Tribe, G. E. *187, 192.*
Trueman, F. S. *194.*
Trumper, V. T. *52.*
Tunnicliffe, J. *7.*
Turnbull, M. J. L. *53, 54, 58, 81-84, 120.*
Tyldesley, G. E. *15, 16, 18-20, 22, 24, 33.*
Tyldesley, J. T. *3.*
Tyldesley, R. K. *10, 42, 44, 46.*

Valentine, B. H. *153-155, 158, 161.*
Valentine, V. A. *82, 84.*
Van der Bijl, P. G. V. *154-159.*
Verity, H. *61, 64, 66, 68, 69, 71, 72, 74, 76, 77, 87, 89-93, 95-97, 106, 108-111, 116, 117, 120, 121, 123, 124, 126, 129, 130, 133, 134, 138, 144, 145, 147, 149, 151, 157-159, 164, 205.*
Viljoen, K. G. *107, 113, 115-118, 154, 156, 159.*

Vincent, C. L. *4, 16-18, 39, 40, 54, 106, 108, 113-118, 153.*
Vivian, H. G. *61, 138-140.*
Voce, W. *53-56, 62-64, 66, 68, 70, 71, 74, 79, 83, 86, 108, 123, 124, 126, 127, 129, 135, 138, 144, 145, 181, 183, 185, 189, 192-194, 196.*

Waddington, A. *12.*
Wade, H. F. *106, 110, 111, 113, 114, 117, 118, 153.*
Wade, W. W. *154.*
Waite, M. G. *149, 150.*
Walker, C. W. *52.*
Wall, T. W. *29, 33, 44, 48, 49, 51, 65, 67, 69, 74, 75, 88, 89, 91, 95, 97, 125.*
Walters, C. F. *81-84, 87-89, 92-94, 96, 98, 107, 120.*
Walters, K. D. *98.*
Ward, F. A. *127, 143.*
Warner, Sir Pelham. *11, 64, 70, 73, 109, 146, 205, 206.*
Washbrook, C. *141, 171, 172, 174-176, 179-181, 184-189, 191, 193-195, 197-201.*
Weekes, E de C. *166.*
Weekes, K. H. *166.*
Weir, G. L. *61.*
Wellard, A. W. *140, 146.*
White, J. C. *21, 24, 25, 30-34, 37, 38, 42, 44, 45, 53, 56.*
White, Hon. L. R. *173.*
Whitington, R. S. *170, 172, 174.*
Whysall, W. W. *49, 50.*
Wight, C. V. *22.*
Wiles, C. A. *82.*
Wilkinson, L. L. *153-155.*
Williams, E. A. V. *164.*
Williams, R. G. *170, 171, 175.*
Wood, A. *148, 150, 162, 164, 165, 167.*
Woodfull, W. M. *26, 27, 29, 30, 32, 34, 43-48, 50, 51, 66, 67, 69-72, 74-76, 87-93, 95-98, 117, 125.*
Workman, J. A. *172, 174.*
Worthington, T. S. *121, 123, 125, 126, 128, 131, 133, 135, 136.*
Wright, D. V. P. *144, 145, 147, 149, 150, 152-154, 156-159, 163, 171, 172, 175, 177, 178, 181, 183, 185-187, 190, 192, 195, 196, 198, 200, 205.*
Wyatt, R. E. S. *17, 40, 48-50, 53-56, 59, 64, 65, 67-70, 77-79, 83-85, 87-94, 96-98, 101-105, 107-118, 120, 125, 126, 135, 136, 148, 204.*

Yardley, N. W. D. *153-155, 185, 186, 188-190, 192, 194-201.*
Young, J. A. *186.*

Zaheer Abbas. *12.*

216